Building Bridges from High Poverty Communities, to Schools, to Productive Citizenship

M. Christopher Brown II
GENERAL EDITOR

Vol. 7

The Education Management series is part of the
Peter Lang Education list.
Every volume is peer reviewed and meets
the highest quality standards for content and production.

PETER LANG
New York • Washington, D.C./Baltimore • Bern
Frankfurt • Berlin • Brussels • Vienna • Oxford

Building Bridges from High Poverty Communities, to Schools, to Productive Citizenship

A Holistic Approach to Addressing Poverty through Exceptional Educational Leadership

Lisa Bass & Susan C. Faircloth
WITH JUANITA G. VARGAS, ROBBIE WAHNEE, & WENDELL WAUKAU

PETER LANG
New York • Washington, D.C./Baltimore • Bern
Frankfurt • Berlin • Brussels • Vienna • Oxford

Library of Congress Cataloging-in-Publication Data
Bass, Lisa.
Building bridges from high poverty communities, to schools,
to productive citizenship: a holistic approach to addressing poverty
through exceptional educational leadership / Lisa Bass, Susan C. Faircloth.
pages cm. — (Education management: contexts, constituents, and communities; vol. 7)
Includes bibliographical references and index.
1. Children with social disabilities—Education—United States.
2. Poor children—Education—United States. 3. School improvement programs—
United States. I. Bass, Lisa. II. Faircloth, Susan C. III. Title.
LC4091.B38   371.826'94—dc23   2013003550
ISBN 978-1-4331-1410-6 (hardcover)
ISBN 978-1-4331-1409-0 (paperback)
ISBN 978-1-4539-1109-9 (e-book)
ISSN 1947-6256

Bibliographic information published by **Die Deutsche Nationalbibliothek**.
Die Deutsche Nationalbibliothek lists this publication in the "Deutsche
Nationalbibliografie"; detailed bibliographic data is available
on the Internet at http://dnb.d-nb.de/.

© 2013 Peter Lang Publishing, Inc., New York
29 Broadway, 18th floor, New York, NY 10006
www.peterlang.com

All rights reserved.
Reprint or reproduction, even partially, in all forms such as microfilm,
xerography, microfiche, microcard, and offset strictly prohibited.

*We would like to dedicate this book
to children striving to attain an education
despite difficult economic circumstances,
and to the educators, families, and communities
who make their dreams a reality.*

Contents

Acknowledgments ix

Introduction 1
    Lisa Bass

1 Contemporary Issues in High Poverty Schools: Can Schools Make a
    Difference in Student Outcomes? Implications for Educational Leadership 13
    Lisa Bass & Susan C. Faircloth

2 The Role of Educational Leaders in High Poverty Schools:
    A Framework for a Revised Job Description 29
    Lisa Bass & Susan C. Faircloth

3 To What Extent Do Schools Have a Moral, Ethical, or Professional
    Imperative to Serve Students from Low Socioeconomic Backgrounds? 45
    Lisa Bass & Susan C. Faircloth

4 Effective Instructional Leadership for Diverse High Poverty Populations:
    The Effect of Instructional Supervision on Principal Trust 63
    Robbie Wahnee

5 Professional Development and Learning in Schools:
    Teaching Institutions as Learning Institutions 91
    Lisa Bass

6 Bringing Together Schools and Communities to Meet the Needs
    of Students from High Poverty Contexts 107
    Susan C. Faircloth & Lisa Bass

7 Re-visioning the Future of Education for Youth from High Poverty Contexts:
    Lessons Learned from Working in the Field of American Indian Education 121
    Susan C. Faircloth

8 Addressing the Needs of High Poverty Latino Students as
    They Navigate the Terrain of Higher Education 131
    Juanita Vargas

9 Importance of Exceptional Leadership: One School Leader's Insight on
    Effective Leadership in a High Poverty School System 149
    Wendell Waukau

10 Bridging High Poverty Schools and Communities—Implications and
    Conclusions: Where Do We Go from Here? 161
    Susan C. Faircloth

Contributors 175

Index 177

Acknowledgments

This book was motivated by our desire to see education work in the best interests of all children, especially those who live in high poverty communities and/or attend high poverty schools. As we bring this project to a close, we are reminded that the work of minimizing the effects of poverty on schools and communities is a lifelong endeavor, thus the work is never completely done. We hope that the information offered in this book will encourage educators and community members to continue this most important work. Although we believe strongly in the power of education to effect change, we also believe that real change cannot be sustained without the collaborative efforts of all stakeholders. This book is dedicated to those who continue to fight the good fight on behalf of our children, schools, families, and communities.

Special Acknowledgments from First Author, Lisa Bass
As noted, the publication of this book by no means marks completion of our work to improve learning conditions for those living in poverty—rather it is a beginning. As we mark this momentous event, I would be remiss if I did not take this opportunity to acknowledge those who have so freely contributed to my personal and professional development. I recognize that without their support, my work would not be possible. I would like to acknowledge those who have inspired me to continue to produce work that promotes the educational interests of disenfranchised children. Before I acknowledge friends and family, I must first acknowledge God who gives me the strength and inspiration to continue—even when I

feel all strength has gone. I would like to thank and acknowledge the memory of my father; Floyd Bass, although he did not live to witness the completion of my Ph.D., he nurtured my love of learning, and planted the seed for me to continue my education. I will never forget how he told me that I would never be satisfied until I earned my Ph.D.! I would also like to thank and acknowledge my mother, Estella Bass, who supplies endless love and support of me in my work. She truly is my biggest promoter and fan. Additionally, I would like to acknowledge Robyn, John, Valorie, and Wayne for being awesome brothers and sisters as I have grown into the woman and scholar that I am becoming. I would like to thank Susan Faircloth, coauthor, mentor, partner, and encourager, for her understanding and support throughout the completion of this endeavor. It has truly been a journey in more ways than one, and she was there—even when the going got tough! I must also acknowledge Linda Tillman and Michelle Young, extraordinary mentors and facilitators of opportunities such as the Barbara Jackson Scholars Mentoring program. Their support and influence has opened many doors of opportunity for me. I would like to thank my 'sister docs', Karen Beard, Cosette Grant-Overton, Sonya Horsford, April Peters-Hawkins, and Latish Reed, who inspire and provide endless amounts of moral support and inspiration. I must also acknowledge my prayer partners and soul mates: Anya Rashid, Sylvia Austin, Karen Powell-Sears, and Josephine Boardman for their ears and their prayers. It is true that it takes a village to raise a child, and even more true that it takes the effort of many to raise a scholar! I acknowledge and am grateful for my 'village of support.'

Special Acknowledgments from Second Author, Susan Faircloth
Thank you to my family for supporting me during this process. To my husband, Lee Brotzman, thanks for lending a critical ear and for serving as an impromptu editor. To my daughter, Journey, thanks for letting Mommy write even when you wanted to play. I promise to spend more time playing with you in the future. To my parents, Gene and Marie Faircloth, thank you for instilling a love of learning and for always believing that your children could do and be anything. My goal in life has always been to make you proud. To Lisa, my coauthor, thanks for inviting me to join you in this project. Your commitment to this work made this book possible.

Note of thanks
Finally, we would like to thank Mary Ann Danowitz, Chair of the Leadership, Policy and Adult and Higher Education department at North Carolina State University. During her tenure, she has been both a mentor and supporter of our efforts to develop this book. Under her leadership, we were able to secure the financial support required to cover the costs of copyediting and typesetting. We are most grateful for her efforts on our behalf.

Introduction

Lisa Bass

We must remember that in almost every conceivable way, the very structure of the U.S. education system denies students in poverty the opportunities and access it affords most other students. We must recognize, too, that people living in poverty are fully aware of these discrepancies. So when we see hopelessness in some of our students' eyes, when we sense a reluctance to engage, a distrust of our intentions, we must recognize that these reactions arise, if they arise at all, from lifetimes of oppression and not from a failure to value education or from an inherent moral deficiency. In fact, we should recognize the resilience of a community that overcomes such insurmountable odds, such savage inequalities, and, despite its maltreatment by schools and society, continues to push, to strive, to learn and achieve. (Gorski, 2007, paras. 10–11)

Poverty is viewed as one of the most formidable barriers to quality education in the United States (Bourdieu, 1977; Breen & Johnson, 2005; Hannon, 2003; Mortenson, 2000; Sullivan, 2001). Failure to provide quality education results in a lack of productive educated citizenry, thereby threatening the nation's potential ability to make and sustain progress. Education holds the key to improving the economic vitality of this nation and its citizens. However, for education to make a positive and lasting impact, it must be restructured to meet the needs of children, youth, and communities who are most at risk for social and economic disasters (e.g., Ladd, 2012). While conversations regarding school reform address issues of poverty and the lack of appropriate funding for schools (Borman, Hewes, Overman, & Brown, 2003), in the United States, these discussions also tend to involve the quality and purpose of education, as well as issues of equity (e.g., Lubienski, 2002; Rodriguez, 2001). One of the points raised in these discussions is that those living in poverty often do not receive a quality education due to differences in the distribution of resources in schools, which is closely linked to the socioeconomic status of children's families and communities. For this reason, there is a sense of urgency toward dismantling the conditions that help to reinforce vast differences in socioeconomic status and perpetuate cycles of poverty in communities across the United States. Socioeconomially "disadvantaged children should not be punished for the circumstances into which they are born, and improved education policy is one of the best ways to prevent this from happening" (Jacob & Ludwig, 2009, p. 61).

In this book, we consider the impact of poverty on education; the unique needs of students from high poverty backgrounds; and strategies that hold promise in successfully educating students from high poverty backgrounds. In writing this book, we grappled with the use of the term "culture of poverty" (e.g., Lewis, 1966, as cited in Harding, Lamont, & Small, 2010; Payne, 2005), which has been used to refer to behavioral and attitudinal variables that contribute to and help to perpetuate the existence of poverty. In doing so, we acknowledge the controversial nature of this term, while simultaneously acknowledging the need to address head-on the potential for social, attitudinal, and institutional structures to influence one's thinking about, and in turn reaction to or coping with, the lack of access to financial and other resources and opportunities. In this way, the term "culture of poverty" may be used more accurately to describe the ways in which many of those in power, including those at the school level, think about and respond to those who live in poverty. For educational leaders, the goal is to think deeply about poverty and the ways in which schools and education at large help either to promote or to diminish the conditions that sustain poverty (see Chapter One, figure 1.1). In many cases, this thinking and reflecting should lead to revised ways of doing and leading in schools serving students from high poverty backgrounds.

In writing this book, we also acknowledge that the complexities surrounding the persistence of poverty in the United States have even confounded economists for decades (Hickey & Bracking, 2005; Karelis, 2009; Venkatesh, 2006). Unfortunately, economic studies have failed to adequately explain why intergenerational poverty continues to exist in a country where economic, educational, and community resources are thought to be abundant (Hulme & McKay, 2005; Karelis, 2009; Seccombe, 2000). The irony lies in the fact that a nation often dubbed "the land of opportunity," a destination to which large numbers of immigrants flock in search of safe harbor and the opportunity to pursue their personal and professional aspirations (Wilson, 2009), struggles with its own issues of social and economic disparity and inequality.

Poverty and Schools

What makes this issue even more difficult is the fact that children and youth are among those most affected by poverty. According to Child Trends (Moore, Redd,

Burkhauser, Mbwana, & Collins, 2009), more than 13 million of this nation's children live in poverty. This is particularly troubling given reported links between poverty, low academic achievement, increased risk of dropping out of school, and high incidences of health, behavioral, and emotional problems (Mistry, Vandewater, Huston, & McLloyd, 2002). These issues are significant, as they impact children's overall well-being. If children's sense of well-being is compromised it is highly likely that their physical, social, and emotional well-being will also be compromised, leading to a negatively impacted quality of life. Although schools alone do not have the power or capability of eradicating poverty, they do have the potential to impact the individual lives of children and their families. Empowering even one child to transcend the bonds of poverty is an accomplishment that should not be minimized, but the goal should be for this impact to be felt by all students within a school.

To focus our efforts only on the school is to negate the complex nature of poverty whose impact is not limited to the external boundaries of the school but which tends to permeate these boundaries. Not only are children affected by poverty within their homes and communities, in fact, the effects of poverty are often also felt within the confines of schools and other educational institutions designed to serve children and youth (e.g., Engle & Black, 2008). More than 16,000 (17%) public schools are identified as high poverty, meaning that at least 75% of the students in these schools are eligible to receive free or reduced price lunch. Approximately 20% of elementary and 6% of secondary students attend these schools. The concentration of high poverty schools is even greater in urban areas, as many districts qualify as Title I districts, or districts in which all schools are composed of 75% or more students who are eligible to receive free or reduced price lunch. Black, Hispanic, and American Indian/Alaska Native students are more likely to attend these schools than are white or Asian/Pacific Islander students. These schools also serve a significant number of students who speak a language other than English at home (Aud et al., 2010).

One of the interesting facets of these schools is the characteristics of those who teach and lead in these schools. Recent data indicate 21% of all elementary and 12% of all secondary school principals are assigned to high poverty schools. Further, high poverty secondary schools[*] tend to attract higher numbers of Black and Hispanic principals than do lower poverty schools and the principals in high poverty secondary schools also tend to have completed lower levels of education than their peers who work in lower poverty schools (Aud et al., 2010). Teachers in these higher poverty schools also tend to have fewer years of teaching experience

---

[*] The school poverty measure used is the percentage of a school's enrollment that is eligible for free and reduced price lunch (FRPL) through the National School Lunch Program (NSLP). High poverty schools are those where 76% to 100% of students are eligible for FRPL; low poverty schools are those where 0% to 25% of students are eligible for FRPL (Aud et al., 2010).

than do their peers in lower poverty schools (Aud et al., 2010; Clotfelter, Ladd, & Vigdor, 2007; Sass, Hannaway, Xu, Figlio, & Feng, 2010).

Location of high poverty schools
Although the largest percentage (40%) of high poverty elementary schools is located in urban areas, high poverty schools are not confined to cities. Fifteen percent of high poverty elementary schools are located in towns, 13% are located in suburban areas, and 10% are located in rural areas. Similar percentages are found among secondary schools, with 20% of all high poverty secondary schools located in cities, and 5% to 8% located in towns and suburban and rural areas (Aud et al., 2010). Across the nation, 24% of elementary schools in the South and West, 16% in the Northeast, and 12% in the Midwest are identified as high poverty. Among secondary schools, 12% in the West, 11% in the Northeast and South, and 5% in the Midwest are designated as high poverty (Aud et al., 2010).

Failure to Provide Educational Equity and Equality for All Students
According to the National Center for Education Statistics (Aud et al., 2010), students attending high poverty schools tend to score lower on the 4th and 8th grade reading and math assessments included in the National Assessment of Educational Progress. These students are also less likely to graduate than those in lower poverty schools, and those who do graduate are less likely to go on to college than their peers (Boyd, Loeb, Wyckoff, Lankford, & Rockoff, 2008; Coleman, 1966; Mistry et al., 2002). Failure to meet the needs of high poverty schools is likely to result in a continual cycle of low academic achievement among students living in high poverty contexts.

Although the mission of schools in the United States has been touted as one of providing an opportunity for all citizens to become educated to improve their life chances (Wilson, 2009), such opportunities have not yet resulted in widespread social or economic parity for all (Datnow, Borman, Stringfield, Overman, & Castellano, 2003). Comprehensive school reform efforts, including the provision of mandatory public schooling, special education programs and services, remedial reading programs, free tutoring, after-school programs, mentoring, free and reduced price lunch programs, charter schools, year-round schooling, and increased accountability measures driven by federal education policies such as No Child Left Behind (NCLB), have not worked to create equality of opportunity or to stop the cycle of poverty in the United States (Cooper & Jordan, 2003).

This failure to eradicate poverty means that schools continue to struggle against the effects of poverty. Not only are schools tasked with addressing the individual needs of their students, but they also must respond to public cries for schools to do more with less. As poverty persists, it remains a central theme in school reform discussions, not so much because administrators and policy makers are concerned about the plight of the poor (Mantsios, 1998), but because the issue of poverty continually emerges as an impediment to improving student achievement. This is particularly important at the school and district levels as school administrators are held accountable for all students' achievement (Wilson, 2009). As a result, administrators from high poverty schools and districts are placed in the position of having to advocate for themselves by demonstrating the myriad of difficulties they encounter as they attempt to educate students from high poverty environments (Noguera, 2003). Such difficulties include a lack of parental involvement (Evans, 2004); single-parent homes (Christian & Barbarin, 2001; Evans, 2004; Seccombe, 2000); the fact that parents from high poverty environments are often undereducated, and lack the ability to adequately support their children's learning at home (Bradley & Corwyn, 2002; Evans, 2004; Guo & Harris, 2000); living conditions that are not conducive to learning (Duncan & Brooks-Gunn, 2000; Mayer, 1997, as cited in Seccombe, 2000); a lack of fiscal, physical, and other resources in both the home and school (National Research Council, 1983, as cited in Eamon, 2001); negative peer pressure (Brody et al., 2001, as cited in Evans, 2004; Duncan & Brooks-Gunn, 2000); a lack of social and cultural capital (Bradley & Corwyn, 2002; Cleaver, 2005; Evans, 2004; Seccombe, 2000); and the list continues. We view these conditions as symptoms of a larger issue that schools can, and must, address holistically if we are to achieve the original purposes of education—to provide all children with an education that serves as the great equalizer, to act as a forum where all children can learn, and to become the place where the foundations of aspirations are built and later realized (e.g., Downey, von Hippel, & Broh, 2004; Mann, 1848, as cited in Scutari, 2009; Oakes, 1985).

Our Purpose

The purpose of this book is not simply to reiterate previous conversations on poverty (Amato & Zuo, 1992; Carlson, 2006; Ravallion, 2007; Sullivan, 2001; Tickamyer & Duncan, 1990), but to prompt readers to move beyond these conventional conversations into a dialogue that facilitates a holistic approach to addressing the relationship between poverty and schools, through the practice of "exceptional educational leadership." For the purposes of this discussion, exceptional educational leadership is defined as leadership that meets the needs of exceptional or challenging contexts (e.g., Goldberg, 2001). Goldberg argues that leadership is situational and that the ability to adapt to unique situations or contexts, such as those found in high poverty schools, is the mark of an exceptional leader. Exceptional educational leaders recognize the nuances and aspects unique to the contexts in which they work and adjust their leadership styles to accommodate these aspects in order to promote a positive school climate while maximizing student achievement.

In framing the concept of exceptional educational leadership, we address the multidimensional nature of school leadership (i.e., instructional leader, professional developer, general building manager, human resources manager, public relations manager, school-community-home liaison), and provide recommendations regarding how various aspects of poverty can be addressed by schools and school leaders working collaboratively and intensively with community members, agencies, and organizations. In essence, we seek to demonstrate that combating the effects of poverty on schools goes much deeper than increasing monetary and other forms of tangible resources (Bradley & Corwyn, 2002; Green & Hulme, 2005); in fact, it goes to the very heart of one's attitudes, beliefs, and behaviors.

We hope this book will motivate readers to recognize the power possessed by school leaders to change conditions for learning and to lead their schools in ways that promote academic achievement and instill a future orientation within students, regardless of their low socioeconomic status. We also aim to introduce and discuss further the concept of "exceptional educational leadership" as a means to address poverty and its effects on student learning. We view this as a proactive and much more productive endeavor than focusing solely on the seemingly insurmountable obstacles associated with poverty. In essence, our goal is to introduce ways to build bridges from the present realities of poverty to future possibilities of increased academic achievement through exceptional educational leadership.

Our hope is that educational leaders will be empowered by the discussions and strategies that emerge from this book and the literature selected for additional reference. A final goal is for school leaders to be reassured that exceptional educational leadership can make a difference in the lives of students by working to improve student achievement and to reduce the cycle of poverty.

As you read this book, we encourage you to think deeply about the following questions:

1. What is poverty?
2. Is there a culture of poverty? If so, how does this culture of poverty influence educational attainment? Who is responsible for dismantling this culture of poverty?
3. What is the role of education in decreasing the cycle of poverty?
4. What is exceptional educational leadership within the context of your school or school district?
5. How can educational leaders be more strategic in linking the purpose of schools with the demands of leadership?
6. How can educational leaders use school and community resources to their maximum benefit to reduce the cycle of poverty?

7. What are the most effective strategies/practices for working with diverse student populations in high poverty contexts?
8. To what extent, and in what ways, might ethical frameworks such as the ethics of care, critique, justice, and the best interests of students serve to reduce the cycle of poverty?
9. How can educational leaders bridge the gap between educational policies at the national and state levels and the realities of educating students from high poverty backgrounds at the local level?

We aim to facilitate discussion around these questions with the information provided in the following chapters. In doing so, we divide the book into ten chapters as outlined below:

Chapter One: *Contemporary Issues in High Poverty Schools: Can Schools Make a Difference in Student Outcomes? Implications for Educational Leadership*

Chapter One provides a brief overview of the literature on high poverty schools. This chapter begins by describing poverty as it relates to the context of schools and schooling. Next, we argue that leadership styles and strategies should be predicated upon the needs, abilities, and desires of the group being led, and that when leadership is tailored to the needs of the people being served (in this case, individuals from high poverty backgrounds), goals can be identified and met more effectively.

Chapter Two: *The Role of Educational Leaders in High Poverty Schools: A Framework for a Revised Job Description*

Chapter Two outlines the knowledge, skills, dispositions, and responsibilities of exceptional educational leaders in high poverty contexts. This chapter stresses the need for educational leaders who possess leadership skills and dispositions outside the realm of what has been traditionally discussed in educational leadership literature. This chapter speaks to the importance of ethical and caring behavior, strong instructional leadership, targeted professional development, the need to collaborate with community partners, and the adoption of high standards and goals for all students. Subsequent chapters discuss these attributes in detail.

Chapter Three: *To What Extent Do Schools Have a Moral, Ethical, or Professional Imperative to Serve Students from Low Socioeconomic Backgrounds?*

Chapter Three discusses the moral and ethical imperatives for school leaders to lead in the best interests of all students, including those from high poverty contexts. This chapter draws upon the ethical frames of care and best interests as described by Noddings (1984, 2005), Stefkovich (2006), and Stefkovich and Begley (2007).

Chapter Four: *Effective Instructional Leadership for Diverse High Poverty Populations: The Effect of Instructional Supervision on Principal Trust*

Establishing our argument for the need for strong instructional leadership in high poverty schools, Chapter Four presents an in-depth review of the literature on instructional leadership. Strong instructional leadership is particularly important in high poverty contexts where families may be unable to sufficiently support their children's academic needs (Lareau & Weininger, 2003; Nadel & Sagawa, 2000) and the teaching force is composed largely of a less seasoned, and potentially more mobile, teaching force than is found in lower poverty schools (Nadel & Sagawa; Wahnee, 2010).

Chapter Five: *Professional Development and Learning in Schools: Teaching Institutions as Learning Institutions*

Chapter Five addresses the importance of tailoring professional development to the needs of individual teachers, as well as the school as a whole. High poverty schools cannot afford ineffective professional development; in fact, they need professional development that trains them how to deal with the unique teaching and learning needs, as well as the physical needs of students from high poverty backgrounds. Unfortunately, many teachers complain that professional development in schools is often not relevant to their needs. Examples of professional development activities that may be successful in the high poverty context can be found in Chapter Five.

Chapter Six: *Bringing Together Schools and Communities to Meet the Needs of Students from High Poverty Contexts*

This chapter outlines the need for coordinated and collaborative relationships between high poverty schools and the communities they serve. In this approach, schools, in collaboration with community members and groups, provide supportive services such as food, clothing, school supplies, after-school programs, tutoring, extended educational opportunities, parent resource rooms, and other necessary supports and services.

Chapter Seven: *Re-visioning the Future of Education for Youth from High Poverty Contexts: Lessons Learned from Working in the Field of American Indian Education*

Chapter Seven expands upon a previously published article written by the second author in response to Michael Corbett's *Learning to Leave: The Irony of Schooling in a Coastal Community*. In this book, Dr. Corbett argues that education in rural communities has historically been used as a tool to prepare students for their eventual departure from their rural communities of origin. In responding to this book, the author argues that education must be re-visioned so that students are given the options to remain in their communities and be successful, leave their communities and be successful, or leave their communities and be successful before returning to their home communities where they are better able to contribute in meaningful and practical ways than they would have been had they chosen not to venture outside these communities.

Chapter Eight: *Addressing the Needs of High Poverty Latino Students as They Navigate the Terrain of Higher Education*

Chapter Eight addresses the need to foster a college-going culture among students from high poverty backgrounds. An essential element of successful high poverty schools is the championing of high academic standards and the belief that all students can achieve. As part of the fastest growing minority population in this nation, many Latino students are also likely to reside in areas of high or concentrated poverty. This chapter cites examples of ways in which a college-going culture may be fostered.

Chapter Nine: *Importance of Exceptional Leadership: One School Leader's Insight on Effective Leadership in a High Poverty School System*

Chapter Nine draws upon lessons learned by a superintendent working in a predominantly American Indian school system. Through his leadership, and the support of the community, this school system has increased graduation rates, decreased dropout rates, and worked to make the school an integral part of the community. This chapter serves as a prime example of how the responsibility for ensuring the successful education of children and youth from high poverty backgrounds rests not only with the school leader, but also with the community at large.

Chapter Ten: *Bridging High Poverty Schools and Communities—Implications and Conclusions: Where Do We Go from Here?*

Chapter Ten concludes with recommendations for policy, practice, and future research.

Conclusion

In writing this book, we acknowledge that the issues surrounding poverty are complex and multifaceted. As such, we neither wish to make light of these complexities, nor to minimize the truth of the lived realities of those living, working, and learning in poverty. To overcome these challenges, students and their schools need collaborative and targeted supports aimed at meeting their individual and collective needs and empowering them to move beyond the boundaries of poverty. We believe strongly that when done right, education has the power to lift individuals and their communities out of the depths of poverty.

Our goal in writing this book is to encourage school leaders to move beyond discussions of the futility of schools and their leaders to lessen or moderate the effects of poverty. We believe that educational leaders have a moral and ethical imperative to work in the individual and collective best interests (Stefkovich, 2006; Stefkovich & Begley, 2007) of their schools, students, and communities. The ideas we propose in this book are small steps toward actualizing the ethical imperatives of care and best interests and developing leadership skills and practices that are truly exceptional.

We hope that after reading this text, practicing school leaders, students of educational leadership and administration, and other educators will have a better understanding of ways in which they can work to improve the educational conditions and subsequent life experiences of students from high poverty backgrounds. Our goal is to encourage ongoing conversation and thought around the concept of exceptional educational leadership and how it might be enacted in such ways that it becomes the catalyst for real and lasting change in the lives of children, youth, their families, and their communities. We know that leading in any school can be challenging, but we firmly believe that committed, collaborative, and visionary leaders will be willing and able to rise above these challenges as they work to re-vision the future of education for students in high poverty schools and communities.

References

Amato, P. R., & Zuo, J. (1992, June). Rural poverty, urban poverty, and psychological well-being. *The Sociological Quarterly, 33*(2), 229–240.

Aud, S., Hussar, W., Planty, M., Snyder, T., Bianco, K., Fox, M., et al. (2010). *The condition of education 2010* (NCES Publication No. 2010-028). Washington, DC: U.S. Department of Education, National Center for Education Statistics, Institute of Education Sciences.

Borman, G., Hewes, G., Overman, L., & Brown, S. (2003, Summer). Comprehensive school reform and achievement: A meta-analysis. *Review of Educational Research, 73*(2), 125–230. Retrieved from http://www.successforall.net/_images/pdfs/Borman_CSR_meta_RER.pdf

Bourdieu, P. (1977). Cultural reproduction and social reproduction. In J. Karabel & A. H. Halsey (Eds.), *Power and ideology in education* (pp. 487–511). New York: Oxford University Press.

Boyd, D., Loeb, S., Wyckoff, J., Lankford, H., & Rockoff, J. (2008). The narrowing gap in New York City teacher qualification and its implications for student achievement in high-poverty schools. *Journal of Policy, Analysis & Management, 27*, 793–818. Retrieved from http://www.teacherpolicyresearch.org/portals/1/pdfs/JPAM%20Narrowing%20the%20Gap.pdf

Bradley, R. H., & Corwyn, R. F. (2002). Socioeconomic status and child development. *Annual Review of Psychology, 53*, 371–399.

Breen, R., & Johnson, J. O. (2005). Inequality of opportunity in comparative perspective: Recent research on educational attainment and social mobility. *Annual Review of Sociology*, 223–243.

Carlson, K. T. (2006). Poverty and youth violence exposure: Experiences in rural communities. *Children & Schools, 28*(2), 87–96.

Christian, M. D., & Barbarin, O. A. (2001). Cultural resources and psychological adjustment of African American children: Effects of spirituality and racial attribution. *Journal of Black Psychology, 27*(1), 43–63.

Cleaver, F. (2005). The inequality of social capital and the reproduction of chronic poverty. *World Development, 33*(6), 893–906.

Clotfelter, C. T., Ladd, H. F., & Vigdor, J. L. (2007). *Teacher credentials and student achievement in high school: A cross-subject analysis with student fixed effects* (NBPR Working Paper No. 13617). Cambridge, MA: National Bureau of Economic Research. Retrieved from http://www.nber.org/papers/w13617.pdf?new_window=1

Coleman, J. S. (1966). Equal schools or equal students? *The Public Interest, 4*, 70-75.

Cooper, R., & Jordan, W. J. (2003). Cultural issues in comprehensive school reform. *Urban Education, 38*(4), 380–397.

Datnow, A., Borman, G. D., Stringfield, S., Overman, L. T., & Castellano, M. (2003). Comprehensive school reform in culturally and linguistically diverse contexts: Implementation and outcomes from a four-year study. *Educational Evaluation and Policy Analysis, 25*(2), 143–170.

Downey, D. B., von Hippel, P. T., & Broh, B. A. (2004). Are schools the great equalizer? Cognitive inequality during the summer months and the school year. *American Sociological Review, 69*(5), 613–635.

Dryfoos, J. G., & Maguire, S. (2002). *Inside full-service community schools*. Thousand Oaks, CA: Corwin.

Duncan G. J., & Brooks-Gunn, G. (2000). Family poverty, welfare reform, and child development. *Child Development, 71*(2), 188–196.

Eamon, M. K. (2001). The effects of poverty on children's socioemotional development: An ecological systems analysis. *Social Work, 46,* 256–266.

Engle, P. L., & Black, M. M. (2008). The effect of poverty on child development and educational outcomes. *Annals of the New York Academy of Sciences, 1136,* 243–256.

Evans, G. W. (2004). The environment of childhood poverty. *American Psychologist, 59*(2), 77–92.

Goldberg, M. F. (2001). *Lessons from exceptional school leaders*. Alexandria, VA: Association for Supervision and Curriculum Development.

Gorski, P. C. (2007, Spring). The question of class. *Teaching Tolerance, 31.* Retrieved from http://www.tolerance.org/magazine/number-31-spring-2007/feature/question-class

Green, M., & Hulme, D. (2005). From correlates and characteristics to causes: Thinking about poverty from a chronic poverty perspective. *World Development, 33*(6), 867–879.

Guo, G., & Harris, K. M. (2000). The mechanisms mediating the effects of poverty on children's intellectual development. *Demography, 37*(4), 431–447.

Hannon, L. (2003, November). Poverty, delinquency, and educational attainment: Cumulative disadvantage or disadvantage saturation? *Sociological Inquiry, 73*(4), 575–594

Harding, D. J., Lamont, M., & Small, M. L. (2010, May). Reconsidering culture and poverty. *Annals of the American Academy of Political and Social Science, 629,* 6–27.

Hickey, S., & Bracking, S. (2005). Exploring the politics of chronic poverty: From representation to a politics of justice? *World Development, 33*(6), 851–865.

Hulme, D., & McKay, A. (2005). *Identifying and measuring chronic poverty: Beyond monetary measures*. Paper presented at the International Conference on the Many Dimensions of Poverty, International Poverty Center, Brasilia, Brazil.

Jacob, B. A., & Ludwig, J. (2009). Improving educational outcomes for poor children. *Focus, 26*(2), 56–61.

Karelis, C. (2009). *The persistence of poverty: Why the economics of the well off can't help the poor*. New Haven, CT: Yale University Press.

Ladd, H. F. (2012). Education and poverty: Confronting the evidence. *Journal of Policy Analysis and Management, 31*(2), 203–227. Retrieved from http://EconPapers.repec.org/RePEc:wly:jpamg r:v:31:y:2012:i:2:p:203-227

Lareau, A., & Weininger, E. B. (2003). Cultural capital in educational research: A critical assessment. *Theory and Society,* 567–606.

Lubienski, S. T. (2002). Research, reform, and equity in US mathematics education. *Mathematical Thinking and Learning, 4*(2–3), 103–125.

Mantsios, G. (1998). What does labor stand for? *WorkingUSA: The Journal of Labor & Society, 2*(4), 24-40. doi: 10.1111/j.1743-4580.1998.tb00111.x

Mistry, R. S., Vandewater, E. A., Huston, A. C., & McLoyd, V. C. (2002). Economic well-being and children's social adjustment: The role of family processes in an ethnically diverse low-income sample. *Child Development, 73,* 935–951.

Moore, K. A., Redd, Z., Burkhauser, M. A., Mbwana, M. P. P., & Collins, A. (2009, April). *Children in poverty: Trends, consequences, and policy options* (Child Trends Research Brief No. 2009-11). Washington, DC: Child Trends. Retrieved from http://www.childtrends.org

Mortenson, T. G. (2000). Educational attainment and state economic welfare. *Postsecondary Education Opportunity, 100*, 9–16.

Nadel, W., & Sagawa, S. (2000). *America's forgotten children. Child poverty in rural America*. Retrieved from http://www.savethechildren.org/afc_pdf_02.shtml

Noddings, N. (1984). *Caring*. Berkeley: University of California Press.

Noddings, N. (2005). Caring in education. *The encyclopedia of informal education*. Retrieved from http://www.infed.org/biblio/noddings_caring_in_education.htm

Noguera, P. A. (2003). *City schools and the American dream: Reclaiming the promise of public education*. New York: Teachers College Press.

Oakes, J. (1985). *Keeping track: How schools structure inequality* (2nd ed.). New Haven, CT: Yale University Press.

Payne, R. K. (2005). *A framework for understanding poverty* (4th ed.). Highlands, TX: aha! Process.

Ravallion, M. (2007). Inequality is bad for the poor. In J. Micklewright & S. Jenkins (Eds.), *Inequality and poverty re-examined* (pp. 37–61). Oxford, England: Oxford University Press.

Rodriguez, A. J. (2001). From gap gazing to promising cases: Moving toward equity in urban education reform. *Journal of Research in Science Teaching, 38*(10), 1115–1129.

Sass, T., Hannaway, J., Xu, Z., Figlio, D., & Feng, L. (2010). *Value added of teachers in high-poverty schools and lower-poverty schools*. CALDER Working Paper 52. Washington, DC: The Urban Institute. Retrieved from http://www.urban.org/UploadedPDF/1001469-calder-working-paper-52.pdf

Scutari, M. (2009). "The great equalizer": Making sense of the Supreme Court's equal protection jurisprudence in American public education and beyond. *Georgetown Law Journal, 97*, 917–943.

Seccombe, K. (2000). Families in poverty in the 1990s: Trends, causes, consequences, and lessons learned. *Journal of Marriage and Family, 62*(4), 1094–1113.

Stefkovich, J. A. (2006). *The best interests of the student: Applying ethical constructs to legal cases in education*. New York: Taylor & Francis.

Stefkovich, J., & Begley, P. T. (2007). Ethical school leadership: Defining best interest of students. *Educational Management, 35*(2), 205–224.

Sullivan, A. (2001). Cultural capital and educational attainment. *Sociology, 53*, 893–912.

Tickamyer, A. R., & Duncan, C. M. (1990). Poverty in rural America. *Annual Review of Sociology, 16*, 67–86.

Venkatesh, S. A. (2006). *Off the books: The underground economy of the urban poor*. Cambridge, MA: Harvard University Press.

Wahnee, R. L. (2010). *The effect of instructional supervision on principal trust*. (Doctoral dissertation). University of Oklahoma, Norman.

Wilson, W. J. (2009). *More than race: Being black and poor in the inner city*. New York: Norton.

CHAPTER ONE

Contemporary Issues in High Poverty Schools

Can Schools Make a Difference in Student Outcomes? Implications for Educational Leadership

Lisa Bass & Susan C. Faircloth

> *Most antipoverty policies focus on lifting adults out of poverty. These policies are often controversial because of an unavoidable tension between the desire to help people who have been unlucky and the motivation to encourage hard work and punish socially unproductive behavior. In contrast, successful education policies can not only help reduce poverty over the long term by making poor children more productive during adulthood, but also foster economic growth that expands the 'pie' for everyone. Educational interventions also benefit from a compelling moral justification. Disadvantaged children should not be punished for the circumstances into which they are born, and improved education policy is one of the best ways to prevent this from happening.* (Jacob & Ludwig, 2009, p. 61)

Chapter One begins by discussing poverty as it relates to the context of schools and schooling. Working definitions are provided in order to contextualize the ways in which we approach the study of poverty and its relationship to schools and the process of schooling. Our goal is to begin to articulate the ways in which the practices of school leaders can and should be shaped to meet the needs of the schools and communities. When leadership is tailored to the needs and desires of those being served (in this case, students and families from high poverty backgrounds), goals can be reached more effectively. We conclude this chapter with implications for schools and school leadership.

Understanding the Complexity of Poverty

In writing this book, we were struck by the difficulty of conceptualizing and defining poverty in concrete terms. Although we recognize that poverty is a complex notion blurred by its multifaceted nature and the multiple perspectives that come into play when defining this term, we acknowledge that poverty is too often defined in terms of dollars or economic earning power. An example of this is the U.S. Census's definition of poverty, which utilizes a combination of income, family size, and relative cost of living when establishing poverty levels (U.S. Census Bureau, n.d.a).

Although numbers have been used to demarcate those living at or below the poverty level, the construct of poverty is complicated by the fact that one's relative position in society is also defined in terms of social status, social standing, and lifestyle. In this way it is measured by the fluidity of one's actions, his or her degree of freedom, and how much power he or she exudes or has access to (http://www.combatpoverty.ie/povertyinireland/whatispoverty.htm#WhatIsPoverty).

Thus, we argue that there are at least two perspectives from which to view poverty—the first, a purely economic perspective, and the other, a socio-cultural-economic perspective. The following definition illustrates this point:

> People are living in poverty if their income and resources (material, cultural, and social) are so inadequate as to preclude them from having a standard of living which is regarded as acceptable by [U.S.] society generally. As a result of inadequate income and other resources people may be excluded and marginalized from participating in activities which are considered the norm for other people in society. (www.combatpoverty.ie, p. 1)

This definition takes into account the fact that those living in poverty experience more differential levels of physical, cultural, and social mobility than do their peers with higher levels of socioeconomic status.

Although it is not realistic to argue that individual schools and school leaders can move generations of families and communities out of poverty, it is realistic to believe that schools and school leaders can work to equip current and future generations of children and youth with the tools needed to moderate or mediate the effects of poverty, thus lessening the likelihood that these children and youth will grow up to live in poverty. We believe that all children and youth have the right to access and accumulate the social and cultural capital (Bourdieu, 1983) that will enable them to be productive citizens. This includes access to after-school activities such as music lessons, supplemental tutoring, and sports; culturally enriching activities; the opportunity to live in a safe neighborhood; involvement of parents, siblings, and community members who understand and can assist with school work; and even the nutritional benefits derived from eating healthy, high-quality, well-balanced meals. All of these factors help to garner a healthy life for children. Ultimately, the availability or lack of these and other resources impacts student learning and achievement. If schools are to be successful in working with students from high poverty backgrounds, school leaders must take into account differences in student socioeconomic status and background as they work to mitigate the effects of these differences. We believe that the narrowing of the achievement gap is dependent upon a real understanding of the effect of poverty on students and their schools and the efforts educational leaders and other educators exert toward meeting the needs of students from high poverty backgrounds.

Characteristics of Intergenerational and Persistent Poverty

As previously indicated, poverty is a complex condition influenced by a multitude of economic, political, societal, and familial variables. Too often, families are impacted by a pattern of poverty that for some seems insurmountable. This seemingly endless cycle of poverty, transmitted from one generation to the next, is termed *intergenerational poverty* (e.g., Corcoran, 1995). This type of poverty is not usually caused by a single catastrophic incident, such as illness, childbirth, death, or job loss, that negatively impacts one's financial standing; in contrast, this term best describes those whose lives have been impacted by poverty due to a combination of causes. According to the Chronic Poverty Research Center (CPRC) at the University of Birmingham, United Kingdom (Moore, 2001), poverty is demonstrated by the absence of transfer of capital in one or more of the following areas: human, sociocultural, socio-political, financial/material, and environmental/natural. Intergenerational poverty occurs when there is a lack of 'capital' passing from one generation to the next, resulting in the transmission of poverty from one generation to the next. The CPRC also notes that intergenerational poverty is used to describe the 'private' transmission of poverty from older generations of individuals and families to younger generations (especially, but not solely, from parents to children).

Poverty and Well-Being
Children who are born in poverty tend to spend intermittent periods of their life both in and out of poverty; however, many of them are unable to break this cycle and as a result spend the bulk of their lives in poverty (Ratcliffe & McKernan, 2010). There are myriad consequences of being poor, including a decline in both physical and psychological well-being (Amato & Zuo, 1992; Hartley, 2004). Those who are born poor are also at risk for dropping out of school, giving birth as a single parent during the teenage years, and having difficulty in obtaining employment (Urban Institute, n.d.). Poverty is highest among those who do not earn a high school diploma, live by themselves, or experience poor health. Although not limited to a particular racial or ethnic group, poverty tends to be concentrated among African Americans and Hispanics (Issa & Zedlewski, 2011).

Factors that Perpetuate the Cycle of Poverty
For many, the effects of poverty are cyclical, as factors associated with poverty are interrelated and interdependent (see Figure 1.1). Factors contributing to the cycle

of poverty include low levels of education, limited access to gainful employment, lack of reliable transportation, and health and psychological disparities. Although these factors may seem distinctly different, they are intricately related and difficult to respond to in isolation in the face of poverty.

The first factor to be discussed is the low level of education typically associated with poverty. Most individuals who come from high poverty backgrounds generally have a lower degree of education than their counterparts from higher socioeconomic contexts (e.g., U.S. Census Bureau, n.d.b). Many individuals in poverty had negative schooling experiences, or their family members recounted reports of negative experiences in school (e.g., Lott, 2001). Regardless of their experience in school, many individuals living in poverty are perceived as uninterested in school or labeled as lagging behind their peers academically. Although this may be true for some, for others the struggle to succeed academically may be related to difficulties in relating to the educational system or to identifying ways in which education is applicable to their own futures (Borman & Overman, 2004; Ceballo, McLoyd, & Toyokawa, 2004). Without positive learning experiences, nurturing educator-student relationships, or a sense of purpose for education, many students from a high poverty context will find it difficult to identify with the mission and purpose of schools. Those who are unable to connect with the educational system may emotionally or physically tune out or drop out of school. Failure to complete school, in turn, contributes to and helps to sustain poverty.

Without the credentials associated with formalized education, many individuals are unable to secure or maintain gainful employment. In challenging economic times, when it is difficult for individuals with college degrees to secure gainful employment in their field of study, it is nearly impossible for those without a high school diploma to secure gainful employment. Access to such employment is further limited by geographic isolation often found in rural areas. Many of these areas are also economically depressed and have lost profitable local businesses, leaving local inhabitants without work (Kusmin & Hertz, 2010).

The lack of gainful employment is also associated with a lack of reliable transportation (Child Trends, n.d.). People experiencing high poverty are often not able to afford cars and the maintenance costs associated with car ownership. Therefore, they are less able to travel to places of employment that are off bus routes or to get to doctors or other important appointments. They are also less able to get to school or to participate in after-school events. The lack of reliable transportation has implications for those living in high poverty contexts, as their mobility is severely limited. Without gainful employment and transportation, those living in poverty are less able to afford quality and safe housing. The absence of highly valued homes also reduces the amount of money that school districts gain from property taxes, which can promote disparities in the quality of education received by students living in wealthy, middle-class, or high poverty contexts (Reber, 2011; Vaught, 2009).

The lack of quality housing, employment, and transportation is also linked to food and water insecurity, especially among the working poor (e.g., Schafft, Jensen, & Hinrichs, 2009). Those living in high poverty conditions often do not have access to quality fruits, vegetables, and other nutrient-dense foods. For example, poorer urban neighborhoods often lack full-service, fully stocked grocery stores. Unfortunately, it is difficult and expensive for those without cars to travel miles to adequate grocery stores. As a result, many settle for what is easiest or most convenient and accessible—fat-laden fast foods and what is offered at corner convenience stores. This results in what some have described as "food deserts" (e.g., Burke, Keane, & Walker, 2010; Morland, Wing, Diez Roux, & Poole, 2002; Schafft et al., 2009). The lack of quality nutrition contributes to obesity and other health disparities among those living in poverty, which can lead to poorer school

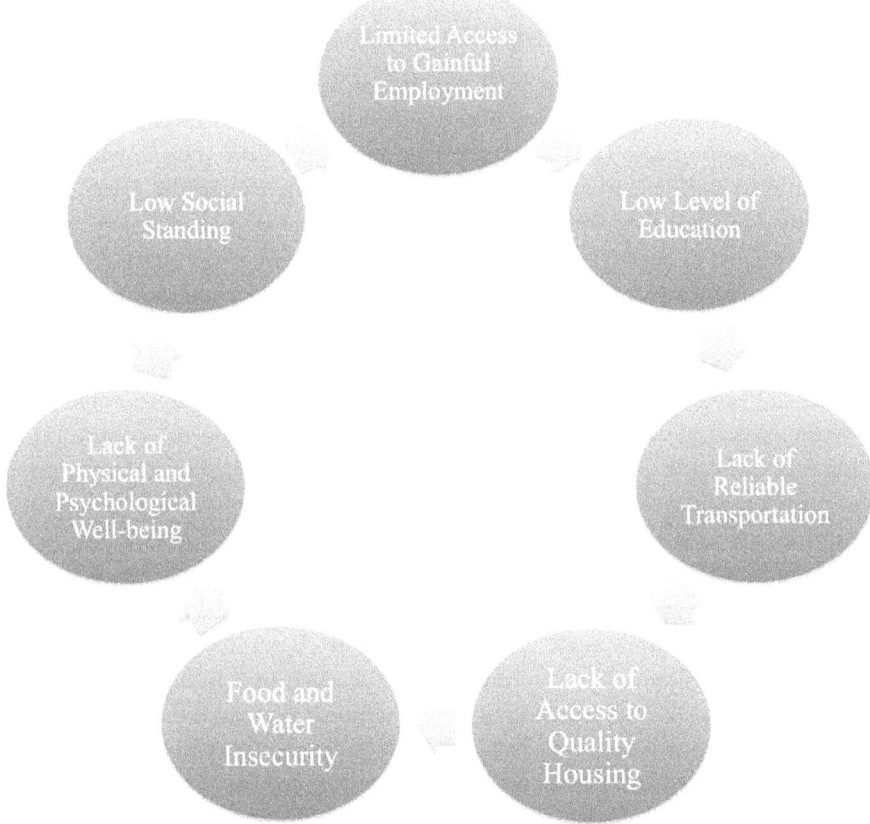

Figure 1.1 Factors Perpetuating the Cycle of Poverty

and work attendance (e.g., Jyoti, Frongillo, & Jones, 2005), further perpetuating the cycle of poverty (Ceballo et al., 2004; Green & Hulme, 2005). Poor diet may result in developmental delays, which often result in poor school achievement as well as emotional and behavioral challenges (e.g., Brooks-Gunn & Duncan, 1997). Individuals living in poverty in urban areas also experience similar difficulties due to long distances to supermarkets and lack of transportation (Blank, 2005; Commins, 2004).

Though no fault of their own, all of these factors, when combined, point to the increased social and resource challenges faced by students living in high poverty contexts, as well as to the inequalities experienced by children and youth in high poverty contexts. These factors not only speak to the increased challenges experienced by students from high poverty contexts but also to challenges that must be confronted and considered by educators and educational leaders if we are to be successful in closing the experience and achievement gaps between students from high poverty backgrounds and their wealthier peers.

The Challenge for School Leaders

In working with students from high poverty backgrounds, school leaders must consider the impact of poverty on children, their learning, and their achievement. School leaders must also consider potential differences in the ways in which poverty manifests itself in urban and rural contexts. Most important, what factors should be considered by educational leaders as they engage in decision-making processes related to their leadership of schools in high poverty contexts? As former public school educators, professors of educational leadership, and individuals who have witnessed the impact of poverty on our own family members and communities, we are intrigued, and often perplexed, by these challenges. Our desire to explore these challenges emanates from our own personal and professional need to better understand, and respond, to the factors that enable the continuation of poverty from one generation to the next. This is an issue of great concern for school leaders and policy makers as they work to create equitable schooling opportunities for all students.

This nation's founders believed that schools would act as "the great equalizer," meaning that after one attained an education she or he would have similar access to the same opportunities as the wealthy and middle classes (Downey, von Hippel, & Broh, 2004; Oakes, 1985). As Mann (1848, as cited in Scutari, 2009, p. 930) wrote, "Education . . . beyond all other devises of human origin, is the great equalizer of the condition of men, —the balance-wheel of the social machinery." Although education has served to open doors for many, it has not functioned as the great equalizer that it was intended to be (e.g., Nieto, 2008; Scutari, 2009). In many cases, education has not empowered children and youth to attain a higher socioeconomic status than their parents and families. As a result, inequalities in wealth and social standing continue to persist, thus exemplifying the potential for social and economic reproduction of inequality vis-à-vis education (e.g., Collins, 2009).

Working to Minimize Intergenerational Poverty
In order for equality of opportunity to be realized, schools must equip students from all socioeconomic groups with the knowledge, skills, and dispositions needed to be successful both within and beyond their current social and economic status. This requires students from all socioeconomic groups to interact within and beyond the confines of schools. Despite the failure of many schools to promote positive relationships with all students, we view schools not only as the natural environment to promote equity among social groups but also as a vehicle through which parity can be reached. What is unique about schools is that all children have access to schooling, thus creating somewhat of a common experience or bond among this nation's children and youth. Schools are one of the few places where students from all socioeconomic backgrounds come together on a daily basis. This requires schools to meet the needs of a wide range of students and their families. Our hope is that this common experience or bond can be made more equitable so that it serves to promote the academic, social, and economic success of our children and youth rather than serving to promote inequities and disparities.

Educational leaders and policy makers can aid students in transcending the potentially negative effects of poverty, but to do so, they must first be willing and able to understand the material, social, and emotional effects of living in poverty, and be committed to ensuring that these effects are significantly lessened, if not eradicated. We believe that educational leaders are in a position to disrupt and discontinue the cycle of low achievement among children and youth from high poverty contexts. Unfortunately, many schools are limited in their understanding of what students need to improve their academic and social standing. Although research (e.g., Foorman, Schatschnieder, Eakin, Fletcher, & Francis, 2006; Taylor, Pearson, Peterson, & Rodriguez, 2003) has been published on how to teach students from high poverty contexts, until recently there has been comparatively less literature that addresses specific aspects of leading schools that service students from high poverty contexts.

Understanding the Contexts in which Poverty Occurs
Educational leaders must understand the terrain in which they work before engaging in visionary (Brown & Anfara, 2003; Hoyle, English, & Steffy, 1998; Sashkin, 1988; SEDL, n.d.; Ylimaki, 2006), transformational (e.g., Cooper, 2009; Finnigan, 2012; Giles, Johnson, Brooks, & Jacobson, 2005; Hallinger, 2003), or transformative (e.g., Shields, 2011) leadership. If not, the vision for the academic environment in which they lead will likely not be based upon principles of leadership that are effective for the environment or context in which they work. In order to be successful, school leaders must know how to lead according to the type of

environment they work in. This requires time on the job and in the school and community. Unfortunately, principal and teacher turnover is significantly higher in high poverty schools (Grissom, 2011; Kraft et al., 2012; Loeb, Kalogrides, & Horng, 2010). The research above suggests this lack of retention is due in large part to the complexities surrounding high poverty schools.

High Poverty Schools in Urban Contexts

As previously mentioned, the shape and form of poverty sometimes differ depending upon the context in which poverty occurs. Urban poverty is discussed widely in education and is often the precursor to conversations concerning low student achievement (e.g., Lippman, Burns, & McArthur, 1996). The conditions that plague many urban environments are said to be a large part of the reason that children coming from high poverty urban backgrounds perform less well than their middle- and upper class counterparts. According to the 2010 Census, *urban* is defined as a densely populated area, having at least 2,500 residents. There are more than 3,500 urban areas in the United States, with a total population of nearly 250 million. This equates to approximately 81% of the total U.S. population. The most densely populated urban areas are located in California, New York, Hawaii, and Nevada. The most populated urban areas are located in New York, New Jersey, Connecticut; California; Indiana; Florida; and Pennsylvania, Delaware, and Maryland (U.S. Census, n.d.b). Causes or antecedents of poverty in urban areas include, but are not limited to: decreased earning potential; decreased value of earnings; segregation; exodus of families who are not considered poor; and the effects of local, state, and federal policies that have failed to take into consideration the impact of these policies on life in urban areas (Gephart, 1997).

High Poverty Schools in Rural Contexts

There is a commonly accepted myth that poverty occurs most often or is most concentrated in urban areas. Tickamyer and Duncan (1990) offer a historical rebuttal to this myth by demonstrating the extent to which poverty occurs in rural areas and the factors that serve to drive poverty in these areas. A report by the National Conference of State Legislatures (2003, as cited in Carlson, 2006) revealed that of the 200 persistently poor counties in the United States, 195 of them were rural. According to this report, "Children living in rural areas are more likely to experience high levels of poverty compared to urban children, are more likely to experience substance abuse, and are more likely to be exposed to substance abuse, and are more likely to lack appropriate health care" (p. 88).

Among the causes of rural poverty are lack of economic opportunity in rural areas, limited opportunities for mobility, and lack of community investment. One of the primary differences between urban and rural poverty is found in the geography or location of poverty within these areas. Rural areas are typically characterized by more open spaces that are farther away from the city center. Rather than densely populated neighborhoods saturated with multiple-family housing projects, rural poverty is characterized by more sparsely populated areas and fewer city amenities. Rural poverty is seen when there is a lack of economic and social resources in areas characterized as rural. Therefore, rural poverty is often less visible than urban poverty. According to Brown, Swanson, and Barton (2003), rural poverty is just as severe as urban poverty but it tends to be hidden. As with high poverty urban areas, there is variation in the level of poverty in rural areas. Further, access to resources varies depending upon location and the severity of the poverty in rural areas. Some rural areas have shopping, restaurants, and other conveniences within a few miles, while other rural areas are far from amenities that urbanites take for granted. Many residents of severely impoverished rural areas lack access to basic utilities and sometimes may not have reliable Internet access or telephone service (e.g., Bissell, 2004) or even electricity and indoor plumbing, depending on the region of the country and area (Green & Hulme, 2005).

Regardless of Location, Poverty Impacts Schools
While rural poverty and urban poverty have the lack of resources in common, the implications for and behind this lack are often different. Similarities in urban and rural poverty include the lack of financial resources to purchase quality food, housing, and medical care. Another unexpected similarity in the lives of impoverished urban and rural youth is the presence of violence. According to a study conducted by Carlson (2006), "Higher levels of poverty are significantly related to higher levels of direct exposure to violence in school, and to dissociation, damaging property of others, and some measures of violence proneness" (p. 87). Carlson attributes the higher incidence of poverty in rural areas to increased access to guns and other weapons.

Additional implications to be considered by educational leaders include sociocultural aspects specific to urban and rural environments, as well as cultural norms and rituals unique to the communities that exist within each of these locales. Becoming familiar with these aspects is important for all schools regardless of the socioeconomic level of the school. Establishing relationships and becoming acquainted with the students, parents, and communities served by the school is one way of establishing a platform of support for the educational leader on which to build and nurture his or her vision for the school. Without this support, the school leader will have to work much harder to achieve this vision and even to accomplish the most basic of tasks.

Considerations for Exceptional Educational Leaders

As noted above, expectations for, as well as actual levels of, academic performance are often different, and in some cases lower, for students who hail from either urban or rural poverty backgrounds. Fortunately, there is no sound reason for lower academic achievement among economically disadvantaged students when educators meet their needs. However, some educators and educational leaders who have been unsuccessful at educating students from high poverty backgrounds reason that the disadvantages faced by these students inhibit their ability to learn and achieve at the highest levels (Clotfelter, Ladd, Vigdorn, & Wheeler, 2006; McGee, 2004). As educators, we recognize the challenges and disadvantages faced by students from high poverty backgrounds, and we acknowledge that these challenges can adversely affect student achievement. However, we believe that if proper measures are taken to meet the unique needs of students in high poverty contexts, the obstacles faced by these students can be overcome. We also believe that the challenges associated with high poverty contexts can be moderated with the support of school leaders who possess the knowledge, skills, and dispositions associated with exceptional educational leadership.

To combat and overcome the adverse effects of poverty, exceptional educational leaders know that they must engage students with care and hope. Carlson (2006) notes that hopelessness can lead to violence and other associated ills. When students do not feel a sense of hope, they are more prone to engage in destructive behaviors that endanger not only themselves but also those around them. This type of reaction can perpetuate a cycle of violence in high poverty contexts. When students engage in violent behaviors, their peers feel less safe. This lack of safety contributes to their carrying weapons, engaging in violence in self-defense, and joining dangerous gangs for protection (Goetz, 2003). Leaders who are successful in working with students who are fearful of violence realize the importance of establishing a safe learning environment for students.

What Sets Exceptional Educational Leaders Apart from Their Peers?

Exceptional leaders recognize that there are no magic bullets or a one-size-fits-all panacea approach to educational leadership—especially in high poverty contexts. They resist the temptation to adopt programs and to practice reform efforts without careful consideration of their context. Exceptional leaders know the environment in which they lead and the implications their environment has on school leadership. As such, they learn their environment and make the necessary exceptions or adaptations to facilitate student learning. For high poverty schools, this means observing what their students lack, as well as the multiple gifts and talents these students bring to schools (e.g., Moll, Amanti, Neff, & Gonzalez, 2001), and providing students with what they need to be successful, whether it is physical, psychological, or psychosocial. Most often, the needs of students from high poverty backgrounds span a delicate mix of all of the above. Effective exceptional educational leaders use their resources, management skills, and social capital to acquire the necessary resources to meet the needs of their students.

Exceptional leaders take into account the level of poverty of their students and the reasons behind their poverty. They note whether the poverty is attributable to individual reasons—reasons that point directly to the behavior or actions of those living in poverty; structural reasons—reasons that point to structural inequality in society; and fatalistic or catastrophic reasons—a string of bad luck, such as the loss of a job due to economics or illness (Bullock, 1999; Feagin, 1975; Furnham, 1982). In our experience, we have found that those leaders who are most successful at establishing an atmosphere conducive to learning in high poverty schools are those who learn the reason behind their students' socioeconomic conditions and adjust their leadership accordingly to meet their students' needs. Such learning occurs as they invest in establishing relationships with their students, their families, and their communities. Exceptional leadership is a framework for educational leadership that explores strategies for meeting individuals' needs—regardless of their socioeconomic standing.

Questions to Consider

1. To what extent is poverty an issue in your current school? What are the factors that contribute to poverty in your community and school? To answer these questions, you will need to conduct an environmental scan. See Johnson and Kruse (2009)[1] for a brief overview of environmental scanning and its use in schools.[2] The goal of environmental scanning is to identify conditions, both internal and external to an organization, that impact the way in which the organization currently functions as well as to prepare the organization to respond to changing conditions in the future. Using the results of the environmental scan, identify three ways in which your school leadership can work to moderate the effects of poverty in your school.

2. Reflecting on Activity 1, what role, if any, does your school leadership currently play in working to reduce poverty in your school and community? To what extent is it the responsibility of school leaders to fight against the conditions that work to sustain poverty in schools and communities?

3. Research has demonstrated that leading schools in high poverty contexts may require a different leadership style than leading schools in middle and upper socioeconomic contexts. Do you believe this to be true? Why or why not? If so, what are the differences in ways that school leaders might approach leadership in high poverty contexts?

4. When poverty in schools is discussed, the issues of poverty are often discussed in general rather than delineating differences between urban and rural settings. Do you see the need to differentiate between high poverty urban and rural settings? Why or why not? What considerations would you make for working with students in each type of setting?

5. Although poverty generally connotes lack, there are multiple ways in which the reasons for poverty have been conceptualized. Do you see a need, as a school leader, to consider the factors that contribute to and work to sustain poverty? Why or why not? How might you respond differently to individuals who come from backgrounds of persistent poverty as opposed to those who find themselves experiencing circumstantial or short-term conditions that place them in poverty?

Notes

1. Johnson, B. L., & Kruse, S. D. (2009). The educational leader as decision maker: Themes, inferences, and conclusions. In B. L. Johnson & S. D. Kruse. *Decision making for educational leaders: Underexamined dimensions and issues* (pp. 205–218). Albany: State University of New York Press.
2. For additional information regarding environmental scans, see: (1) Thomas, P. S. (1980). Environmental scanning: The state of the art. *Long Range Planning, 13,* 20–25. (2) Morrison, J. L. (1985). Establishing an environmental scanning process. In R. Davis (Ed.), *Leadership and Institutional Renewal: New Directions for Higher Education, 49* (pp. 31–37). San Francisco: Jossey-Bass.

References

Amato, P. R., & Zuo, J. (1992, Summer). Rural poverty, urban poverty, and psychological well-being. *The Sociological Quarterly, 33*(2), 229–240.

Barrett, C. B. (2010). A century-long perspective on agricultural development. *American Journal of Agricultural Economics, 92*(2), 447–468.

Bissell, T. (2004). The digital divide dilemma: Preserving Native American culture while increasing access to information technology on reservations. *Journal of Law, Technology & Policy, 1,* 129–150.

Blank, R. M. (2005). Poverty, policy, and place: How poverty and policies to alleviate poverty are shaped by local characteristics. *International Regional Science Review, 28*(4), 441–464.

Borman, G. D., & Overman, L. T. (2004). Academic resilience in mathematics among poor and minority students. *Elementary School Journal, 104*(3), 177–195.

Bourdieu, P. (1983). The forms of capital. In J. G. Richardson (Ed.), *Handbook of theory and research for the sociology of education* (pp. 241–258). New York: Greenwood Press.

Brooks-Gunn, J., & Duncan, G. J. (1997, Summer–Fall). The effects of poverty on children. *Children and Poverty, 7*(2), 55–71.

Brooks-Gunn, J., Duncan, G. J., & Aber, J. L. (Eds.). (1997). *Neighborhood poverty: Context and consequences for children.* New York: Russell Sage Foundation.

Brown, K. M., & Anfara, V. A., Jr. (2003). Paving the way for change: Visionary leadership in action at the middle level. *NASSP Bulletin, 87*(635), 16–34.

Brown, D. L., Swanson, L. E., & Barton, A. W. (2003). *Challenges for rural America in the twenty-first century.* University Park: Pennsylvania State University Press.

Bullock, H. E. (1999). Attributions for poverty: A comparison of middle-class and welfare recipient attitudes. *Journal of Applied Psychology, 29,* 2059–2082.

Burke, J. G., Keane, C. R., & Walker, R. E. (2010). Disparities and access to healthy food in the United States: A review of food deserts literature. *Health and Place, 16(5),* 876–884.

Carlson, K. T. (2006). Poverty and youth violence exposure: Experiences in rural communities. *Children & Schools, 282*, 87–96.

Ceballo, R., McLoyd, V. C., & Toyokawa, T. (2004). The influence of neighborhood quality on adolescents' educational values and school effort. *Journal of Adolescent Research, 19*(6), 716–739.

Child Trends Data Bank. (n.d.). Parental involvement in schools. Retrieved from http://www.childrensdatabank.org

Clotfelter, C., Ladd, H. F., Vigdor, J., & Wheeler, J. (2006). High-poverty schools and the distribution of teachers and principals. *North Carolina Law Review, 85*, 1345.

Collins, J. (2009). Social reproduction in classrooms and schools. *Annual Review of Anthropology, 38*, 33–48. Retrieved from http://www.annualreviews.org

Commins, P. (2004). Poverty and social exclusion in rural areas: Characteristics, processes, and research issues. *Sociologia Ruralis, 44*(1), 60–75.

Cooper, C. W. (2009). Performing cultural work in demographically changing schools: Implications for expanding transformative leadership frameworks. *Educational Administration Quarterly, 45*(5), 694–724.

Corcoran, M. (1995). Rags to rags: Poverty and mobility in the United States. *Annual Review of Sociology, 21*, 237–267. Retrieved from http://links.jstor.org/sici?sici=0360-0572%281995%2921%C237%3ARTRPAM%3E2R.0.CO%3B2-L

Downey, D. B., von Hippel, P. T., & Broh, B. A. (2004). Are schools the great equalizer? Cognitive inequality during the summer months and the school year. *American Sociological Review, 69*(5), 613–635.

Feagin, J. (1975). *Subordinating the poor*. Englewood Cliffs, NJ: Prentice-Hall.

Finnigan, K. S. (2012, March). Principal leadership in low-performing schools: A closer look through the eyes of teachers. *Education and Urban Society, 44*(2), 183–202.

Foorman, B. R., Schatschnieder, C., Eakin, M. N., Fletcher, L. C., & Francis, D. J. (2006, January). The impact of instructional practices in grades 1 and 2 on reading and spelling achievement in high poverty schools. *Contemporary Educational Psychology, 31*(1), 1–29.

Furnham, A. (1982, November). Why are the poor always with us? Explanations for poverty in Britain. *British Journal of Social Psychology, 21*(4), 311–322.

Gephart, M. A. (1997). Neighborhoods and communities as contexts for development. In J. Brooks-Gunn, G. J. Duncan, & J. L. Aber (Eds.), *Neighborhood poverty: Context and consequences for children* (pp. 1–43). New York: Russell Sage Foundation.

Giles, C., Johnson, L., Brooks, S., & Jacobson, S. L. (2005, September). Building bridges, building community: Transformational leadership in a challenging urban context. *Journal of School Leadership, 51*(5), 519–545.

Goetz, E. (2003). *Clearing the way: Deconcentrating the poor in urban America*. New York: Urban Institute Press. Retrieved from http://www.urban.org/uipress/

Green, M., & Hulme, D. (2005). From correlates and characteristics to causes: Thinking about poverty from a chronic poverty perspective. *World Development, 33*(6), 867–879.

Grissom, J. A. (2011). Can good principals keep teachers in disadvantaged schools? Linking principal effectiveness to teacher satisfaction and turnover in hard-to-staff environments. *Teachers College Record, 113*(11), 2552–2585.

Hallinger, P. (2003). Leading educational change: Reflections on the practice of instructional and transformational leadership. *Cambridge Journal of Education, 33*(3), 329–351.

Hartley, D. (2004). Rural health disparities, population health, and rural culture. *American Journal of Public Health, 94*(10), 1675–1678

Hoyle, J. R., English, F. W., & Steffy, B. W. (1998). *Skills for successful 21st century school leaders: Standards for peak performers*. Arlington, VA: American Association of School Administrators.

Issa, P., & Zedlewski, S. R. (2011, February). *Poverty among older Americans, 2009*. Retirement Security Data Brief. Urban Institute, Program on Retirement Policy.

Jacob, B. A., & Ludwig, J. (2009, Fall). Improving educational outcomes for poor children. *Focus, 20*(2), 56–61.

Jyoti, D., Frongillo, E., & Jones, S. (2005). Food insecurity affects school children's academic performance, weight gain, and social skills. *Journal of Nutrition, 135,* 2831–2839.

Kraft, M. A., Papay, J. P., Charner-Laird, M., Johnson, S. M., Ng, M., & Reinhorn, S. K. (2012). Committed to their students but in need of support: How school context influences teacher turnover in high-poverty, urban schools. Cambridge, MA: Harvard Graduate School of Education. Retrieved from http://scholar.harvard.edu/mkraft/publications/committed-their-students-need-support-how-school-context-influences-teacher-turn

Kusmin, L., & Hertz, T. (2010). *Rural America at a glance, 2010 edition* (Economic Information Bulletin EIB–68). Washington, DC: Economic Research Service, U.S. Department of Agriculture.

Lippman, L., Burns, S., & McArthur, E. (1996). *Urban schools: The challenge of location and poverty*. Washington, DC: U.S. Department of Education, Office of Educational Research and Improvement, National Center for Educational Statistics.

Loeb, S., Kalogrides, D., & Horng, E. L. (2010). Principal preferences and the uneven distribution of principals across schools. *Educational Evaluation and Policy Analysis, 32*(2), 205–229.

Lott, B. (2001). Low-income parents and the public schools. *Journal of Social Issues, 57*(2), 247–259.

McGee, G. W. (2004). Closing the achievement gap: Lessons from Illinois' golden spike high-poverty high-performing schools. *Journal of Education for Students Placed at Risk, 9*(2), 97–125.

Moll, L., Amanti, C., Neff, D., & Gonzalez, N. (2001, Spring). Funds of knowledge for teaching: Using a qualitative approach to connect homes and classrooms. *Theory Into Practice, 31*(2), 132–141.

Moore, K. (2001). *Frameworks for understanding the inter-generational transmission of poverty and well-being in developing countries* (Chronic Poverty Research Centre Working Paper 8). Birmingham, England: International Development Department, School of Public Policy, University of Birmingham. Retrieved from http://www.chronicpoverty.org/uploads/publication_files/WP08_Moore.pdf

Morland, K., Wing, S., Diez Roux, A., & Poole, C. (2002). Neighborhood characteristics associated with the location of food stores and food service places. *American Journal of Preventive Medicine, 22*(1), 23–29.

Nieto, S. (2008). Public education in the twentieth century and beyond: High hopes, broken promises, and an uncertain future. *Harvard Educational Review, 75*(1), 43–64.

Oakes, J. (1985). *Keeping track: How schools structure inequality* (2nd ed.). New Haven, CT: Yale University Press.

Picucci, A. C., Brownson, A., Kahlert, R., & Sobel, A. (2002). *Driven to succeed: High-performing, high-poverty, turnaround middle schools: Vol. 1. Cross-case analysis of high-performing, high-poverty, turnaround middle schools*. Austin: Charles A. Dana Center, University of Texas at Austin.

Ratcliffe, C., & McKernan, S-M. (2010, June). *Childhood poverty persistence: Facts and consequences*. Urban Institute. Brief 14. Retrieved from http://www.urban.org

Reber, S. J. (2011). From separate and unequal to integrated and equal? School desegregation and school finance in Louisiana. *The Review of Economics and Statistics, 93*(2), 404–415.

Sashkin, M. (1988). The visionary principal: School leadership for the next century. *Education and Urban Society, 20*(3), 239–249.

Schafft, K. A., Jensen, E. B., & Hinrichs, C. C. (2009). Food deserts and overweight schoolchildren: Evidence from Pennsylvania. *Rural Sociology, 74*(2), 153–177.

Scutari, M. (2009). "The great equalizer": Making sense of the Supreme Court's equal protection jurisprudence in American public education and beyond. *Georgetown Law Journal, 97,* 917–943.

SEDL. (n.d.). Leadership characteristics that facilitate school change. Retrieved from http://www.sedl.org/change/leadership/character.html

Shields, C. M. (Ed.). (2011). *Transformative leadership: A reader. Counterpoints: Studies in the postmodern theory of education. Volume 409.* New York: Peter Lang.

Taylor, B. M., Pearson, D., Peterson, D. S., & Rodriguez, M. C. (2003). Reading growth in high-poverty classrooms: The influence of teacher practices that encourage cognitive engagement in literacy learning. *Elementary School Journal, 104*(1), 3–28.

Tickamyer, A. R., & Duncan, C. M. (1990). Poverty and opportunity structure in rural America. *Annual Review of Sociology, 16,* 67–86.

Urban Institute. (n.d.). Born poor? Half of these babies will spend most of their childhood in poverty; significantly more likely to be poor 30 years later. Retrieved from http://www.urban.org/publications/901356.html

U.S. Census Bureau. (n.d.a). Poverty: How the Census Bureau measures poverty. Retrieved from www.gov/hhes/www/poverty/about/overview/measure.html

U.S. Census Bureau. (n.d.b). Historical income tables. Table F–18: Educational attainment of householder—families with householder 25 years old and over by median and mean income. Table F–19: Years of school completed—families with householder 25 years old and over by median and mean income. Retrieved from http://www.census.gov/hhes/www/income/data/historical/families/index.html

Vaught, S. E. (2009). The color of money: School funding and the commodification of black children. *Urban Education, 44*(5), 545–570.

Ylimaki, R. M. (2006). Toward a new conceptualization of vision in the work of educational leaders: Cases of the visionary archetype. *Educational Administration Quarterly, 42*(4), 620–651.

CHAPTER TWO

The Role of Educational Leaders in High Poverty Schools

A Framework for a Revised Job Description

Lisa Bass & Susan C. Faircloth

> *Research tells us that principals are the linchpins in the enormously complex workings, both physical and human, of a school. The job calls for a staggering range of roles, psychologist, teacher, facilities manager, philosopher, police officer, diplomat, social worker, mentor, PR director, coach, cheerleader. The principalship is both lowly and lofty. In one morning, you might deal with a broken window and a broken home. A bruised knee and a bruised ego. A rusty pipe and a rusty teacher.* (Sherman, 2000, p. 1)

In Chapter Two, we attempt to outline the knowledge, skills, and dispositions, as well as the philosophies and practices, of exceptional leaders in high poverty contexts. Research demonstrates that principals play an integral role in schools, particularly those that are designated as high poverty schools (e.g., Leithwood, Louis, Anderson, & Wahlstrom, 2004; Louis, Leithwood, Wahlstrom, & Anderson, 2010). We believe that exceptional educational leaders are those who operate out of an ethic of care, engender trust, possess strong interpersonal skills, exhibit flexibility and resourcefulness, assume effective instructional leadership, and work to facilitate school-community engagement. These leaders view themselves as responsible not only for the academic and intellectual development of their students and their schools, but also for the social, emotional, and physical well-being of these students and schools, and ultimately of their communities.

The Knowledge, Skills, and Disposition of Successful School Leaders in High Poverty Contexts

Above all other qualities qualities, principals of schools in high poverty contexts must be **caring** and **compassionate** (Leithwood & Riehl, 2003; Noddings, 2006;

Peterson & Deal, 1998; Sebring & Bryk, 2000). As is discussed in Chapter Three, educational leaders face an ethical and moral imperative to provide a suitable learning environment for their students—regardless of the socioeconomic characteristics of the student population they serve (Noddings, 1988). In the case of students from high poverty contexts, this will likely mean that school leaders will be required to go above and beyond what is generally expected to best meet the needs of their students. In order for principals to be motivated to take on these added roles and responsibilities, they must be caring leaders who are moved to act when they see injustices and inequality perpetrated against students in their schools. The key to their motivation to meet the unique needs of their students emanates from the way in which they view their responsibility to serve their students, combined with a moral and ethical calling to ensure the needs of students from socially and economically disadvantaged backgrounds are met. According to Noddings (1988), educators must care enough to be moved to corrective action. Though Noddings writes mostly about caring in the behaviors of teachers, the same is true for principals and other school personnel whose work touches the lives of students.

Although care is typically demonstrated in personal interactions with individuals and groups, the school leader must go beyond this basic form of caring to ensure that care and compassion are embedded within the policies and practices enacted within the school. Siddle-Walker and Snarey (2004), Noddings (1988), and Cassidy and Bates (2005) describe this as a form of institutional caring that requires school leaders and their staff to go beyond the espoused notion of caring to a more authentic and visible form of enacted caring in which the school is structured as a change agent, with the ultimate goal of assisting students and their families in moving beyond the constraints and challenges of poverty.

When leaders care, they learn the backgrounds and needs of their student body. They take the extra time required to understand where their students come from; the social and political dynamics of the communities in which their schools are located; and how best to relate to their students, their parents, and the communities in which they reside. In their study on the traits of effective leaders in high poverty contexts, Kannapel, Clements, Taylor, and Hibpshman (2005) found that this investment in students, parents, and the surrounding community is a trait of effective leaders in high poverty contexts.

Meeting the needs of students and their families not only calls for care and compassion, this also calls for strong **interpersonal skills and the establishment of trust**. As Lunenberg (2010) argues, principals must also be able to effectively communicate with their students, parents, families, and staff. According to Lunenberg, principals spend 70% to 80% of their time engaged in interpersonal communication (p. 5). Effective interpersonal skills foster trust and effective communication. The development of strong interpersonal skills is directly related to one's level of interpersonal intelligence, or the ability to decipher what spoken and unspoken cues, such as action or inaction and body language, mean. This level of interpersonal competence can result from one's innate ability, but is most often honed with practice and time spent with students and their parents, during which time the school leader comes to understand their circumstances. For many, interpersonal skills are often developed as the result of learning from mistakes made in working with individuals from diverse backgrounds. In the case of schools, when students and parents feel comfortable with and trust the school leader, he is better able to garner increased involvement and support from both parents and students. This is critically important as the principal works to secure buy-in and support for programs or services he wishes to implement.

Trust is also important to overall school improvement efforts (Bryk & Schneider, 2003). Trust is discussed at length in Chapter 4. During changes in programs or project implementation, it is also important that teachers be communicative and cooperative. When a principal introduces new programs or initiatives for the school, it is imperative that teachers and other faculty and staff support the building leader in his or her efforts. If he lacks the support of building faculty, harmful dissension and toxicity can result and is easily detectable by students, parents, and the community (Peterson, 2002). When outside stakeholders detect strife in the school, trust is eroded, and support can wane on behalf of both parents and the community. Principals can avoid this by drawing upon their interpersonal skills while working with teachers and community stakeholders. (A discussion of school-community relations is presented in Chapter Six.) At the school level, school leaders must get to know their teachers on a professional level, being careful not to unduly cross the boundaries between their personal and professional lives in and out of school. Although teachers may desire for their principals to be their friend, principals should first build a strong foundation of mutual *professional* respect (Bird, Wang, Watson, & Murray, 2012; Cosner, 2009).

Principals can get to know their teachers professionally as they provide principal-led professional development, and also through their formal and informal observations and resulting discussions. Principals who regularly 'partner' with their teachers to improve their teaching and classroom environment, rather than those who seek to 'catch them' doing something wrong, position themselves to forge positive professional relationships (see Brewster & Railsback, 2003, for an overview of literature on principal-teacher trust and relationships). In other words, principals who seek to catch the teachers in their charge doing something right and who work with them to improve their instruction and classroom environment provide fertile ground for stronger, more positive professional interpersonal relationships with their teachers. As strong professional relationships are forged, principals will inevitably get to know their teachers (and parents and students) on a more personal level. This type of knowing makes way for increased understanding and empathy, as well as intercultural competence.

Establishing authentic and meaningful relationships requires school leaders to engender a sense of trust between themselves, their colleagues, students, parents, and community members. The establishment of trust is a critically important responsibility for schools leaders (e.g., Bryk & Schneider, 2003), especially when it involves working with parents from low socioeconomic and urban areas (e.g., Comer et al., 1996, as cited in Bryk & Schneider, 2003). A comprehensive review of literature by Tschannen-Moran and Hoy (2003) identified five elements of trust involving schools. These included benevolence—the school leader is concerned with the best interests of his or her students, faculty, and staff; reliability—the school leader acts in a dependable and consistent manner; competence—the school leader is capable of doing the job he or she has been tasked with doing; honesty—the school leader acts honorably; and openness—the school leader acts in a transparent manner. In a subsequent publication, Vodicka (2006) argued that there are four essential elements of principal trust. These include consistency, compassion, communication, and competency. Building on these notions of trust, Bryk and Schneider (2003) identified two unique aspects of what they describe as relational trust, a type of trust evident in organizations, such as schools, in which the relationships between and among members of the school community are critical to the functioning and success of the organization. Key to relational trust is the principle of respect. With this respect comes a willingness to engage others in open and ongoing dialogue even when they disagree on certain issues or points. The second aspect of relational trust is personal regard or genuine care and concern for others. In Chapter Four, Wahnee expands upon these notions of trust by describing ways in which teacher trust of principals is fundamental to the principal's establishment of strong and effective instructional leadership.

As Wahnee illustrates in Chapter Four, exceptional educational leaders serve as **the instructional leaders of their schools** (e.g., Jacobson, 2008). In this role, they not only champion high academic expectations for their students, but also ensure teachers receive high-quality **professional development**, mentoring, and guidance needed to ensure that students have the opportunity and resources necessary to learn and achieve on par with (or by exceeding) their peers. If principals are to be viewed as the instructional leaders of their schools, it is imperative that they establish and maintain good working relationships with teachers. Teachers also need to feel understood and valued by their principals (Supovitz, Sirinides, & May, 2010). **Connecting with teachers** helps principals accomplish their objectives as school leaders (Grissom & Loeb, 2011). Unfortunately, time away from the classroom can create a professional gulf between principals and teachers. Out of the classroom and in the administrative realm, principals are encumbered with a multiplicity of non-instructional responsibilities associated with being a building leader. As a result, they often lose sight of what it is like to be a teacher. The pressure experienced by principals as they are caught between the demands of the school, the school district, parents, teachers, and students can serve to dampen their memories of the issues most important to classroom teachers. Successful principals are able to reach into the recesses of their memory to recall what it was like to be a part of the teacher culture so that they can take this into account as they communicate with teachers, and establish building policies that concern them. When a principal is sensitive to the needs and experiences of teachers, he is more likely to gain their favor and support.

As is true with teachers and other school staff, one of the most important relationships involving the school leader is the relationship with parents and families. Principals who are trusted help to pave the way for **facilitating parent involvement**. By including parents in educational decision-making, principals demonstrate the importance of active parental involvement, as well as their desire to promote positive parent-school relationships (e.g., Tschannen-Moran, 2001). One way to do this is to talk with parents about their children and their goals for their children's education. Reaching out to parents in meaningful ways requires some level of understanding of the parent's perspective. To do so, the principal must invest time learning where parents come from—geographically and ideologically—and how their perspectives have been formed. To obtain this information, principals should take time to speak with parents as they visit the school, observe parent patterns of behavior in school-related events and activities, and talk with teachers regarding their experiences with parents. The information attained by taking the time to learn basic information about parents will be appreciated, and also save the principal from embarrassing and costly mistakes during interactions with parents. If principals attempt to learn the types of challenges faced by the families in their school, basic facts regarding their lifestyle, disciplinary practices, and prior experiences with schooling, they will likely be perceived as more connected and caring by parents (e.g., Epstein, 1995). Again, this perceived caring, and willingness to actively engage parents, will help to establish trust and lay the foundation for more authentic partnerships between parents and students.

Once trust is established, the principal must also work to maintain ongoing parental involvement (Hoerr, 2005). This can be achieved in part by providing parent information and training workshops; inviting parents to fulfill specific roles within the school (parents are more likely to help when the requests for help are clearly defined); supporting school-parent groups, such as the PTA or PTO; and by meeting with parents to discuss their concerns regarding their child's well-being, even when students are faring well (Blankstein, 2004; Christenson, 2004; Constantino, 2003; Hoerr, 2005). Principals who are able to connect and partner with parents make their jobs easier, as they are not as encumbered with firefighting and handling discipline problems—which frees them to devote a greater percentage of their time to instructional leadership.

In addition to establishing trust and connecting with teachers, staff, and parents and families, exceptional leaders in high poverty schools must be **flexible and resourceful**—even if resources are less than abundant. Principals in high poverty schools are often underfunded and called to maximize already limited resources (Jacobson, Brooks, Giles, Johnson, & Ylimaki, 2004). As a result, principals who work in under-resourced environments are required to be flexible enough to function effectively, even if their best-laid plans are altered on short notice. When funding is limited and budgeting is tight, plans are sometimes interrupted, as administrators are forced to juggle resources to simultaneously meet the learning needs of students and unanticipated operational emergencies, such as maintenance costs, teacher shortages, or other pressing needs. In addition to financial shortfalls at the school level, financial shortages among parents and students create added difficulties for the school, especially when students and their parents are unable to afford their part of school-related expenses.

As demonstrated above, flexibility and resourcefulness are clearly two characteristics that contribute to the success of principals in high poverty schools (e.g., Charles A. Dana Center, 1999). These principals must think and act strategically on behalf of their students and their life situations as well as those situations that occur in their schools. Just as school leaders may face a higher incidence of emergencies and unexpected situations where they are called to stretch funds, their students face similar challenges due to their families' limited financial resources. Students and their families living in high poverty situations are more likely to experience crisis situations that they are unable to prevent or control due to their lack of money, which often equates to a lack of social power. Though problems are certainly not limited to students in high poverty contexts, many of these students do not have the resources available to them that their middle-class peers do to protect against financial and other emergencies. As a result, some of the situations that principals in high poverty schools encounter include a shortage of food (Brown & Pollitt, 1996) in students' homes, homelessness, abuse, and increased rates of teenage pregnancy and parenting (e.g., Brooks-Gunn & Duncan, 1997; Shanks & Danziger, 2010). Unintended, circumstances surrounding poverty can result in instability and trauma, which can enter and interrupt the learning environment. Such outside forces (i.e., food insecurity, homelessness, abuse, increased pregnancy), as noted by the research indicated (Brooks-Gunn & Duncan, 1997; Brown & Pollitt, 1996; Shanks & Danziger, 2010), can infiltrate the educative process and schooling. It is difficult, if not impossible, for children to shed their home lives at the schoolhouse door; thus, exceptional principals in high poverty contexts may be called upon, and should thus be prepared, to assist their students and their families through some of their difficulties.

Awareness and understanding of the environment in which he or she works is another skill or area of competency that a principal who seeks to be successful in a high poverty environment must possess. For many principals this will entail becoming culturally aware and responsive (Bustamante, Nelson, & Onwuegbuzie, 2009; Lindsey, Roberts, & Campbell-Jones, 2004); having the ability and willingness to get to know the linguistic and cultural diversity of students, their families, and communities; and acting in ways that honor and respect such diversity. However, for principals in socioeconomically challenged schools, this level of competence often extends beyond a simple awareness of the diversity represented among their schools' students, teachers, and staff. Acting in a culturally competent manner means that one is aware of, attempts to understand, appreciates, and incorporates diversity into the teaching and learning processes within one's school. These principals are charged with understanding and responding to the factors that place these schools and their communities at risk as well as those factors that can be harnessed as potential mediators of the socioeconomic and other societal risks these students and communities face both within and outside of the school. These principals must strive to understand and honor their students', parents', and teachers' perspectives when engaged in decision-making activities, professional conversations, and even during casual interactions. A principal who is mindful with respect to individuals' differing perspectives takes into account how their identities and backgrounds impact their learning or teaching styles as well as the extent to which they participate in school in academic and non-academic ways. For example, this may include anything from being mindful of students' religious holidays and celebrations; students' need to have access to technology to support their learning experiences; or parents' reluctance to actively engage in the schooling process due to their own negative schooling experiences.

While understanding the cultural backgrounds of teachers, students, and parents is critically important (Ladson-Billings, 1995), understanding the conditions that contribute to students and their families living in poverty is also paramount to being successful at working with children and their parents from high poverty backgrounds. **Understanding factors that contribute to intergenerational poverty** will assist principals in knowing how best to structure their leadership style toward reducing the effects of poverty. In doing so, the school leader will help to establish a school community and culture that operates in ways that are counterintuitive toward the continuance of generational poverty. In fact, a principal who considers the factors contributing to intergenerational poverty in his leadership style has the power to minimize the cycle of poverty by promoting equally high expectations for all students (Kannapel et al., 2005). Kannapel and colleagues studied effective high poverty schools and found that principals who led effective schools in high poverty communities held the same high expectations for all students regardless of their socioeconomic status. Although they took the time to get to know and support students from lower socioeconomic backgrounds, they expected just as much from these students as they did from their more socioeconomically advantaged students. What this tells us is that principals can influence the attitudes and academic and social identities of their students by holding high expectations for all of them, regardless of socioeconomic status. Exceptional educational leaders envision their students in preparation for living lives out of poverty—even before the actual shift occurs. This means treating students with respect and exposing them to quality educational experiences previously reserved for more advantaged or privileged students. As such, principals should seek a wide array of funding and supportive services to ensure their schools have the resources necessary to expose their students to the best possible education. Geoff Canada of the Harlem Children's Zone is a prime example. The Harlem Children's Zone is a full service community charter school in which Geoff Canada planned and organized a high poverty school community in which students would receive advantages such as a high quality education, including extended days, tutoring, and exposure to quality cultural capital. The Harlem Children's Zone and other full service community schools are discussed further below. Mr. Canada has successfully embedded these principles within that school (Page & Stone, 2010).

As noted above, parents and principals should partner in working to improve students' outcomes. When principals are able to partner with parents, parents can then work toward aligning the home experience with their child's school experience. This alignment simplifies the educative process for students, parents, and teachers, and promotes an easier transition between home and the school for children. When principals, teachers, and parents work together, the resulting consistency helps students to know what to expect, and to fulfill these expectations. For many students, these partnerships are sufficient; however, for students from high poverty backgrounds, schools may be called upon to meet needs that go beyond academics. For these students, **community-school partnerships** are essential. One such example is the Harlem Children's Zone (HCZ), a charter school system in which students are accepted at the elementary school level, and are provided an education through high school and support through college, creating, in a sense, a pipeline for successful educational opportunities for students, mostly from high poverty backgrounds, who might have otherwise failed. HCZ is exceptional in that the school provides wraparound educational, social, and medical services in which students are cared for from birth through college. The school provides a longer school day and after-school support, summer support, tutoring services, and even parent training. The school, much like a community school, is connected to the community and seeks to provide for students so that they are fully supported in their educational endeavors.

As the school leader, Geoffrey Canada boasts high expectations of all students, as all students are expected to go to college, and there are mechanisms set in place from beginning to end to ensure that students do not fall through the cracks. For example, supportive services such as programs for expectant mothers and young children are provided in the community, separate from the school, so that *all interested community members* can take advantage of them. Consequently, most community members desire for their children to be admitted to HCZ, but only a select number of students who are accepted into the school through a lottery process have the privilege of enrolling. Guiding principles, such as high expectations, the provision of services that meet the needs of students and support them, and parental education and involvement, influence the development of rules and policies, as well as the administrative practices at HCZ. As a result, many students in the HCZ pipeline program are successful in school as well as have a plan and desire to succeed post-graduation (Page & Stone, 2010).

Many students from high poverty backgrounds desire to do well and have the hope of a prosperous future; however, they often do not have the direction or support needed to assist them in framing and accomplishing their goals. This is where the exceptional educational leader can make a difference. Economically disadvantaged students need to have access to the highest quality curricula and textbooks, as well as supplemental educational and cultural experiences before school, after school, and during extended breaks from school. They also need the opportunity to participate in activities that will bolster their social (e.g., Noguera, 2001) and cultural capital (Hardaway & McLloyd, 2009). Further, academic supports, such as effective tutoring programs and targeted academic counseling, should be in place to ensure that students are aware of the range of educational options and opportunities available to them. It is this type of intensive support that will aid in lessening the gap between the quality of educational experiences of students from diverse economic backgrounds. When principals facilitate the delivery and availability of a wide range of services provided by the school to assist in the growth of students from high poverty contexts, this demonstrates to students and parents that the principal believes in the students' possibilities for prosperous futures, and that he has invested in resources to ensure their best possible outcomes. In turn, students are more likely to exert effort toward the success of their own future when they see this level of investment in their lives early on. One model that provides such wraparound support is the **community schools model**, which is discussed in brief in Chapter Six.

We believe that the community schools model is potentially less stratifying and isolating than other traditional models of serving students from socioeconomically disadvantaged backgrounds. For example, students from lower socioeconomic backgrounds, such as those who are eligible for free or reduced price lunch, have been traditionally singled out as beneficiaries of certain school-based programs (e.g., Mirtcheva & Powell, 2009; Wong & Meyer, 1998). In contrast, the community schools model benefits the entire school by making a wide range of supports and services available to students and their families regardless of income level. Rather than stigmatizing students and making them feel branded or labeled, they simply become one of many students who receive supportive services.

In addition to bringing supports and services to students, we believe strongly that **exceptional educational leaders promote an ethic of reciprocity**, a commitment to giving back to their schools and communities. Reciprocity is empowering and affirming for students and their communities. Service learning is a prime example of how school leaders can promote this ethic. Other ways are through formal and informal community projects, and by openly rewarding students who are 'caught serving others.' Instilling an ethic of reciprocity can be seen as a means of fighting back against deficit thinking, which attempts to minimize the potential contributions of individuals from socioeconomically disadvantaged backgrounds. In effect, exceptional educational leaders and their staff model for their students the importance of giving back, which in turn helps to promote this ethic of reciprocity.

Although traditional job descriptions may not explicitly cite the need to espouse an ethic of reciprocity, school leaders who desire to promote civic engagement and to minimize the effects of poverty on their students, schools, and communities will pay attention to this important role and include it as part of their school leadership strategies (Zaff & Lerner, 2010). Not only does advancing an ethic of reciprocity promote self-sufficiency and self-efficacy, but it also promotes increased academic connectedness and self-esteem (Karcher, 2009). As educators, we have a moral and ethical responsibility to shield our students from the damaging effects of forces such as poverty and to equip our students with the knowledge and skills necessary to live productive lives in and outside of school. By showing them their potential to make an impact on the well-being of their schools and communities, we demonstrate to students that they are much more than the sum of their socioeconomic status. This is a difficult challenge for school leaders as they balance their duty to provide supports and services within the school with their duty to ensure students are not negatively labeled or tracked as a function of where they come from or what they have in terms of financial resources. As leaders, we must have it be our goal to provide equitable learning experiences and environments for students. Yet, in many cases, equity is reached through provision of supplemental programs and supports designed specifically for economically disadvantaged students. While meeting their nutritional and other needs, such programs can serve to set these students apart from their peers in ways that are potentially damaging to their self-esteem and emotional well-being. We are certainly not suggesting that these programs and services not be provided; we are simply suggesting that these services be provided in ways that are not stigmatizing to students.

If students are to overcome the barriers of poverty, they will need to view themselves as self-sufficient and capable; as givers rather than receivers; as advantaged rather than disadvantaged. This way of thinking can be promoted as students are encouraged to see their worth and value and their ability to contribute to the greater society. Students' ability to identify as important contributors to society can result from experiencing what it is like to act in the role of the 'giver' or the 'benefactor.' In effect, students are taught to embrace the ethic of reciprocity, or giving back (Deckop, Cirka, & Anderson, 2003). Principals who facilitate activities and programs that allow their students to give back to their communities demonstrate to students that they have much to give and that their gifts are valued. Service learning is one way principals can facilitate such a culture of contributing (Billing, 2000; Furco & Root, 2010). Through service learning, Billing found that students not only learned to give back, they also improved their interpersonal skills and their ability to relate to diverse groups. This experience also had a positive impact on their career exploration and aspirations.

School leaders' ability to **connect to, relate to, and leverage community resources** is imperative for the accomplishment of the objectives noted above (Catano & Stronge, 2006). Community partnerships will assist and support the principal as he attempts to connect to parents, as well as in providing resources to students. The support and resources provided by community partnerships will vary by community; however, the principal's ability to identify valuable community resources, to gain community buy-in, as well as to negotiate working relationships with community partners is an important skill for principals of high poverty schools. After identifying prospective community members, principals must reach out to them in ways that they will be receptive to. After they have community members' buy-in, principals must lay out clear expectations of their partners. When community partners are not sure how to assist schools, they often do nothing—despite their desire to improve schools. Negotiating the rules of engagement for relationships with community partners is achieved through the interpersonal communication skills discussed above.

Principals who involve community partners and who provide wraparound services in their buildings help to enact a model known as community schools (Bass, 2010; Dryfoos & Maguire, 2002; Epstein, 2001). As such, principals who implement the community schools model can be called **community schools facilitators**. This schooling model was developed on the premise that students from high poverty backgrounds lack many of the services and supports provided to their wealthier counterparts. Therefore, educational and social services must be provided in collaboration with schools (Bass, 2010; Dryfoos & Maguire, 2002; Epstein, 2001). Services provided by community schools vary depending upon the resources of the schools, external funding, and the resources available in the community, but generally include before- and after-school clubs and programs, tutoring, medical care, counseling, food and clothing programs, school gardens, and parent resources rooms. These services are designed to close the cultural, social, and achievement gaps between students from high poverty contexts and their wealthier counterparts (Bass & Gerstl-Pepin, 2011). Implementing a community schools model requires skilled coordination as well as the ability to manage a wide range of activities and programs. Whether a principal employs a full-service community school model, a more traditional design, or a blend, he needs to effectively manage the building and human resources at his disposal.

Finally, principals who are effective at leading high poverty schools must also demonstrate proficiency at **general building management** (e.g., personnel and budget) (Grissom & Loeb, 2011). Interestingly, in their study of principal effectiveness, Grissom and Loeb examined 42 functions of the principal role, and found that organization management, or general building management, was the only factor that could predict student achievement growth and other success measures. All of the above roles and responsibilities are part of general building management. When resources are limited and conditions are ripe for chaos, principals must have strategies and support systems in place to proactively address the ebbs and flows that can occur in high poverty schools. Stability, which students from high poverty contexts need, is the result of effective general building management. Principals who are proficient at general building management have a vision of how they want their buildings to function, as well as proactive strategies for handling the problems that regularly occur in schools, especially in the high poverty context.

Conclusion

Given the high level of commitment required to lead high poverty schools, not all school leaders are suited for this work. Therefore, principals should not be assigned to high poverty schools if they do not have the heart and disposition, skill set, and competence in interpersonal communication for working with students who need extra time and attention; do not demonstrate institutional care though the policies and practices they develop; or are not able or willing to devote the time and work necessary to ensure that the school operates smoothly and successfully in the high poverty context. Identifying appropriate leaders for schools in the high poverty context is the first step in ensuring that these schools are staffed with individuals who are positioned to make a positive, sustained impact on the lives of their students, their families, and their communities.

Questions to Consider

1. This chapter gets to the heart of the complexity of the role of the principal in a high poverty school. To what extent do the knowledge, skills, and dispositions outlined in this chapter accurately reflect the role of the principal in a high poverty school? How might these knowledges, skills, and dispositions be expanded or changed to better reflect exceptional leadership in a high poverty school?

2. If you could design a school with all of the supports and services you deem necessary for a successful school, what would this school look like? Develop an organizational chart, including brief descriptions of the roles and responsibilities for each of the positions in this school. (Use your imagination! Include roles and responsibilities that go beyond those found in traditional schools.)
3. How can education leadership programs better prepare principals (theoretically and experientially) who will work in high poverty contexts?

References

Bass, L. (2010). Refining tradition in education: Invoking an ethic of community. *Journal of School Public Relations, 31*, 68–90.

Bass, L., & Gerstl-Pepin, C. (2011). Declaring bankruptcy on educational inequity. *Educational Policy, 25*(6), 908–934.

Billing, S. H. (2000). Research on K–12 school-based service learning: The evidence builds. *Phi Delta Kappan, 81*(9), 658–664.

Bird, J. J., Wang, C., Watson, J., & Murray, L. (2012). Teacher and principal perceptions of authentic leadership: Implications for trust, engagement, and intention to return. *Journal of School Leadership, 22*(3), 425–461.

Blankstein, A. (2004). *Failure is not an option*. Thousand Oaks, CA: Corwin.

Brewster, C., & Railsback, J. (2003). *Building trusting relationships for school improvement: Implications for principals and teachers*. Portland, OR: Northwest Regional Education Laboratory.

Brooks-Gunn, J., & Duncan, G. J. (1997, Summer–Fall). The effects of poverty on children. *The Future of Children,* 55–71.

Brown, J. L., & Pollitt, E. (1996). Malnutrition, poverty and intellectual development. *Scientific American, 274*(2), 38–43.

Bryk, A. S., & Schneider, B. (2003, March). Trust in schools: A core resource for school reform. *Educational Leadership, 60*(6), 40–45.

Bustamante, R. M., Nelson, J. A., & Onwuegbuzie, A. J. (2009). Assessing schoolwide cultural competence: Implications for school leadership preparation. *Educational Administration Quarterly, 45*(5), 793–827.

Cassidy, W., & Bates, A. (2005, November). "Drop-outs" and "push-outs": Finding hope at a school that actualized the ethic of care. *American Journal of Education, 112,* 66–102.

Catano, W., & Stronge, J. H. (2006). What are principals expected to do? Congruence between principal evaluation and performance standards. *NASSP Bulletin, 90*(3), 221–237.

Charles A. Dana Center. (1999). *Hope for urban education: A study of nine high performing, high poverty, urban elementary schools*. Austin: University of Texas at Austin.

Christenson, S. L. (2004). The family school partnership: An opportunity to promote learning competency of all students. *School Psychology Review, 33*(1), 83–104.

Constantino, S. (2003). *Engaging all families*. Lanham, MD: Scarecrow Education.

Cosner, S. (2009). Building organizational capacity through trust. *Educational Administration Quarterly, 45*(2), 248–291.

Deckop, J. R., Cirka, C. C., & Anderson, L. M. (2003). Doing unto others: The reciprocity of helping behavior in organizations. *Journal of Business Ethics, 47*(2), 101–113.

Dryfoos, J., & Maguire, S. (2002). *Inside full-service community schools*. Thousand Oaks, CA: Corwin.

Epstein, J. L. (1995, May). School-family-community partnerships: Caring for the children we share. *Phi Delta Kappan, 76*(9), 701–712.

Epstein, J. L. (2001). *School, family and community partnerships: Preparing educators and improving schools.* Boulder, CO: Westview Press.

Furco, A., & Root, S. (2010). Research demonstrates the value of service learning. *Phi Delta Kappan, 91*(5), 8–15.

Grissom, J. A., & Loeb, S. (2011). Triangulating principal effectiveness: How perspectives of parents, teachers, and assistant principals identify the central importance of managerial skills. *American Educational Research Journal, 48*(5), 1091–1123.

Hardaway, C. R., & McLoyd, V. C. (2009). Escaping poverty and securing middle class status: How race and socioeconomic status shape mobility prospects for African Americans during the transition to adulthood. *Journal of Youth and Adolescence, 38*(2), 242–256.

Hoerr, T. R. (2005). *The art of school leadership.* Alexandria, VA: Association for Supervision and Curriculum Developments.

Hoy, W. K., & Tschannen-Moran, M. (2003). The conceptualization and measurement of faculty trust in schools. In W. K. Hoy & C. G. Miskel (Eds.), *Studies in leading and organizing schools* (pp. 181–207). Greenwich, CT: IAP.

Jacobson, S. L. (2008). Leadership for success in high poverty elementary schools. *Journal of Educational Leadership, Policy and Practice, 23*(1), 3–17.

Jacobson, S. L., Brooks, S., Giles, C., Johnson, L., & Ylimaki, R. (2004, December). *Successful school leadership in high poverty schools: An examination of three urban elementary schools.* Buffalo, NY: Graduate School of Education, University of Buffalo.

Kannapel, P. J., Clements, S. K., Taylor, D., & Hibpshman, T. (2005). *Inside the black box of high-performing high-poverty schools* [Report]. Lexington, KY: Prichard Committee for Academic Excellence.

Karcher, M. (2009). Increases in academic connectedness and self-esteem among high school students who serve as cross-age peer mentors. *Professional School Counseling, 12*(4), 292–299.

Ladson-Billings, G. (1995). Toward a theory of culturally relevant pedagogy. *American Educational Research Journal, 32*(2), 465–491.

Leithwood K. A., & Riehl, C. (2003, January). *What we know about successful school leadership.* Philadelphia, PA: Laboratory for Student Success, Temple University. Retrieved from http://csuphd.pbworks.com/w/file/fetch/62848668/what_we_know_about_school_leadership.pdf

Leithwood, K., Louis, K. S., Anderson, S., & Wahlstrom, K. (2004). *How leadership influences student learning.* New York: Wallace Foundation.

Lindsey, R. B., Roberts, L. M., & Campbell-Jones, F. (2004). *The culturally proficient school: An implementation guide for school leaders.* Thousand Oaks, CA: Corwin.

Louis, K. S., Leithwood, K., Wahlstrom, K. L., & Anderson, S. E. (2010*). Investigating the links to improved student learning. Final report of research findings.* Center for Applied Research and Educational Improvement, University of Minnesota and Ontario Institute for Studies in Eduction, University of Toronto.

Lunenberg, F. C. (2010). The principal and the school: What do principals do? *National Forum of Educational Administration and Supervision Journal, 27*(4), 1–12.

Mirtcheva, D. M., & Powell, L. M. (2009, October). Participation in the National School Lunch Program: Importance of school-level and neighborhood contextual factors. *Journal of School Health, 79*(10), 485–494.

Noddings, N. (1988). An ethic of caring and its implications for instructional arrangements. *American Journal of Education, 96*(2), 215–230

Noddings, N. (1992). *The challenge to care in schools: An alternative approach to education: Vol. 8. Advances in contemporary educational thought.* New York: Teachers College Press.

Noddings, N. (2006). Educational leaders as caring teachers. *School Leadership and Management, 26*(4), 399–345.

Noguera, P. A. (2001). Transforming urban schools through investments in the social capital of parents. In S. Saegert, J. P. Thompson, & M. R. Warren (Eds.), *Social capital and poor communities* (pp. 189–212). New York: Russell Sage Foundation.

Page, E. E., & Stone, A. M. (2010, January). *From Harlem Children's Zone to Promise Neighborhoods: Creating the tipping point for success.* Paper presented at the Family Impact Seminar, Washington, DC. Retrieved from http://www.familyimpactseminars.org/s_dcfis36report.pdf

Peterson, K. D. (2002). Positive or negative. *Journal of Staff Development, 23*(3), 10–15.

Peterson, K. D., & Deal, T. E. (1998). How leaders influence the culture of schools. *Educational Leadership, 56,* 28–31.

Printy, S. M., Marks, H. M., & Bowers, A. J. (2009). Integrated leadership: How principals and teachers share transformational and instructional influence. *Journal of School Leadership, 19*(5), 504–532.

Sebring, P. B., & Bryk, A. S. (2000). School leadership and the bottom line in Chicago. *Phi Delta Kappan, 81*(6), 440–443.

Shanks, T. R. W., & Danziger, S. K. (2010). *Social policy for children and families: A risk and resilience perspective.* Thousand Oaks, CA: Sage.

Sherman, L. (2000, Spring). The new principal. *NW Education.* Retrieved from http://www.educationnorthwest.org/webfm_send/1236

Siddle-Walker, V., & Snarey, J. (2004). *Race-ing moral formation: African-American perspectives on care and justice.* New York: Teachers College Press.

Supovitz, J., Sirinides, P., & May, H. (2010). How principals and peers influence teaching and learning. *Educational Administration Quarterly, 46*(1), 31–56.

Trail, K. (2000). Taking the lead: The role of the principal in school reform. *CSRD Connections, 1*(4), 1–4.

Tschannen-Moran, M. (2001). Collaboration and the need for trust. *Journal of Educational Administration, 39*(4), 308–331.

Vodicka, D. (2006, November). The four elements of trust. *Principal Leadership,* 27–30.

Wong, K. K., & Meyer, S. J. (1998, Summer). Title I schoolwide programs: A synthesis of findings from recent evaluation. *Educational Evaluation and Policy Analysis, 20*(2), 115–136.

Zaff, J. F., & Lerner, R. M. (2010). Service learning promotes positive youth development in high school. *Phi Delta Kappan, 91*(5), 21–23.

CHAPTER THREE

To What Extent Do Schools Have a Moral, Ethical, or Professional Imperative to Serve Students from Low Socioeconomic Backgrounds?

Lisa Bass & Susan C. Faircloth

> *Few would argue that the business of education is to ethically prepare all children to become responsible adults and productive citizens.* (Normore & Blanco, 2006, p. 229)

In this chapter, we argue that schools have a moral (Frick, 2009; Frick & Gutierrez, 2008), ethical (Starratt, 1991), and professional imperative to develop the educational capital of all students, regardless of their socioeconomic backgrounds (Bass, 2010; Bourdieu, 1984, as cited in Kelly, 2009; Coleman, 1994; Schultz, 1961). This requires schools to address the needs of the whole child, not just his or her academic needs. According to Jacobson (2008), effective school leaders are not only concerned with students' test scores and grades, but are also passionate, persistent, and committed to improving students' futures.

Meeting the disparate needs of children from different socioeconomic backgrounds can be taxing to the already limited resources of schools and school leaders (e.g., Kraft et al., 2012; Masumoto & Brown-Welty, 2009). Regardless, school leaders are charged with providing equitable programs and services for all students (e.g., Frick & Faircloth, 2007). To do this in high poverty schools requires school leaders who are knowledgeable of and comfortable in dealing with the sometimes heart-wrenching circumstances of their students and their families. Ultimately, the school leader's goal is to act in the best interests (Stefkovich, 2006; Stefkovich & Begley, 2007) of the children in his/her school, and to do so in a manner that is in accordance with his/her personal and professional moral and ethical principles.

The Ethic of Profession, an Ethical Imperative to Act in the Best Interest(s) of Children

Stefkovich discusses the professional ethics of educational leaders in her 2006 text, *The Best Interests of the Student: Applying Ethical Constructs to Legal Cases in Education*. In this text, Stefkovich establishes the ethical responsibility of the school leader to consider the best interests of students in all decision-making. The ethic of the profession for educational leaders posits that educational leaders lead with students in mind, aim to do them no harm, and allow students' needs to guide their leadership practice. This ethic asserts, "The focus on the student is the backbone of the profession and that students deserve zealous representation" (Shapiro & Stefkovich, 2010, p. 23). This ethical perspective is particularly relevant when leading in high poverty contexts. In a study of high performing, high poverty schools, Kannapel, Clements, Taylor, and Hibpshman (2005) found that successful leaders ensure alignment between curriculum and instruction, which requires time for individual student data analysis, while ensuring that their students receive individualized, tailored instruction; that teachers receive regular, targeted professional development; that there are consistent high expectations for all students; and that faculty work diligently to meet the academic and nonacademic needs (e.g., transportation, clothing, health care, and other services) of all students. This is an example of successful school leaders, and their staff, making administrative and managerial decisions in the best interests of the students in their charge.

Getting to Know Students, Their Families, and Their Communities

In order to lead in the best interests of students (e.g., Stefkovich & Begley, 2007) from high poverty backgrounds, it is important that school leaders understand the conditions that have resulted in these students, their families, and their communities living in poverty. Rather than espousing a deficit view of students and their families as living in poverty as a function of a culture of poverty, which Payne (2005) has described as resulting primarily from the way in which people think and act, getting to know students and their families on a personal level helps schools to understand, in a more nuanced way, the real reasons behind conditions of poverty. This is an essential part of understanding the issues and challenges students encounter in their daily lives (Kannapel et al., 2005). This level of familiarity also allows for the development and implementation of policies and practices aimed at building a more nurturing and welcoming school culture (e.g., Saifer, Edwards, Ellis, Ko, & Stuczynski, 2005), and enacting policies and practices that are sensitive to the unique needs of students from high poverty contexts (e.g., Kannapel et al., 2005; Masumoto & Brown-Welty, 2009; National Center for Children in Poverty, 2007).

Building Caring and Welcoming School Culture

If schools are to meet the needs of all students, school leaders must work to develop a school culture that is welcoming to and caring for all students. Research demonstrates that students, especially those from high poverty contexts, experience a greater sense of school identification and connectedness to school and achieve at higher rates when school leaders foster a caring school climate (Brand, Felner, Shim, Seitsinger, & Dumas, 2003; Cohen, McCabe, Michelli, & Pickeral, 2009; Libbey, 2004) that seeks to meet students' needs. A student-centered climate can be developed through the implementation of school policies, services, and practices that support the development of students from high poverty contexts (Fusarelli, 2011). In some cases, this requires policy changes and reform that match the unique contexts of the school (Skiba, 2000, 2008; Tebo, 2000). A prime example is the abolishment of punitive practices, such as zero tolerance policies, that run contrary to the democratic dispositions we aim to instill in children. Such policies suggest a lack of forgiveness and an inability to recognize the potential for change. Even more, these policies negate student voice. If a goal of education is to support the development and growth of children and youth as morally literate citizens (e.g., Bennett, 1988), then purely punitive policies may not be developmentally appropriate for schools as they do not allow students to grow and learn from their mistakes (e.g., McNeely, Nonemaker, & Blum, 2002).

Tebo (2000) argues that zero tolerance policies are counterintuitive to the demonstration of caring and the development of conflict resolution and coping strategies, especially when there is a conflict between students' home environment and the school environment. Rather than impose overly restrictive policies and practices, schools are encouraged to enact policies and practices that aid students in feeling valued and in turn assist them in adjusting more favorably to the school culture and environment. This is apt to occur when school leaders allow time for students to learn the school culture and when they create an open, democratic forum in which students are invited to discuss their issues and challenges, as well as given an opportunity to present situations from their perspectives (Dewey, 1914; Schultz, 1961).

Programming that demonstrates a commitment by school leaders to address students' diverse needs indicates to students that they are cared for by the adults in their school (Arroyo, Rhoad, & Drew, 1999). In meeting students' needs, it is critically important for school leaders not to focus only on the academic needs of their students, but to pay attention to students' social, emotional, and physical needs as well. After-school programs that include tutoring and food are examples of caring service offerings that express to students that they are of value and that school leadership cares enough to provide services to assist them along their journey toward attaining an education (Kannapel et al., 2005). Principals and teachers taking time to greet and welcome students each morning is another practice that can help to facilitate a positive school climate. These types of practices require minimal financial costs; however, they do require a time commitment each day on the part of school faculty. Each of these acts, no matter the cost, provides an opportunity for students to recognize and appreciate educators' attempts to connect and establish relationships with them.

The Ethic of Care: Educating from the Heart

Caring educators are committed to doing the work required to ensure all students' academic, social, emotional, and physical needs are met. This commitment is not something that can simply be taught, but in most cases emanates from an intrinsic disposition toward the care and nurturing of all students. Noddings posits caring as a moral imperative as she charges educators to care because it is the right thing to do (Noddings, 1992, 2005). Care theorists describe care as the motivating factor behind educating students from all socioeconomic backgrounds (Bass, 2009, 2012; Bass & Gerstl-Pepin, 2011; Noddings, 1984, 2005; Siddle-Walker & Snarey, 2004).

When educators and educational leaders choose to educate students because they care for them, they naturally go beyond basic job requirements or the call of duty to ensure the best possible education for students. In fact, educational leaders and educators who are motivated by an ethic of care are not acting out of a sense of duty, nor do they keep count of their good deeds or follow quotas for what they should do for students. Motivation for their actions is pure, as they sincerely want to do what is best for their students because they genuinely care for them. Such leaders have been known to pursue justice on behalf of their students (Bass, 2012), despite rules or outside expectations that may not be in the best interest of their students. An example of this is described in a study by Bass (2009), who found that the ethic of caring trumped the ethic of justice on behalf of African American women principals. In this qualitative study, participants shared several accounts of situations in which they prioritized caring in the best interest of students over following rules (the ethic of justice). Specifically, the principals in this study disagreed with the practice of zero tolerance policies because such policies did not allow their students to express themselves or to provide an explanation of their behaviors; further, these policies were so harsh that they could permanently damage the futures of students who they felt deserved another chance (Casella, 2003; Skiba, 2000, 2008; Skiba & Knesting, 2011). This study also demonstrated that when principals believe that a student will be harmed as a result of exercising a zero tolerance policy, they may choose to ignore zero tolerance policies, instead opting to act on an ethic of care, thereby addressing student infractions in other ways.

The foregoing demonstrates that while caring administrators care because they feel that it is the right thing to do, they also extend the act of caring from obligation to action (Bass, 2009; Noddings, 1992). Out of this ethic of care, there is a sense of obligation that dictates, "I must do what is right for my students." Caring school leaders foster an atmosphere conducive to student achievement by establishing a climate in which students from high poverty backgrounds can thrive. Actions that promote student achievement in high poverty schools include hiring caring teachers who believe in teaching all students; continuously training teachers on the identification and use of best practices in dealing with their students; implementing institutional care (Bass, 2010; Siddle-Walker & Snarey, 2004) by establishing rules and practices that serve the best interests of students by encouraging students to perform academically, rather than causing them to feel negatively, or to discourage them from coming to school; and demonstrating their belief in students by treating them fairly and maintaining high expectations. We also believe that school leaders demonstrate care by recognizing the importance of learning to provide for students' needs in ways that students appreciate, rather than imposing one's own view of what it means to care about others.

Holding High Expectations for All Students

The ethic of care is demonstrated when educational leaders and other educators have high expectations of all students (Mistry, White, Benner, & Huynh, 2009; Rubie-Davies, Peterson, Irving, Widdowson, & Dixon, 2010). This is especially important in high poverty contexts where expectations may be low (Kannapel et al., 2005; Rubie-Davies et al., 2010). Schools most successful in improving the learning experiences of children from high poverty contexts do not distinguish between what is expected of students with greater monetary resources, and those without (Kannapel et al., 2005). That is, students from high poverty backgrounds are more likely to achieve at levels on par with their wealthier peers when there is no wall of separation between students from different socioeconomic backgrounds. High expectations are also communicated to students by educators who do not engage in negative or deficit thinking directed toward students from lower socioeconomic backgrounds (Bomer, Dworin, May, & Semingson, 2009). According to Bomer et al. (2009), deficit thinking damages relationships between teachers and students, and also promotes lower level, lower quality instruction. This ultimately leads to lower achievement. If the ethic of care is to be enacted and demonstrated to students, educational leaders must engage in ethical professional practices (Frick & Faircloth, 2007; Stefkovich, 2006) and commit to treating all students equitably and with high expectations.

Role of the School Counselor in Providing Caring and Supportive Academic and Career Guidance

As the leader of the school, the principal is tasked with the responsibility to utilize school faculty in ways that most benefit students. Guidance and counseling form a resource that should be available for all students. According to the American

School Counselor Association (n.d.), "Professional school counselors participate as members of the educational team and use the skills of leadership, advocacy and collaboration to promote systemic change as appropriate" (p. 9). As such, school counselors are specially trained and have earned graduate degrees to learn how to meet the needs of their students. Since it is the principal's responsibility to provide an educational experience that promotes the best interests of students, the assurance of thoughtful, targeted counseling services is in order. Given the increasing demands of testing and accountability, along with other administrative pressures, in many cases the role of the school counselor has become less focused on the social and emotional needs of students and more focused on administrative and academic support duties (Reiner, Colbert, & Perusse, 2010). This is unfortunate, because counseling services are especially necessary in high poverty contexts in which school might be the only place where students receive much needed counseling and other supportive services (e.g., Amatea & Est-Olatunji, 2007; Dahir, Burnham, & Stone, 2009).

We argue that inasmuch as a central purpose of schooling is to prepare and equip all students for successful lives and careers after graduation from high school (Rury, 2002; Watras, 2002), school leaders should be intentional when establishing plans and processes to prepare individual students for life beyond school. To ensure that talent loss does not occur, principals need to implement effective programs, such as mentoring (Portwood, Ayers, Kinnison, Waris, & Wise, 2005), enhanced counseling services* (House & Sears, 2002), and career exploration. Students need to be introduced to these services as part of their schooling experience in order to fully benefit from them. Although students may opt to choose from a wide range of professions, all students should be prepared for the journey from school to personal and professional productivity and fulfillment. When school leaders fully support students from socioeconomically disadvantaged backgrounds, they nurture and support a hope for their futures that they might not otherwise encounter. To ensure that students are prepared for life post-school, schools must make students aware of the training and/or education necessary to further themselves in their chosen careers, and equip them with the necessary information to pursue the required education and training. Examples of this type of programming include mentoring programs, enhanced counseling services (House & Sears, 2002), targeted visits from professionals who mirror the student population as closely as possible, and numerous field trips that include exposure to high quality academic and professional experiences (Perry, Liu, & Pabian, 2010; Stern, Dayton, & Raby, 2010). Without purposeful exposure to such opportunities and resources, students from high poverty contexts are less likely to reach their academic and professional potential.

---

* This includes socioemotional and career counseling.

Students who have had the benefit of these types of educational experiences emerge from school better able to identify their strengths and weaknesses, and are equipped with the knowledge, skills, and dispositions required to successfully pursue an array of academic and career paths that match their interests and skill sets. This is the level of preparedness envisioned by those who first established the common school. We believe that this preparation should begin in elementary school, as students are introduced to a number of academic and career options, and continue through the completion of secondary school. The earlier that students identify their purpose and focus, the more likely they are to successfully complete their education.

Beginning academic and career exploration in elementary and middle schools can serve several important purposes. For example, students begin to see themselves in and consider academic and career options they may not have considered if they had not been exposed to them at an early age. Students may begin identifying with the positive behaviors and attitudes associated with their chosen career. Career exploration may also offer opportunities for students to be assigned to, or at least become acquainted with, positive role models in their chosen field. This early exposure enables students to have adequate time to prepare themselves for the field(s) they are interested in. An essential element of academic and career exploration involves learning the type of skills and preparation required to qualify for certain professions, as well as to perform the job. It also enables students, particularly those who are older, to intern or volunteer in the professions they are interested in. Not only should students be exposed to a diverse number of careers, and shown models of professions from diverse backgrounds, they should also be taught the level of training and education required to engage in their ideal professions. For example, if students are interested in a highly technical field, or a field such as medicine that requires high levels of science and mathematics, students should learn the relevance of math and science courses as early as possible. Academic and career exploration will not only expose students to a diverse array of professionals but will also facilitate their understanding of the necessity of excelling academically. Students also learn important information such as the benefits of scoring well on required college entrance exams or the need to complete advanced math and science courses in high school in order to be prepared for the intensive math and science courses that will be required in college.

In addition to academic and career counseling, students also benefit from personal counseling to address social and emotional issues they face. For some students, this incudes one-on-one mentoring and role modeling. For example, some students may have difficulty dealing with their emotions in constructive and socially acceptable ways. While some students will act out, others will direct their feelings inwardly. As a result, this latter group of students may fall through the cracks (Jackson, 2010). These students need and can benefit from constructive feedback regarding their behavior and performance. Feedback regarding students' behavior and performance will serve to coach them toward more effective academic and social behaviors, increasing their chances of success both in and out of school. Therefore, all students should be taught to recognize their strengths and weaknesses so that they can use this knowledge as they explore various academic and career options. As students become more self-aware, they can be taught to strengthen their weaker points, as well as to highlight their strengths through the academic and career choices they make. This type of constructive analysis and introspection is made possible as a result of strong mentoring relationships between students, educators, and other positive role models.

Educators can teach students how to assess their strengths and weaknesses as they help them to utilize the feedback they receive from others. They can ask students questions such as the following: "What do you think Mr. Brown meant when he said, 'If you pay more attention to directions on assignments you will earn better grades?'" Or, "You have a lot of potential, but you are sometimes impulsive in your behavior. How can you change that?" Or, "Your creativity is a great asset. How can you focus on that?" Although this type of feedback sounds basic, the student may not have processed what these comments mean in terms of his/her behavior or performance. A teacher might probe and ask if the student has received this type of feedback before, if he/she thinks the statement(s) is true, or how might he/she work to change others' perceptions of their behavior. Teachers have significant power to help mold the behavior of students as they praise positive behaviors and encourage more of such behaviors from students. Teachers may provide students with feedback such as, "That is the type of behavior that will earn you respect from adults and other students." Or, "That is the level of responsibility required if you want to become a doctor, lawyer, engineer, teacher, etc." Teachers may also encourage students academically by statements such as, "You do well in math, but you do better with more practice. Practice is what separates those who are good from those who are great." Or, "There are no great writers, only great re-writers. Your writing will improve as you take the time to re-read and edit your work before handing it in." It may take students years to fully understand the connection between their behavior and the consequences that follow; however, teachers who form relationships and provide constructive feedback can make significant and immediate contributions to their students' development—contributions that pay large dividends to their student' short- and long-term futures.

Making School Relevant to Students

Perhaps the most important justification for academic and career exploration at early ages is to increase the likelihood that students' education is driven by real and meaningful purpose rather than the seemingly burdensome and often un-purposeful rules and requirements of schools. When education is relevant to students' goals and interests, the more likely it will be that students are not simply attending school because they are required to attend, but are motivated to attend and do well in school because they have a strong desire to attain their goal(s). One of the most frequently asked questions by students is, Why do we need to know this? When students and their families understand that they will indeed need what they are learning in school, that is, when school is made relevant to student experience, the groundwork is laid for students and their families to assume increased responsibility for their role in learning (Yamauchi, 2003). Increased motivation for learning equates to higher levels of student effort, connectedness to the curriculum, student interest, and academic performance (e.g., Emmett & McGee, 2013; Tschannen-Moran, Mitchell, & Moore, 2013). Increased time on task and motivation to learn will likely contribute to fewer discipline problems within school (McKissick, Hawkins, Lentz, Hailley, & McGuire, 2010), and likely a narrowing of the achievement gap. These are all goals school leaders and other educators deal with regularly. Educators struggle with how to motivate and improve academic performance, particularly among students they view as challenging. Focusing earlier on students' identification of an academic or professional goal for their future lives may help to decrease the challenge of motivating students.

As discussed above, school leaders have the challenge of preparing students for their academic and professional lives beyond school. Though many families from high poverty contexts do an adequate job of preparing their children for life and work, some families may rely on the school to prepare and counsel their children in academic matters, as well as life beyond school (Lee & Bowen, 2006). Before assuming leadership of a high poverty school, school leaders must understand that effective leadership is often contingent upon the leader's willingness and ability to accommodate the needs of the students, families, and communities with which he or she is charged to work. In high poverty communities, the school leader has a unique opportunity to build a strong academic and career exploration program that enables students to clearly see their "possible selves" both within and outside their communities. Part of this challenge is preparing students who are able to leave their communities in pursuit of their academic and career goals, remain in their communities while pursuing their academic or career goals, or leave and later return to their communities if they so choose.

We strongly believe that no student should reach high school without having considered multiple academic and career paths. In doing so, schools must explicitly demonstrate to students how their education is preparing them for life beyond school (Morrow-Taylor, Foltz, Ellis, & Culbertson, 1999). This knowledge adds relevance, appreciation, and value to their education. This is even more important in high poverty settings, where parents and families are less likely to have the education, skills, or the social and cultural capital necessary to model varied career options for their children (Lee & Bowen, 2006).

Ethical Imperative to Promote Equality of Opportunity

As discussed in the chapter, caring school leaders are concerned with the academic, social, emotional, and physical well-being of their students, both in and beyond school. While the act of caring is an essential element of successful schooling for students from high poverty backgrounds, school leaders must also work to ensure all students have equal and equitable access to educational opportunities. We argue that this is an ethical imperative for school leaders. As previously noted, one of the original purposes of schools in the United States was to educate the masses in order to produce a democratic, educated citizenry (Bass & Gerstl-Pepin, 2011; Dewey, 1914; Watras, 2002). The idea was that an educated citizenry would benefit individuals, as well as the larger society, as citizens experienced an improved standard of living (Mann, 1891). Ideally, higher numbers of educated citizens would equate to a higher level of social order and simultaneously lessen the burden on society to care for the disenfranchised, as more citizens emerged as self-sufficient. With certain exceptions (e.g., African Americans, American Indians, and in some cases women), the aim was to use education as a vehicle for improving the economic and social conditions of all (Goodlad, Klein, & Associates, 1970). Education policy makers, and other key stakeholders in education, understood that a democratic minded, well-educated citizenry would benefit all of society.

Unfortunately, the original goals of education have been thwarted by societal, political, and other forces that have enabled, and some might argue have purposely created, a lack of equity of opportunity among communities, schools, and individuals across the nation. Regardless of our failure to do so, we believe school leaders have a moral, ethical, and professional responsibility to promote and sustain learning environments that ensure equality of opportunity for all students. We believe that school leaders can do this by promoting a caring learning environment in which faculty and staff work to identify, assess, and meet the needs of the students in their charge. This entails the provision of necessary counseling and other supportive services to meet the psychosocial needs of students, as well as the provision of career and higher education exploration programs to prepare students for life beyond school. This is congruent with the work of authors such as Furman and Shields (2005), who argue that

> while we advance the claim that learning is the fundamental purpose of schooling, we are painfully aware that learning is too often equated with narrow definitions of intellectual development, separating it from basic emotional, social, physical, and spiritual development. Moreover, narrow conceptions taken to the extreme are often tied exclusively to test scores thought to represent achievement and learning. (p. 127)

We realize that school leaders bear the responsibility for providing an academic environment for their students, and for ensuring that a rigorous curriculum is in place with high quality teachers to deliver it. However, we also believe that students should be prepared to meet the non-academic demands of life both within and outside of school. If children are not emotionally and psychologically ready to learn, no amount or intensity of instruction alone can positively impact these students' academic achievement (Bryk, Sebring, Allensworth, Luppescu, & Easton, 2010).

Contextualizing the Need for Supports and Services for Students from High Poverty Backgrounds

To ensure equality of opportunity for all students, a number of sociopolitical factors must be considered. Equality of opportunity suggests leveling the playing field for all players. However, the playing field cannot be effectively leveled if educators do not understand the sociopolitical contexts of education and the history of how current policy came to be. Fusarelli (2011) notes that context is often a forgotten aspect of decision-making with regard to school reform. He asserts that a concrete understanding of the impact and importance of place—social context—as well as the ways in which context impacts schooling is missing from many of these reforms, and the discussions surrounding them. Fusarelli further states that the over-used phrase 'educational reform' is demonstrative of the narrow manner in which the problem of failing schools is conceptualized and discussed. As Fusarelli argues, we can no longer disregard context in the operation of schools if we want to see increased student efficacy, student engagement, sense of student identification with school, and student achievement. School leaders and policy makers should take the socioeconomic, racial, and ethnic composition of the student body into consideration as they make decisions regarding the education of these students. Economic and social diversity calls for leadership that has a finger on the pulse of the student base, and who is sensitive to the needs of all students. Schools are more likely to be effective if they are tailored to meet the needs of their students, and appropriate, effective leadership practices are implemented (e.g., Hallinger, Bickman, & Davis, 1996; Leithwood, Louis, Anderson, & Wahlstrom, 2004). In other words, schools must be relevant to their contexts in order to reach the students they serve.

In the same vein, if one is to be a successful school leader, his or her leadership style must be appropriate for the context in which he leads (Fusarelli, 2011), rather than defaulting to a pre-conceived or standard set of ideals of what it means to be a principal. This is true even when it means going above and beyond to provide enhanced counseling services, or a continuous career exploration program. According to the ethic of the profession, principals prioritize and employ the best interest of the child framework (Stefkovich & Begley, 2007). If we are to follow a 'best interest of the child' framework, this means that the needs of children are at the center of leadership and decision-making. Individualized attention to students in need, as provided through career and personal counseling, will serve to assist students in need of extra support, and to point individual students in the right direction to maximize life opportunities. As educators nurture the talents of their students, their gifts and talents will be discovered and will lead those who work with them toward pursuit of the optimal goals for their students' lives, just as they might in their own children's lives.

Meeting the Needs of Students from High Poverty Backgrounds: A Moral Imperative

Researchers and policy makers alike have historically drawn the connection between successful schools, an educated citizenry, and a productive society. As early as 1828, a group of New York philanthropists declared the need for successful schools to forestall the need for more prisons (Rury, 2002). Likewise, researchers and policy makers also draw a parallel between failing schools, underachieving students, students with higher dropout and truancy rates, and high rates of incarceration (Darensbourg, Perez, & Blake, 2010). Unfortunately, for too many of our children, the educational system serves as a pipeline to prison rather than a pipeline to prosperity. Given our belief in the power of education to make deep and lasting positive impacts on the lives of children, youth, and adults, we join those who ask, "Why are we, as a nation, still investing so much in prisons, and comparatively so little in improving schools?" As Ladson-Billings (2006) so aptly asks, why is it that the achievement gap, or more precisely the education debt, is still so clearly drawn along poverty and racial and ethnic lines? As educators, we have a moral obligation to acknowledge the inequitable and unequal conditions encountered by students living in poverty, as well as the implications this has for educational achievement and student outcomes. Once we as researchers, policy makers, school leaders, and educators acknowledge these injustices, whether or not we perceive ourselves to have personally perpetuated them, we have a professional, moral, and ethical obligation to improve learning conditions for all students. If not, we are complicit in maintaining the status quo, and can be named co-conspirators with those who allow policies and practices known to harm students to persist, while doing nothing to improve student learning.

Starratt (1991) and Stefkovich (2006) agree that to assume a leadership role in a school is akin to taking the Hippocratic oath, as is practiced in the medical profession. The ethic of the profession of education/school leadership dictates that school leaders willingly agree to do their students no harm as well as to preserve their lives at any cost. Although the Hippocratic oath taken by physicians refers to the physical lives of their patients, principals who understand what it means to serve the whole child essentially agree to protect their students' physical, mental, social, emotional, and educational well-being. In order for students to perform at their optimal levels, they must feel safe from harm and they must be given the opportunity to discover and to explore their intellectual interests. Successful school leaders in high poverty contexts, then, understand that they must undergo necessary preparation of themselves and their staff in order to accommodate the needs of their students. For many educators, this will require a combination of on-the-job training, professional development, and sustained engagement with parents, families, and community members. Although educational leadership programs can teach effective leadership skills, certain dispositions toward caring need to be present in order for caring leadership practices to flourish.

Questions to Consider

1. What are the professional and ethical codes that govern the profession of school leadership?

2. To what extent did your educational leadership training prepare you to address the ethical and moral dilemmas of school leadership?

3. Describe the ethic of the profession (educational leader), from your perspective.

4. What does the term 'moral leadership' mean to you as an educational leader, or an aspiring educational leader? Does it mean something different in a high poverty context? If so, how?

5. Is it ethical, as a school leader, to designate increased funds toward programs and services designed specifically for students from high poverty backgrounds? Is it ethical to use school funds toward students' unmet non-academic needs (e.g., food, clothing, extra counseling)? Or, should all students receive the same supports and services regardless of their socioeconomic status? Explain how you arrived at your answer.

6. What role does the school counselor play in your school? How might this role be revised to better support the needs of students from high poverty backgrounds? What are the unique needs of the students, parents, and communities served by your school? To what extent are these needs being met by your school?

7. To what extent does your school offer career and technical counseling?

8. What ethical or moral responsibilities do schools have to prepare students for life beyond school? To what extent is your school or district embracing these responsibilities?

References

Amatea, E. S., & West-Olatunji, C. A. (2007). Joining the conversation about educating our poorest children: Emerging leadership roles for school counselors in high-poverty schools. *Professional School Counseling, 11*(2), 81–89.

American School Counselor Association. (n.d.). ASCA position statements. Retrieved from http://www.schoolcounselor.org

Arroyo, A. A., Rhoad, R., & Drew, P. (1999). Meeting diverse student needs in urban schools: Research-based recommendations for school personnel. *Preventing School Failure, 43*(4), 145–153.

Bass, L. (2009). Fostering an ethic of care in leadership: A conversation with five African American women. *Advances in Human Resources, 11*(5), 619–632.

Bass, L. (2012). When care trumps justice: The impact of black feminist caring in educational leadership. *International Journal of Qualitative Research in Education, 25*(1), 73–87.

Bass, L., & Gerstl-Pepin, C. (2011). Declaring bankruptcy on educational inequity. *Educational Policy, 25*(6), 908–934.

Becker, G. S. (1967). *Human capital and the personal distribution of income: An analytical approach.* Ann Arbor, MI: Institute of Public Administration.

Bennett, W. J. (1988, December). Moral literacy and the formation of character. *NASSP Bulletin, 72,* 29–34. doi:10.1177/019263658807251208

Bomer, R., Dworin, J., May, L., & Semingson, P. (2009). What's wrong with a deficit perspective? *Teachers College Record.* Retrieved from http://www.tcrecord.org (ID No. 15648)

Brand, S., Felner, R. D., Shim, M., Seitsinger, A., & Dumas, T. (2003). Middle school improvement and reform: Development and validation of a school-level assessment of climate, cultural pluralism, and school safety. *Journal of Educational Psychology, 95,* 570–588.

Bryk, A. S., Sebring, P. B., Allensworth, E., Luppescu, S., & Easton, J. Q. (2010). *Organizing schools for improvement: Lessons from Chicago.* Chicago: University of Chicago Press.

Casella, R. (2003). Zero tolerance policy in schools: Rationale, consequences, and alternatives. *Teachers College Record, 105*(5), 872–892.

Cohen, J., McCabe, L., Michelli, N. M., & Pickeral, T. (2009). School climate: Research, policy, practice, and teacher education. *Teachers College Record, 111*(1), 180–213.

Coleman, J. S. (1994). *Social capital in the creation of human capital.* Chicago: University of Chicago Press.

Dahir, C. A., Burnham, J. J., & Stone, C. (2009). Listen to the voices: School counselors and comprehensive school counseling programs. *Professional School Counseling, 12*(3), 182–192.

Darensbourg, A., Perez, E., & Blake, J. (2010). Overrepresentation of African American males in exclusionary discipline: The role of school-based mental health professionals in dismantling the school to prison pipeline. *Journal of African American Males in Education, 1*(3), 196–211.

Dewey, J. (1914). Experimental studies in kindergarten theory and practice: Reasoning in early childhood. *Teachers College Record, 15*(1), 9–15.

Emmett, J., & McGee, D. (2013). Extrinsic motivation for large-scale assessments: A case study of a student achievement program at one urban high school. *The High School Journal, 96*(2), 116–137.

Frick, W. C. (2009). Principals' value-informed decision making, intrapersonal moral discord and pathways to resolution: The complexities of moral leadership praxis. *Journal of Educational Administration, 47*(1), 50–74.

Frick, W. C., & Faircloth, S. C. (2007). Acting in the collective and individual best interest of students: When ethical imperatives clash with administrative demands. *Journal of Special Education Leadership, 20*(1), 21–32.

Frick, W. C., & Gutierrez, K. J. (2008). Those moral aspects unique to the profession: Principals' perspectives on their work and the implications for a professional ethic for educational leadership. *Journal of School Leadership, 18*(1), 32–61.

Furman, G. C., & Shields, C. M. (2005). How can educational leaders promote and support social justice and democratic community in schools? In W. A. Firestone & C. Riehl (Eds.), *A new agenda for research in educational leadership* (pp. 119–137). New York: Teachers College Press.

Fusarelli, L. D. (2011). School reform in a vacuum: Demographic change, social policy, and the future of children. *Peabody Journal of Education, 86*(3), 215–235.

Gati, I., & Saka, N. (2001). High school students' career-related decision-making difficulties. *Journal of Counseling & Development, 79*(3), 331–340.

Goodlad, J. L., Klein, M. F., & Associates. (1970). *Behind the classroom door*. Worthington, OH: Charles A. Jones.

Hallinger, P., Bickman, L., & Davis, K. (1996). School context, principal leadership, and student reading achievement. *The Elementary School Journal, 96*(5), 527–549.

House, R. M., & Sears, S. J. (2002). Preparing school counselors to be leaders and advocates: A critical need in the new millennium. *Theory Into Practice, 41*(3), 154–162.

Jackson, R. R. (2010). Flagged for success. *Educational Leadership, 68*(2), 18–21.

Jacobson, S. L. (2008). Leadership for success in high poverty elementary schools. *Journal of Educational Leadership, Policy and Practice, 23*(1), 3–17.

Johnson, J., Rochkind, J., Ott, A. N., & DuPont, S. (2010). *Can I get a little advice here? How an overstretched high school guidance system is undermining students' college aspirations*. A Public Agenda report prepared for the Bill & Melinda Gates Foundation. Retrieved from http://www.publicagenda.org/files/pdf/can-i-get-a-little-advice-here.pdf

Kannapel, P. J., Clements, S. K., Taylor, D., & Hibpshman, T. (2005). *Inside the black box of high-performing high-poverty schools* [Report]. Lexington, KY: Prichard Committee for Academic Excellence.

Kelly, H. (2009). What Jim Crow's teachers could do: Educational capital and teachers' work in under-resourced schools. *The Urban Review, 42*(4), 329–350. doi:10.1007/s11256-009-0132-3

Kraft, M. A., Papay, J. P., Charner-Laird, M., Johnson, S. M., Ng, M., & Reinhorn, S. K. (2012). *Committed to their students but in need of support: How school context influences teacher turnover in high-poverty, urban schools*. Retrieved from http://scholar.harvard.edu/mkraft.

Ladson-Billings, G. (2006). From the achievement gap to the education debt: Understanding achievement in U.S. schools. *Educational Researcher, 35*(7), 3–12.

Lee, J., & Bowen, N. (2006). Parent involvement, cultural capital, and the achievement gap among elementary school children. *American Educational Research Journal, 43*, 193–218.

Leithwood, K., Louis, K. S., Anderson, S., & Wahlstrom, K. (2004). *Review of research: How leadership influences student learning*. New York: Learning from Leadership Project. Retrieved from http://www.wallacefoundation.org/knowledge-center/school-leadership/key-research/Documents/How-Leadership-Influences-Student-Learning.pdf

Libbey, H. P. (2004). Measuring student relationships to school: Attachment, bonding, connectedness, and engagement. *Journal of School Health, 74*(7), 274–283.

Mann, H. (1891). *Life and works of Horace Mann*. Boston: Lee and Shepard.

Masumoto, M., & Brown-Welty, S. (2009). Case study of leadership practices and school-community interrelationships in high-performing, high-poverty rural California high schools. *Journal of Research in Rural Education, 24*(1), 1–18.

McKissick, C., Hawkins, R. O., Lentz, F. E., Hailley, J., & McGuire, S. (2010). Randomizing multiple contingency components to decrease disruptive behaviors and increase student engagement in an urban second-grade classroom. *Psychology in the Schools, 47*(9), 944–959.

McNeely, C A., Nonemaker, J. M., & Blum, R. W. (2002, April). Promoting school connectedness: Evidence from the national longitudinal study of adolescent health. *Journal of School Health, 72*(4), 138–146.

Miles, K. H., Ware, K., & Roza, M. (2003). Leveling the playing field: Creating funding equity through student-based budgeting. *Phi Delta Kappan, 85*(2), 114–119.

Mistry, R. S., White, E. S., Benner, A. D., & Huynh, V. W. (2009). A longitudinal study of the simultaneous influence of mothers' and teachers' educational expectations on low-income youths' academic achievement. *Journal of Youth and Adolescence, 38*(6), 826–838.

Morrow-Taylor, C., Foltz, B. M., Ellis, M. R., & Culbertson, K. (1999). A multicultural career fair for elementary school students. *Professional School Counseling, 2,* 241–243.

National Center for Children in Poverty. (2007, November). *Who are America's poor children? The unofficial story.* New York: Columbia University, Mailman School of Public Affairs.

Noddings, N. (1984). *Caring.* Berkeley: University of California Press.

Noddings, N. (1992). *The challenge to care in schools: An alternative approach to education: Vol. 8. Advances in contemporary educational thought.* New York: Teachers College Press.

Noddings, N. (2005). Caring in education. *The encyclopedia of informal education.* Retrieved from http://www.infed.org/biblio/noddings_caring_in_education.htm

Normore, A. H., & Blanco, R. I. (2006). Leadership for social justice and morality: Collaborative partnerships, school-linked services and the plight of the poor. *International Electronic Journal for Leadership in Learning, 10.* Retrieved from http://iejll.synergiesprairies.ca/iejll/index.php/ijll/article/view/627/289

Payne, R. K. (2005). *A framework for understanding poverty* (4th ed.). Highlands, TX: aha! Process.

Perry, J. C., Liu, X., & Pabian, Y. (2010). School engagement as a mediator of academic performance among urban youth: The role of career preparation, parental career support, and teacher support. *The Counseling Psychologist, 38*(2), 269–295.

Portwood, S. G., Ayers, P. M., Kinnison, K. E., Waris, R. G., & Wise, D. L. (2005). YouthFriends: Outcomes from a school-based mentoring program. *Journal of Primary Prevention, 26*(2), 129–188.

Reiner, S. M., Colbert, R. D., & Peruse, R. (2010). Teacher perceptions of the professional school counselor role: A national study. *Professional School Counseling, 12*(5), 324–332.

Rubie-Davies, C. M., Peterson, E., Irving, E., Widdowson, D., & Dixon, R. (2010). Expectations of achievement: Student, teacher and parent perceptions. *Research in Education, 83*(1), 36–53.

Rury, J. (2002). *Education and social change: Themes in the history of American schooling.* Mahwah, NJ: Lawrence Erlbaum.

Saifer, S., Edwards, K., Ellis, D., Ko, L., & Stuczynski, A. (2005, December). *Classroom to community and back: Using culturally responsive standards-based teaching to strengthen family and community partnerships and increase student achievement.* Portland, OR: Northwest Regional Educational Laboratory. Retrieved from http://oregonpirc.org/webfm_send/19

Schultz, T. (1961, March). Investment in human capital. *American Economic Review, 51,* 1–17.

Shapiro, J. P., & Stefkovich, J. A. (2010). *Ethical leadership and decision making in education: Applying theoretical perspectives to complex dilemmas.* New York: Routledge.

Siddle-Walker, V., & Snarey, J. (2004). *Race-ing moral formation: African American perspectives on care.* New York: Teachers College Press.

Skiba, R. J. (2000). *Zero tolerance, zero evidence. An analysis of school discipline practice* (Indiana Education Policy Center Policy Research Report No. SRS2). Retrieved from http://www.indiana.edu/~safeschl/ztze.pdf

Skiba, R. J. (2008). Are zero tolerance policies effective in the schools? An evidentiary review and recommendations. *American Psychologist, 63*(9), 852–862.

Skiba, R. J., & Knesting, K. (2011). Zero tolerance, zero evidence: An analysis of school disciplinary practice. *New Directions for Mental Health Services, 2001*(92), 17–43.

Starratt, R. J. (1991). Building an ethical school: A theory for practice in educational leadership. *Educational Administration Quarterly, 27*(2), 185–202.

Stefkovich, J. A. (2006). *The best interests of the student: Applying ethical constructs to legal cases in education.* New York: Taylor & Francis.

Stefkovich, J., & Begley, P. T. (2007). Ethical school leadership: Defining best interests of students. *Educational Management Administration & Leadership, 35*(2), 205–224.

Stern, D., Dayton, C., & Raby, M. (2010). Career academies: A proven strategy to prepare high school students for college and careers. *UC Berkeley Career Academy Support Network Working Paper.* Retrieved from http://casn.berkeley.edu/resource_files/Proven_Strategy_2-25-1010-03-12-04-27-01.pdf

Tebo, M. G. (2000). Zero tolerance, zero sense. *ABA Journal, 86*(4), 40. Retrieved from Hein On Line 86 A.B.A. J. 40.

Tschannen-Moran, M., Mitchell, R. M., & Moore, D. (2013). Student academic optimism: A confirmatory factor analysis. *Journal of Educational Administration, 51*(2), 150–175.

Watras, J. (2002). *The foundations of educational curriculum and diversity: 1565 to the present.* Boston: Allyn & Bacon.

Wimberly, G. L., & Noeth, R. J. (2005). *College readiness begins in middle school* (ACT Policy Report). Washington, DC: ACT. Retrieved from http://www.act.org/research/policymakers/pdf/CollegeReadiness.pdf

Yamauchi, L. A. (2003). Making school relevant for at-risk students: The Waiʻanae High School Hawaiian Studies Program. *Journal of Education for Students Placed at Risk, 8*(4), 379–390.

CHAPTER FOUR

Effective Instructional Leadership for Diverse High Poverty Populations

The Effect of Instructional Supervision on Principal Trust

Robbie Wahnee

Instructional supervision has transitioned into a school-based activity, practice, or process that engages teachers in meaningful, non-judgmental, and ongoing instructional dialogue for the purpose of improving teaching and learning. (Glanz & Sullivan, 2003, p. 8)

Chapter Four highlights the importance of what we term *exceptional instructional supervision*, a characteristic necessary for working effectively with students from socioeconomically disadvantaged backgrounds. The role of instructional leadership and supervision is particularly important in high poverty contexts due to a number of factors, including the potential for a lack of high academic press and the predominance of a younger, less experienced, and often more mobile teaching force. Drawing on our belief in the importance of the interpersonal nature of leadership, this chapter focuses on the relationship between effective instructional supervision and trust. The author concludes with a discussion of research-based strategies for effective instructional leadership in high poverty contexts.

Introduction

Research consistently suggests that principals play a critical role in schools regardless of the school's overall socioeconomic status (Forsyth, Adams, & Hoy, 2011; Hallinger & Heck, 1996a, 1996b; Hallinger & Leithwood, 1994; Marks & Printy, 2003; Quinn, 2002). The ideal school climate is open and collegial, and one in which teachers share ideas and provide feedback to the principal and the principal reciprocates. Along with meeting state and federal mandates, the principal's task is to help teachers improve teaching. Teachers and principals collaboratively functioning together can improve student performance. However, there are situations and interpersonal exchanges where power between principals and teachers becomes unbalanced due to differences in role expectations and responsibilities. One of the primary roles where confusion is prevalent is that of teacher-principal interaction during the principal's role as instructional supervisor.

As austere as it may seem, instructional supervision is a complex, multifaceted role. Prior research (Cogan, 1973; Garman, 1986; Goldhammer, 1969; Goldhammer, Anderson, & Krajewski, 1980) generally acknowledges instructional supervision as a subtle but circumspect task of the principal. In many instances, supervision is synonymous with power, control, command, and hierarchy. Contemporary definitions treat instructional supervision as a learning and development process shaped by the principal, and not solely limited to teacher-principal interactions. Blase and Blase (2002b) note, "Instructional supervision is often defined as a blend of several leadership tasks such as supervision of classroom instruction, staff development, and curriculum development" (p. 8). Glickman, Gordon, and Ross-Gordon (2007) agree that instructional supervision is a comprehensive process that consists of supervisory tasks including direct assistance, group development, professional development, curriculum development, and action research to improve teaching and learning. Kochanek (2005) emphasizes that no reform can succeed without a principal who is willing to perform skillful instructional supervision that supports improved teaching, positive interactions, and trusting relationships. Instructional supervision in the context of this research is defined as the direct assistance of the principal in principal-teacher interactions that promote reflective practice and professional growth (Blase & Blase, 2000).

Principal trust is based primarily on teachers' perceived intentions of the principal. The quality of interpersonal exchanges can reinforce power asymmetry between teachers and principals, whereas power symmetry reduces vulnerability (Blase & Blase, 2002b). Disparities between the two perceived purposes of instructional supervision necessitated measurement to determine the effect on principal trust. To gain a better understanding of the relationship between instructional supervision and principal trust, this chapter's study, conducted in an urban school district, situates the formation of principal trust within the context of the principal's direct, instructional assistance.

The Relationship between Trust and Instructional Leadership

As noted below, confidence in the principal is an important component of trust (Tschannen-Moran & Hoy, 2000). Faculty trust in principals is inextricably related to instructional leadership behaviors. Wahnee (2010) found in a sample of 56 urban elementary schools that principals who were perceived as providing direct instructional assistance and supporting the professional growth of teachers engendered greater trust. In contrast, lower faculty trust in principals was associated with behaviors perceived as detrimental to instructional improvement. Direct instructional assistance and support for professional growth of teachers have consequences for healthy teacher-principal interactions.

Conditions that Foster Principal-Teacher Trust

Interpersonal trust is an indistinct phenomenon as opposed to a tangible artifact. Behavioral, affective, and cognitive components (McAllister, 1995) compose trust. Cognition-based trust exists when another is perceived as reliable or dependable. Affective trust involves emotion and evolves from another's reciprocal care and concern (McAllister, 1995). Interpersonal or behavioral trust in the workplace has been found to influence productivity, individual performance, team or work group performance and outcomes, and organizational citizenship (Dirks & Ferrin, 2001; Rousseau, Sitkin, Burt, & Camerer, 1998).

Trust conceptualizations evolved over time and across disciplines. A number of different scientific lenses influenced the evolution of empirical trust definitions, such as: (1) the researcher's discipline; (2) the individual, group, or organization analyzed; and (3) the type of trust studied (Lewicki & Bunker, 1995). Trust is described as occurring laterally (e.g., peer relationships), vertically (e.g., supervisor and subordinate relationships), and externally (e.g., organizational relationships between clients or customers), which adds complexity to understanding and conceptualizing this phenomenon (Fox, 1974). Length (Bigley & Pearce, 1998; Rotter, 1967) and history (Boon & Holmes, 1991) of a relationship are also elements that add dimensionality to understanding and defining trust.

In the context of schools, trust may be an individual affective state or more of a collective orientation of role groups that include students, parents, teachers, principals, and the outside school community (Forsyth, Barnes, & Adams, 2006). Trust, depending on context, is based on the individual's beliefs and behaviors, as well as another's beliefs and behaviors (Golembiewski, 1979, 1985; McAllister, 1995), focuses on individuals or objects, depends on reciprocity, and, when aggregated, is a logical archetype. As such, trusting behavior is a latent construct with measurable indicators, such as openness, honesty, reliability, competence, and benevolence (Hoy & Tschannen-Moran, 1999, 2003). *Principal trust* is defined as a teacher's willingness to be vulnerable based on the confidence that the principal is benevolent, reliable, competent, honest, and open (Hoy & Tschannen-Moran, 1999, 2003). The seminal work of Hoy and his colleagues (Goddard, Tschannen-Moran, & Hoy, 2001; Hoy, Gage, & Tarter, 2006; Hoy & Kupersmith, 1985; Hoy, Smith, & Sweetland, 2002; Hoy & Tarter, 1997; Hoy &

Tschannen-Moran, 1999, 2003; Tarter, Bliss, & Hoy, 1989; Tarter, Sabo, & Hoy, 1995; Tschannen-Moran & Hoy, 1998, 2000) has contributed to the understanding of the formation and effects of trust in schools. This literature suggests that social exchanges between teachers and principals are the primary mechanism by which teachers discern the trustworthiness of principals (Adams, 2008; Bryk & Schneider, 2002). Discussions of teaching practice and instructional strategies are examples of both formal and informal exchanges that may begin with broad suggestions and conclude with an evaluation conference (Bryk & Schneider, 2002; Darling-Hammond, 1997; Forsyth et al., 2006). Principals are challenged to find equilibrium during informal and formal interactions with teachers. Hoy et al. (2002) suggest that "the principal treats teachers as colleagues, is open, egalitarian, and friendly, but at the same time sets clear expectations and standards of performance" (p. 42).

Many principals are required to balance the two roles of colleague and formal supervisor. The two roles intersect within the micropolitical, hierarchical context of instructional supervision where uneven power distribution results (Blase & Blase, 1999, 2000). Direct and effective assistance to teachers requires collaborative and collegial relationships between principals and teachers; however, the formal authority of the principal can affect power symmetry. Finding an effective balance between relational leadership and task-oriented behaviors is tricky and critically important for principals. The practice of teacher supervision minimally includes face-to-face discussions, pre- and post-conferencing, and the principal's role as instructional supervisor. The formal authority of principals as supervisor intersects with technical expertise, creating a social dynamic that has the potential to influence teacher trust.

Interdependence, Risk, and Vulnerability in Complex School Structures
Highly complex structures, mainly organizations with varying levels of hierarchy and problematic political activity, require elevated interdependence. Such high-risk interdependence requires an increased need for trust. "Given total knowledge, there is no need to trust, and given total ignorance, there is no basis upon which to rationally trust" (McAllister, 1995, p. 26). Public schools defined by mission, size, complexity, hierarchy of authority, and funding structures are highly interactive organizations where trust is found necessary to enable collaboration, cohesiveness, and improved educational goals (Adams, 2008, 2010; Hoy, Gage, & Tartar, 2006; Hoy & Tschannen-Moran, 1999, 2003; Tschannen-Moran, 2003).

School environments that foster flexible alternatives, effective principal-teacher interaction about instruction, and dynamic processes, such as inquiry, reflection, exploration, and experimentation, result in increased trusting behavior. Until school restructuring eliminates hierarchical, power asymmetry, Hoy and Sweetland (2001) suggest proactive attempts be made to change the manner of hierarchy rather than eliminate it. The notion of bureaucracy, hierarchy, and power affects school administrators, teachers, and the community when perceived as coercive, rigid, or unresponsive (Hoy & Forsyth, 1986; Hoy & Sweetland, 2000, 2001). In their conceptual model that analyzed bureaucratic school properties, Hoy and Sweetland (2001) did not dispel the inadequacies of bureaucracy. Consequently, enabling school structures incorporate trustworthy principals and embrace administrative efficiencies while allowing innovative, fluid teaching performance (Hirschhorn, 1997; Hoy & Sweetland, 2000, 2001). Productive schools' research, where the quality of teaching and learning are robust, continues to influence the prevalent model, and perhaps a necessary model hierarchical school structure (Murphy, 1990). Enabling structures endorse interactive dialogue, value differences, and view mistakes as a learning opportunity, and collaboratively problem solve. Enabling, productive schools require principals and teachers trusting each other and collegially working together.

In an era in which global accountability is imperative to achieve results, analysis of school structure is requisite. Robust learning and reciprocal enterprise across school roles, cultures, socioeconomic status, age, gender, and other possible incompatible demographics are redoubtable. Trust is a vital social lubricant, which functions as a precondition to social interaction and cooperation, and in schools, it is crucial (Bryk & Schneider, 2002; Fukuyama, 1995; Gambetta, 1988).

Types of Trust

Educational research provides school principals with empirical data that have insightful implications for their schools. Lewicki and Bunker (1996) identify three types of trust: calculus based, deterrence based, and identity based. The three bases or levels of trust may emerge at different stages in a relationship. Each level may also be developed or undermined through specific individual exchanges. Calculus-based trust is "sustained to the degree that the deterrent or punishment is clear, possible, and likely to occur if the trust is violated" (Lewicki & Bunker, 1996, p. 119). Knowledge-based trust evolves through a history of successful interactions and is characterized by behavioral predictability. Identification-based trust exists when each of the parties understands and appreciates the other's intentions and a sense of shared values and collective identity exists. Repeated interaction is necessary for the manifestation of each trust level. Each level of trust serves its own purpose (Lewicki & Bunker, 1996).

Trust conceptualizations address conditional and unconditional states (Jones & George, 1998). Conditional trust, according to Jones and George, exists when parties are willing to interact without risk of personal detriment or long-term commitment. There is little chance of shared value development. Unconditional trust evolves through repeated, trustworthy interactions. Shared values, interdependence, cooperation, and goal synergy are apparent when unconditional trust exists.

McAllister's (1995) findings support research that cognition-based trust precedes affect-based trust and levels of cognition-based trust positively correlate with levels of affect-based trust. Moreover, affect-based trust based on informal relationships between managers is found to "facilitate effective coordinated action" (p. 25), which McAllister describes as essential to the real work of organizations.

Mayer, Davis, and Schoorman (1995) developed an organizational model that clarifies the role of interpersonal trust in risk taking. This model describes interpersonal trust characteristics of both the trustor and the trustee. The researchers' trust conceptualization considers two types of trust antecedents: (1) a propensity to trust, a trait that remains stable across situations, and (2) three perceptions, ability, benevolence, and integrity, regarding the other person's trustworthy attributes. Mayer and colleagues focus on trust as a willingness to be vulnerable to another. The researchers suggest, "Trust is not taking risk *per se*. But rather it is a *willingness* to take risk" (p. 730) (author's emphasis). Hierarchical relationships create issues of vulnerability when either person feels the other's motives contradict his or her perceptions of trustworthiness.

Principal or leader authenticity, as described by Henderson and Hoy (1982), is defined as "a general and consistent pattern of behavior in which subordinates perceive their leader as demonstrating acceptance of organizational and personal responsibility for actions, outcomes, and mistakes; being non-manipulative of subordinates; and exhibiting a salience of self over role" (p. 81). Hoy and Kupersmith's (1985) research suggests that trust is not a generalized perception or affect based but is referent specific. Target variables encompass persons, concepts, or institutions and in complex environments. Trustors are selective about whom or what they trust (Clark & Payne, 1997; Dirks & Ferrin, 2001; Mayer et al., 1995).

Critical trust-building mechanisms for schools are behaviors that promote an academic emphasis (Geist & Hoy, 2004; Hoy et al., 2002; Hoy & Sweetland, 2001), cognitive discernments of collective efficacy (Goddard et al., 2001), and affective role perceptions (Adams & Forsyth, 2007). Environmental characteristics, social and contextual conditions, such as economic status, ethnicity, and school size, also affect trust maturation and sustainability. Aggregated, the divergent sources and types of trust mechanisms allow individuals to become intuitive auditors of another's trustworthiness (Kramer, 1999). However, the literature neglects the effect that instructional supervision may have on principal-teacher trust.

Components and Facets of Principal Trust

The definition of trust used for this study identifies openness, honesty, reliability, competence, and benevolence as characteristics of trustworthiness (Hoy & Tschannen-Moran, 1999). Each empirically explored facet is a requisite element of trusting school relationships. The literature iterates that "one's willingness to risk vulnerability is shaped by individual discernments of trust facets" (Adams, 2008, p. 48).

Interdependence and risk are requisite to trust. Without risk, there is no need to trust (Cummings & Bromiley, 1996; Deutsch, 1958; Gambetta, 1988; Hoy & Tschannen-Moran, 1999, 2003; Lewis & Weigert, 1985; Luhmann, 1988; Tschannen-Moran & Hoy, 1998, 2003). Risk involves making oneself vulnerable to another with the confidence that the other will not act in ways that are detrimental to the trusting party even when the opportunity exists to do so (Cummings & Bromiley, 1996; Deutsch, 1958; Hoy & Tschannen-Moran, 1999, 2003; Lewis & Weigert, 1985; Luhmann, 1988; Tschannen-Moran & Hoy, 1998, 2000). Interactions or situations that rise to the level of an individual's willingness to risk vulnerability find the trustor assessing if the potential for loss in the relationship exceeds the potential for gain (Deutsch, 1962, 1973; Luhmann, 1979; Mishra, 1996; Zand, 1971).

Hoy and Tschannen-Moran's (1999, 2003) empirical research indicates a teacher's belief that his or her principal will act in the teacher's best interest determines teacher trust in the principal. In situations of instructional supervision and evaluation, teachers trust principals to supervise fairly and competently. Therefore, a teacher is confident that a principal will act professionally, and the principal will treat the teacher not only with fairness but also with respect and collegiality.

Organizations, by their hierarchical nature and power asymmetry, create situations of risk and vulnerability. Similarly, schools are complex organizations where distinct role relationships create situations of obligations that result in risk and vulnerability. In schools, teachers discern their willingness to take risks based on the principal's behavior.

The rigid, directive principal may focus on compliance and criticism, producing power asymmetry, whereas the supportive, empowering principal is informative, open, and collaborative, and engenders trust building and sustainability. The evidence that trust is required for well-functioning schools is empirically cogent and is dependent upon principals and teachers meeting and exceeding role obligations.

Confidence, Interdependence. Cook and Wall (1980) define trust as "the extent to which one is willing to ascribe good intentions to and have confidence in the words and actions of other people" (p. 39). "There is a growing consensus that trust resides in the degree of confidence one holds in the face of risk rather than in the choice or action that increases one's risk" (Tschannen-Moran & Hoy, 2000, p. 557). Deutsch (1958, 1960) suggests that individuals might act in ways that place them in situations of vulnerability to another, even if the consequences are potentially negative. Tschannen-Moran and Hoy (2000) contend that confidence must build over a period of time. The time frame begins when a commitment is made and extends until results occur. This period of uncertainty and confidence is the degree to which a person trusts (Kee & Knox, 1970; Tschannen-Moran & Hoy, 2000). For example, a teacher has some confidence that his or her performance will be assessed fairly and accurately by the principal regardless of the number of informal interactions that have occurred between them over the course of the year.

Principal's Benevolence. Benevolence is a widely accepted component of trust (Baier, 1986; Butler & Cantrell, 1984; Cummings & Bromiley, 1996; Deutsch, 1958; Frost, Stimpson, & Maughan, 1978; Gambetta, 1988; Hosmer, 1995; Hoy & Kupersmith, 1985; Hoy & Tschannen-Moran, 1999, 2000; Mayer et al., 1995; Mishra, 1996; Zand, 1971). Mayer and colleagues' (1995) definition of benevolence between a trustee and a trustor includes whether the trustee has some attachment to the trustor to "the extent [that] a trustee is believed to want to do good to the trustor, aside from an egocentric profit motive" (p. 718).

Benevolence is a confidence in or an assessment of another party to protect one's best interests and cause without causing harm to the other party (Baier, 1986; Butler & Cantrell, 1984; Cummings & Bromiley, 1996; Deutsch, 1958; Frost et al., 1978; Gambetta, 1988; Hosmer, 1995; Hoy & Kupersmith, 1985; Mayer et al., 1995; Mishra, 1996). Benevolence is important to organizational, interpersonal, and hierarchical relationships. Without trust in the benevolence of the other party, organizations suffer costs in productivity and individuals use emotional and physical energy considering alternatives (Kramer, 1999). For instance, if teachers do not perceive principals as benevolent or caring for their well-being and needs, trust is found to be negatively affected (Hoy & Tschannen-Moran, 1999).

Principal's Reliability. Reliability is said to exist when there is an optimistic belief or confidence that an individual's needs will be addressed or met timely and predictably based on consistency in the words and actions of the other party (Butler & Cantrell, 1984; Gabarro, 1978; Hosmer, 1995; Lewis & Weigert, 1985). In situations of interdependence, reliability refers to the extent to which an individual can depend upon another party to behave consistently and fairly, and to follow through (Butler & Cantrell, 1984; Hoy & Miskel, 2008; Mishra, 1996). Good principals can be relied upon to engage teachers in instructional dialogue and reflective practice aimed at improved instructional strategies and student academic improvement (Glanz, 2005). Reliable principals behave consistently with all teachers and do not play favorites.

Principal's Competence. Competence is synonymous with ability (Butler, 1991). Competence includes the skills or characteristics an individual possesses based on education, experience, or aptitude "that enable a party to have influence within some specific domain and to perform a task" (Mayer et al., 1995, p. 717). In situations of interdependence, competence is the belief in another party's ability to perform the tasks required by his or her position (Gabarro, 1987). For example, teachers expect competent principals, and principals rely on competent teachers. Principals and teachers depend on one another to accomplish the teaching and learning goals of the school. Incompetence, if not managed, can diminish school-wide trust (Bryk & Schneider, 2002). If performed effectively and with reciprocity, the instructional supervision of teachers by principals allows acknowledgment of satisfactory competencies as well as those that need improvement.

Principal's Honesty. Rotter (1967) defines trust as "the expectancy that the word, promise, verbal or written statement of another individual or group can be relied upon" (p. 651). Integrity, character, and authenticity define honesty and are inclusive facets of trust (Hoy & Tschannen-Moran, 1999). A relationship between a person's statements and deeds demonstrates integrity. Moreover, acceptance of responsibility for one's actions and not distorting the truth in order to shift blame to another exemplifies authenticity (Tschannen-Moran & Hoy, 1998). Scholars and researchers continue to define honesty as a pivotal trust characteristic (Baier, 1986; Butler & Cantrell, 1984; Cummings & Bromiley, 1996).

Principal's Openness. Openness is the extent to which relevant information is shared (Butler, 1991). The information alone may not be important, but the delivery of the information is. The process of sharing is one of vulnerability. Sharing requires giving of oneself (Butler & Cantrell, 1984; Mishra, 1996; Tschannen-Moran & Hoy, 2000). Openness occurs when both the receiver and the sender of information are confident that no advantage is lost or gained between them. Without open and honest communication, suspicion, distrust, or even mistreatment result. "Unfortunately, even small, avoided conflicts, derived, for example, from insensitivity in interpersonal relationships or from mere misunderstandings, often escalate into huge, debilitating crises" (Blase & Blase, 2002a, p. 721). However, if principals must guard every communication or withhold information from teachers or teachers from principals, neither individual nor school goals are achieved (Hoy & Sweetland, 2001). Open, nonthreatening communication between teachers and principals allows for collaboration and constructive problem solving (Blase & Blase, 2002a, 2002b).

The combined facets of trust are observable behavior characteristics that lead a party to risk vulnerability (Hoy & Tschannen-Moran, 1999). Each scientific examination of trust provides another piece to the complex puzzle of how individuals discern and monitor others in trusting relationships.

School Role Trust Development

There are many bases for trust formation. In terms of hierarchical trust, the referent is the leader or administrator, or in schools, the principal. Teacher-principal trust, for the most part, is hierarchical. Formal structures and contextual conditions, such as regulations and contracts, and informal structures, such as communication, norms, and trust, help moderate interpersonal interactions (Williamson, 1993; Kramer & Tyler, 1996). Kochanek (2005) discusses factors that contribute to school trust development in terms of social similarity, contracts, proxies, and repeated exchanges.

Social Similarity. Zucker (1986) proposes three modes of trust building that include (1) character-based trust, or trust in others with whom a person or persons share homogeneous characteristics such as physical, cultural, and social similarities; (2) institution-based trust, or trust tied to broad-based societal institutions; and (3) process-based trust, which is tied to the past or expected change. Similarly, Lewicki and Bunker (1996) propose three bases of trust: (1) calculus-based or the rational calculations of rewards and punishments; (2) knowledge-based or predictability of the other party based on a history of interactions; and (3) identification-based, which is identifying with the other party to the point that one will protect and promote the best interests of the other. McAllister (1995) proposes cognitive-based and affective-based trust. Mayer and colleagues (1995) suggest character-based trust in terms of leaders and followers. A leader's authority for decision-making about the follower's pay or promotional opportunities is viewed in terms of impact on the follower's level of vulnerability.

Generally, trust development is multidimensional and takes many forms depending upon variable conditions. Global issues such as diversity, transience, and socioeconomic differences challenge twenty-first-century organizations to build and maintain character-based trust (Zucker, 1986). Although social similarity does not guarantee higher levels of school trust, respect, competence, integrity, and personal regard positively influence trust maturation and sustainability (Bryk & Schneider, 2002; Kochanek, 2005).

Contracts. Research indicates that the absence of a formal contract allows for vulnerability and uneven power distribution (Blau, 1964). Many teachers belong to unions that define work hours, pay, additional duties outside of work hours, and professional development hours. However, teachers spend extra time attending after-school events, meeting with parents, working on special projects for classes, or keeping abreast of state and federal mandates. Increasingly, meeting school goals requires shared understanding and mutual respect, which arise from observed behaviors. For example, Bryk and Schneider (2002) discuss how personal regard, which includes integrity and respect, prevails beyond a contract. Their study, conducted at Holiday Elementary School, a low-income school with an African American population, elicited parent and teacher testimony about the principal's open and caring personal style. The overall conclusion was that the White, male principal's behavior resulted in a similarly conscientious school climate. Bryk and Schneider's extensive work indicates that trust, based on contracts, does not work well for schools and that respect extends beyond expectations on a piece of paper.

Proxies. Proxies, such as rules, handbooks, contracts, and other documents, have been found to influence trust. Trust in a proxy is dependent upon the trustor's expectations or assessment of the trustee's credentials, ethnicity, socioeconomic status, or other similarity or tangible consideration. Individuals become dependent upon and envisage fair or just outcomes based on institutional-based trust (Brockner, Siegel, Daly, Tyler, & Martin, 1997; McKnight, Cummings, & Chervany, 1998; Sitkin & Roth, 1993; Zucker, 1986). For example, principals supervise teachers. On many levels, teachers may feel equal. However, performance evaluation is a time of power asymmetry. Although teachers may be uncomfortable preparing for or being engaged during the evaluation conference, they also feel there are process safeguards. Any violation of this proxy-based trust may find a teacher assessing the competence and integrity of not only the principal but also the school.

Successful institutional-based trust enables the development of knowledge-based trust (Hoy & Tschannen-Moran, 2000; Zucker, 1986). According to Zucker, this type of institutional-based trust is the least effective structure on which to maintain complex societies.

Repeated Exchanges. Kochanek (2005) indicates that social similarity, contracts, and proxy types of trust may be short lived. However, these types of trust are influenced by repeated social exchanges, referred to by Zucker (1986) as knowledge-based trust. Although short-term contracts and proxies prove necessary to achieve immediate outcomes and produce ephemeral trust, long-term contracts continue based on repeated, trustworthy interactions. As one individual finds another reliable and dependable, knowledge-based trust emerges (Zucker, 1986). The result is predictability of another's intentions (Creed & Miles, 1996; Zucker, 1986). Through positive communication and benevolent behavior, each party respects the other during repeated exchanges that require risk-taking, prediction of the other's intent, and confidence in outcomes without violating each other's trust (Creed & Miles, 1996; Hoy & Tschannen-Moran, 2000; Lewicki & Bunker, 1996; Zucker, 1986).

Rationale and Hypothesis
Adams (2008) advances a model of trust formation that specifies behavioral, affective, and cognitive conditions as social antecedents of trust in schools. Teacher trust in a principal's supportive, mutually respectful, and open leadership practices is positively related to higher levels of principal trust (Adams, 2008; Adams, Forsyth, & Mitchell, 2009; Bryk & Schneider, 2002; Forsyth et al., 2006; Goddard et al., 2001; Hoy et al., 2002; Hoy & Tschannen-Moran, 1999, 2003; Tschannen-Moran, 2001, 2003, 2009). In contrast, authoritative leadership behaviors diminish principal trust (Adams, 2008). One of the primary roles where confusion is prevalent is that of teacher-principal interaction during the principal's role as instructional supervisor. The formal authority of principals as supervisor intersects with technical expertise, creating a social dynamic that has the potential to influence teacher trust. Because instructional supervision empowers teachers through interactions that are professional and collaborative, it is predicted that *the practice of instructional supervision within a school would explain principal trust after accounting for the effects of teacher and school characteristics.*

Research Methods

Introduction
The primary purpose of this chapter's research was to examine the relationship between instructional supervision and principal trust within the context of urban elementary schools. It was hypothesized that a principal's instructional supervision practices explain significant variance in principal trust after accounting for teacher and school factors. The design of this study allowed for the unique effect of instructional supervision on principal trust to be tested.

Research Design
An ex post facto correlational design was used to determine the strength of the relationship between teacher perceptions of the principal's instructional supervision behaviors and principal trust. The reliability of the instructional supervision scale was estimated with Cronbach's alpha. Data were collected at one time period from a cross section of elementary schools in an urban district. Both the independent variable of instructional supervision and the dependent variable of principal trust were measured on a continuous scale. Hierarchical Linear Modeling (HLM) was employed to partition an outcome's variability into within-school and between-school components and to test the school-level effects on teacher trust of the principal.

Sample and Data Collection
The study involved multilevel data: teachers nested within schools. Data were collected from 248 teachers representing 56 Title I elementary schools from an urban

school district in a Midwestern state. Teachers were treated as the first level unit of analysis to test the relationship between instructional supervision and principal trust at the individual teacher level.

Because the interest of the researcher was to study the relationship between instructional supervision and principal trust within the context of an urban elementary school, criterion sampling was used (Mertens, 1998). Permission to submit an electronic survey to elementary teachers was obtained from the district. Teachers understood that participation was voluntary and confidentiality was ensured.

Because this study involved nested data, teachers nested within schools, all schools with at least five teacher responses were retained and used for the nested analysis. A power analysis using optimal design 2.0 was conducted to determine the ideal number of schools for the multilevel model. Results suggested that with a sample of 56 schools and an average of five respondents per school, and an expected medium effect size, the estimated power of the sample was 88, which is strong for the sample size of the study population. A power assessment estimates the ability of the sample to detect a statistically significant difference, if one exists, in the overall population. A strong power controls for making type two errors (Aron, Aron, & Coups, 2006). The data suggested that there was an 88% chance that the sample was capable of detecting a significant relationship between instructional supervision and principal trust.

School demographic data were gathered from the state department of education. These data are public and accessible through the department of education's website. Data were collected during late spring 2009. Teachers associated themselves with a school using a coding method employed by the online survey. Teachers' responses were anonymous. Two follow-up emails were sent to improve the number of usable surveys for the analysis. The result was a final sample of 248 teachers and 56 schools. Of the teachers participating, the educational levels were as follows: 106 BA/BS; 45 BA/BS = 30; 63 master's degrees; and 3 doctorate degrees. With regard to teaching experience, 30 had 1 to 3 years, 24 had 4 to 6 years, 19 had 7 to 9 years, and 175 had greater than 9 years. There were 227 female participants, and 21 male participants.

Measures

One purpose of the study was to develop a valid and reliable measure of instructional supervision that captured teachers' perceptions of the principal's behaviors when providing direct instructional assistance. Results of the instrument and variables are discussed briefly in the following section.

Instructional Supervision. Items for the scale were developed from the theoretical and empirical evidence on effective instructional supervisory practices (Blase

& Blase, 1999, 2000; Glickman et al., 2007). Specifically, Blase and Blase's (1999) qualitative identification of effective direct instructional assistance to teachers was the guiding framework for the survey items. Direct assistance consisted of two primary themes (i.e., principal behaviors), talking strategies and promoting professional development (Blase & Blase, 1999, 2000). Twelve items were initially developed that captured teachers' perceptions of principals' direct instructional assistance in the context of instructional supervision.

The researcher submitted the 12 items to a group of 11 principals and asked them to critique items for clarity and alignment with effective supervisory practices. This action assessed construct validity. The panel of principals removed two items to prevent a lack of clarity and lack of fit with the practice of instructional supervision: "The principal offers opportunities for me to implement well-researched ideas" and "The principal encourages teachers to identify and reflect on the relationship between teaching and outcomes." Based on feedback from the panel, three items, "The principal gives teachers choices in addressing instructional issues during post-observation conferences," "The principal provides helpful feedback in a non-evaluative manner," and "The principal empowers teachers to identify instructional concerns," were rewritten to better capture principal behaviors when providing direct instructional assistance. This scale resulted in 10 items that measured direct instructional assistance.

Submitting the 10 items to an exploratory factor analysis assessed internal structure validity. Statistical Package for the Social Sciences (SPSS) was used to run an exploratory factor analysis with principal axis extraction. Data patterns can be explored among the interrelationships of the Instructional Supervision Scale items and identify a common factor and determine the fit of the items. A principal axis approach extracts both common and unique variance (Fabrigar, Wegener, MacCallum, & Strahan, 1999). This approach reduces plausible factor combinations to the factor or factors that explain the most common variance (Fabrigar et al., 1999). Factor loadings were strong, with a range of .70 to .89. Item 8, "The principal provides feedback only when I sign my annual evaluation," had a factor loading of .247, and as a result it was eliminated. The final analysis of nine items yielded a one-factor design with loadings ranging from .72 to .93 (see table 4.1).

Concurrent validity tests for the Instructional Supervision Scale (ISS) were performed through correlational analysis using Enabling School Structure (ESS) survey (Hoy & Sweetland, 2000) and Program Coherence (PC) (Newmann, Smith, Allensworth, & Bryk, 2001).

Principal Trust. Principal trust was measured utilizing the teacher trust of principal subscale of the Omnibus Trust Scale (Hoy & Tschannen-Moran, 2003). Eight questions numbered 1, 4, 7, 9, 11, 15, 18, and 23 of the Omnibus T-Scale assess teacher trust of the principal. The principal trust subscale utilizes a 6-point Likert response set ranging from "strongly disagree" (coded as 1) to "strongly agree" (coded as 6). Example items include "Teachers in this school can rely on the principal" and "The teachers in this school have faith in the integrity of the principal." Three of the items are negatively worded and, as a result, are reverse coded. The construct validity of the Principal Trust Scales was supported by a factor analytic study and alpha values for principal trust calculated at .98 (Hoy & Tschannen-Moran, 2003), as well as its repeated use in other research (Bryk & Schneider, 2002; Forsyth & Adams, 2007; Forsyth et al., 2006; Goddard et al., 2001; Hoy et al., 2002; Hoy & Tschannen-Moran, 2003; Tschannen-Moran, 2001). In the current sample, the Cronbach alpha coefficient of reliability was .96.

Enabling School Structure Survey. The Enabling School Structure (ESS) survey (Hoy & Sweetland, 2000) was used to measure teachers' perceptions of how school leaders exercise administrative authority. The scale ranges on a continuum from enabling formalization and centralization to hindering formalization and centralization (Hoy & Sweetland, 2000, 2001). ESS is a 12-item Likert-type scale that measures the degree to which school structure is enabling. Half the items were negatively worded, which requires reverse scoring. Sample items included "Administrative rules in this school enable authentic communications between teachers and administrators" and "In this school the authority of the principal is used to undermine teachers" (Hoy & Sweetland, 2001).

The Enabling School Structure (ESS) survey consists of six items that capture formalization and six that measure centralization. Validity is supported by strong factor loadings (Hoy & Tschannen-Moran, 1999) and use in other studies (Adams & Forsyth, 2007; Tschannen-Moran, 2009) in addition to the Hoy and Sweetland (2000, 2001) studies. The reliability of the scale is consistently high, usually .90 or higher (Hoy & Sweetland, 2001). For purposes of this study, three items were omitted: "The administrative hierarchy obstructs student achievement," "Administrative rules in this school are guides to solutions rather than rigid procedures," and "In this school the authority of the principal is used to undermine teachers." In the current sample, the alpha coefficient of reliability for this subscale was .92.

Results

The primary purpose of this research was to examine the relationship between instructional supervision and principal trust within the context of urban elementary schools. Results from the HLM analysis tested the following hypothesis: *The practice of instructional supervision within a school explains principal trust after accounting for the effects of teacher and school characteristics.*

Descriptive statistics were calculated to describe the sample of 248 teachers who were nested within 56 urban elementary schools. Contextual and achievement

Table 4.1. Factor Loadings for Instructional Supervision Survey

Item	Statement	Factor Loading	Communalities
1	The principal listens to teachers' instructional problems.	0.88	0.78
2	The principal conducts post-observation conferences.	0.72	0.66
3	The principal gives teachers choices in addressing instructional issues during post-observation conferences.	0.87	0.77
4	The principal encourages creativity in teaching.	0.81	0.71
5	The principal offers professional literature as a resource for instructional improvement.	0.74	0.57
6	The principal provides helpful feedback in a non-evaluative manner.	0.93	0.85
7	The principal provides helpful feedback after instructional observations.	0.92	0.83
8	The principal provides praise that is focused on concrete teacher behaviors.	0.86	0.74
9	The principal visits classrooms on a regular basis.	0.75	0.60
10	The principal empowers teachers to identify instructional concerns.	0.88	0.78

Percentage of Variance = 73%
Alpha = .97

data from the schools in the sample are also included. The proportion of students with schools participating in subsidized meals (SES) varied from 9 to 98 with a mean of 81%. School size varied from 92 to 973 with a mean of 396. The sample API ranged from 603 to 1,500. The state average during the same year was 1,107. The sample totaled 248 teachers and consisted of 21 males and 227 female teachers. Degrees earned by the teachers were 106 BA/BS; 45 BA/BS, plus 30 hours; 63 master's degrees; 31 master's degrees, plus 30 hours; and 3 EdD/PhD.

An existing measure of instructional supervision was not identified or used in the literature. One purpose of this study was to develop a valid and reliable measure of instructional supervision. The 10-item instructional supervision scale was assessed for its factor stability, validity, and reliability. A principal-axis factoring method was performed on the scale to test the instrument's item structure. The results were encouraging. Factor loadings ranged from .72 to .93. One factor explained 73% of the variance among all 10 items, indicating that the Instructional Supervision (IS) Scale is a one-factor measure. The conceptual identifiers of IS clustered around this one dominant factor. High communalities of the factors indicate the strong relationship among all the items. Item consistency, measured by Cronbach's alpha, was strong at .97, which suggests sound internal consistency among the items. In short, the 10-item instructional supervision survey is a valid and reliable measure that incorporates and is representative of instructional supervision.

Discussion

Similar to other organizations, trust within schools is a subjective condition that influences organizational and school effectiveness (Forsyth, 2008). For this reason, understanding the formation of trust was an important objective of this research.

Principal Trust and Role Obligations
Principal trust building largely depends on a principal's ability to create a healthy environment. How the principal manages and communicates goals and expectations either creates barriers or reduces vulnerability. The literature suggests that power symmetry is a necessary goal for effective schools (Bryk & Schneider, 2002; Kochanek, 2005). This theory holds true for the present study. Although no direct measure of power symmetry was introduced, research indicates that any imbalance of power is quickly demonstrated by distrust of those less empowered (Blase & Blase, 2002a; Tschannen-Moran & Hoy, 2000).

Commitment to professional learning communities includes competent principals who are change management specialists and who can guide the top-down culture in a school toward a facilitative, inspired, and transitionally shared vision. Teacher-principal trust leads to collective engagement of teachers, which results in collaborative, healthy school environments. Teachers in the schools surveyed appreciated the principal's direct assistance behaviors. Based on the literature, this is an indication that principals are making strides to promote reflective practice and teacher professional growth. Creating a learning community environment involves action research processes, such as reflection, teacher-teacher interaction, collective discussion, and practice-based learning. Principals must allow teachers time to be involved. Based on this study, the principal's feedback is instrumental and his or her support builds trust. Without time set aside for teacher interaction and sharing of ideas, trust cannot grow or be sustained.

The more pessimistic views assert that not much has changed since the late 1800s and many principals cling to supervision by inspection, oversight, command, and control (Holland & Garman, 2001). The positive end of the continuum indicates that instructional supervision has transitioned into a "school-based or school-college based activity, practice, or process, [that] at its best, engages teachers in meaningful, non-judgmental, and ongoing instructional dialogue for the purpose of improving teaching and learning" (Glanz, 2000, p. 11). Glickman (1985) recognized the impossibility of one person, the principal, to manage all the responsibilities associated with the position and behave as expected by teachers, parents, and the community. Shared and distributed responsibilities increase trust and provide teachers the opportunity to attain self-efficacy as well as feel empowered (Glickman, 1985). Research continues to find that transactional supervisors do not have the successes of transformational supervisors (Blase & Blase, 2001, 2002a, 2002b). Bureaucracies do not have the successes of enabling structures (Hoy & Sweetland, 2001). The measure of instructional supervision supports styles that are more person centered, relationship oriented, supportive (Hoffman, Sabo, Bliss, & Hoy, 1994; Hoy, Tarter, & Witkoskie, 1992; Tarter, Bliss, & Hoy, 1989; Tarter, Sabo, & Hoy, 1995), collegial (Hoy et al., 2002; Tschannen-Moran & Hoy, 1998; Tschannen-Moran, 2001), and transformational (Tschannen-Moran, 2003) and was found to be a powerful and independent predictor of principal trust (Adams, 2008).

Principals and Instructional Supervision
This chapter's study contributes to the literature by providing a reliable and valid instructional supervision measure as well as establishing a relationship between the practice of instructional supervision and principal trust. Results of the study confirmed the hypothesis that instructional supervision is a strong predictor of principal trust after accounting for other school conditions such as school size, API, and SES.

Educational researchers and reformers agree that successful twenty-first-century schools must have strong instructional leaders who can balance the goal of high-quality instructional improvement and trusting relationships (Adams, 2008; Darling-Hammond, 1997). Effective schools, equality, innovation, and accountability are no longer simply visions of state and federal mandates. These mandates are now reality and form the social environment in which current principals operate. The job of leading schools requires a balanced and collaborative approach to coordinate quality teaching and learning. Added to a principal's responsibilities in recent decades has been the growing need to facilitate cooperative relationships with parents, students, community partners, and policy makers. A principal's role obligations are extensive. As such, the principal is expected to be proficient in fiscal management, cultural awareness, facilities management, interpersonal exchanges, and teaching and learning. Balancing a proliferation of rules and regulations with collegial, informative, and supportive behaviors requires highly respected principals who demonstrate the facets of trust.

With the growing demands and accountability pressures confronting principals, it is easy to understand how instructional supervision could be neglected for simpler, but less effective, performance management approaches such as evaluation (Acheson & Gall, 2003). Results of the present research add to the evidence on the importance of instructional supervision. Without principal trust, it is hard to imagine that a principal would be successful at leading improvement efforts. As the evidence from this study suggests, instructional supervision is an effective mechanism to build principal trust.

Direct instructional assistance to teachers included, but was not limited to, behaviors such as making suggestions, pre- and post-conference feedback, reflective discussion, and collaborative decision-making (Blase & Blase, 1999, 2000; Hallinger & Heck, 1996a, 1996b; Leithwood, Jantzi, & Steinbach, 1999). Other functions and purposes of instructional supervision included development of teachers' self-awareness to improve classroom practice (Goldhammer, 1969), development of professionally responsible teachers who understand self-analysis (Cogan, 1973), promotion of interactive and democratic processes aimed at teacher professional development (Acheson & Gall, 1997), facilitation of teachers' self-direction and reflective capacity, and promotion of decision-making competence (Glickman, 1985; Glickman et al., 2007). Each of these processes functioned to enhance professional autonomy and instructional responsibility, two imperative conditions that undergird effective practice and promote trust (Ryan & Deci, 2000). Instructional supervision is a critical component of schools. As this study suggests, higher levels of perceived direct instructional supervision behaviors of the principal are linked to higher levels of principal trust.

Implications for Practice

The focus of this research was on the relationship between instructional supervision and principal trust. Use of the facets of trust continues to suggest that trust is a vital component in well-functioning organizations and school communities. There is demonstrated significance that the empirical measure of instructional supervision developed for this research is also a role that requires further study. Principals are challenged by the inherent hierarchical structure of schools, rules that hinder as well as help him or her to manage, and preparedness, in some instances. Added to the daily routines, principals must motivate teachers, provide support and leadership on one hand, and on the other, discipline or possibly terminate those teachers who cannot or do not succeed. "Clearly, the principal has a critical role to play in establishing an atmosphere of trust within the school, particularly at the elementary school level" (Forsyth & Mitchell, 2004, p. 30). Standards-based and accountability-oriented school reform efforts necessitate hierarchy and principals must also be innovative enough to build an enabling structure. "Adverse consequences of hierarchy are not inherent in structure itself but rather are due to the decisions of administrators in implementing their authority" (Hoy & Sweetland, 2001, p. 301). Although strong perceptions and practice of the traditional hierarchical bureaucratic school structure exists in some districts, the top-down approach is drawing to a close in this virtual society. This is not to say that principals cannot manage, discipline, and hold teachers accountable. However, caution should be highly considered if principals rely on rigid bureaucratic methods of command and control as the only mechanisms to coordinate teaching and learning.

Results from the instructional supervision scale used in this study indicate that a principal's practice of instructional supervision has consequences for principal trust. This finding has implications for both the practice of and further research on instructional supervision. Results indicate that instructional supervision is a variable important to building and maintaining trust. This finding is significant considering the literature that has negatively aligned supervision with evaluation. It is imperative for teachers to feel empowered, as empowerment has been linked to self-efficacy, collective efficacy, and job satisfaction.

Summary

This chapter's study utilized empirically tested facets of trust relative to instructional supervision to gain a better understanding of the evolving concept of principal trust and any influence instructional supervision may have. By framing the survey candidly as an examination of instructional supervision and allowing teachers to respond based on individual perceptions, this study offered a glimpse into teacher-principal interactions. Results from this study suggest that instructional supervision is one of many responsibilities that should not be neglected by school leaders. Improving teacher effectiveness in schools will not result from external policies but instead through internal processes such as instructional supervision that enhance social and human capacity. Greater trust between principals and teachers has consequences for successful school reform, school improvement, student achievement, and school effectiveness (Forsyth, 2008). Instructional supervision can be used as a mechanism to facilitate trust within the school.

Questions to Consider

1. Although the instructional leadership role is at the center of principals' responsibilities, some principals may place this responsibility lower on their list of priorities due to the need to "fight fires" that often occur in high poverty schools. To what extent does instructional leadership play a role in your current or previous school? What factors contribute to the enactment of strong instructional leadership in your school?

2. Should instructional leadership look different in high poverty schools than in higher wealth schools? If so, how? How can you be sure that the necessary level and type of instructional leadership occurs in high poverty schools?
3. To what extent, and in what ways, are trust (teacher to student, leader to teacher, teacher to teacher) and teacher effectiveness impacted by the quality of the principal's instructional leadership?

References

Acheson, K. A., & Gall, M. D. (1997). *Techniques in the clinical supervision of teachers: Preservice and inservice applications* (4th ed.). New York: Longman.

Acheson, K. A., & Gall, M. D. (2003). *Clinical supervision and teacher development: Preservice and inservice applications* (5th ed.). New York: Wiley.

Adams, C. M. (2008). Building trust in schools: A review of the empirical evidence. In W. K. Hoy & M. DiPaola (Eds.), *Improving schools: Studies in leadership and culture* (pp. 1–27). Charlotte, NC: Information Age.

Adams, C. M. (2010). Social determinants of student trust in high poverty elementary schools. In W. K. Hoy & M. DiPaola (Eds.), *Analyzing school contexts* (pp. 255–280). Greenwich, CT: Information Age.

Adams, C. M., & Forsyth, P. B. (2007). Promoting a culture of parent collaboration and trust: An empirical study. *Journal of School Public Relations, 28*(1), 32–56.

Adams, C. M., & Forsyth, P. B. (2009). The nature and function of trust in schools. *Journal of School Leadership, 19*(2), 126–152.

Adams, C. M., Forsyth, P. B., & Mitchell, R. M. (2009). The formation of parent-school trust: A multilevel analysis. *Educational Administration Quarterly, 45*(1), 4–33.

Aron, A., Aron, E. N., & Coups, E. (2006). *Statistics for psychology* (4th ed.). Upper Saddle River, NJ: Prentice Hall.

Baier, A. (1986). Trust and antitrust. *Ethics, 96*, 231–260.

Bigley, G. A., & Pearce, J. L. (1998). Straining for shared meaning in organization science: Problems of trust and distrust. *Academy of Management Review, 23*, 405–452.

Blase, J. (1987). Dimensions of effective school leadership: The teachers' perspective. *American Educational Research Journal, 24*, 598–610.

Blase, J. (1988). The everyday political perspectives of teachers: Vulnerability and conservatism. *Qualitative Studies in Education, 1*(2), 125–142.

Blase, J. (1990). Some negative effects of principals' control-oriented and protective political behavior. *American Educational Research Journal, 27*, 727–753.

Blase, J. (1991a). Analysis and discussion: Some concluding remarks. In J. Blase (Ed.), *The politics of life in schools: Power, conflict, and cooperation* (pp. 237–255). Newbury Park, CA: Sage.

Blase, J. (Ed.). (1991b). *The politics of life in schools: Power, conflict, and cooperation*. Newbury Park, CA: Sage.

Blase, J., & Anderson, G. L. (1995). *The micropolitics of educational leadership: From control to empowerment*. New York: Teachers College Press.

Blase, J., & Blase, J. (1997). The micropolitical orientation of facilitative school principals and its effects on teachers' sense of empowerment. *Journal of Educational Administration, 35*(2), 138–164.

Blase, J., & Blase, J. (1998). *Handbook of instructional leadership: How really good principals promote teaching and learning*. Thousand Oaks, CA: Corwin.

Blase, J., & Blase, J. (1999). Principals' instructional leadership and teacher development: Teachers' perspectives. *Educational Administration Quarterly, 35*(3), 349–378.

Blase, J., & Blase, J. (2000). Effective instructional leadership: Teachers' perspectives on how principals promote teaching and learning in schools. *Journal of Educational Administration, 38*(2), 130–141.

Blase, J., & Blase, J. (2001). *Empowering teachers: What successful principals do!* (2nd ed.). Thousand Oaks, CA: Corwin.

Blase, J., & Blase, J. (2002a). The dark side of leadership: Teacher perspectives of principal mistreatment. *Educational Administration Quarterly, 38*(5), 671–727.

Blase, J., & Blase, J. (2002b). The micropolitics of instructional supervision: A call for research. *Educational Administration Quarterly, 38*(1), 6–44.

Blau, P. M. (1964). *Exchange and power in social life.* New York: Wiley.

Boon, S. D., & Holmes, J. G. (1991). The dynamics of interpersonal trust: Resolving uncertainty in the face of risk. In R. A. Hinde & J. Groebel (Eds.), *Co-operation and prosocial behavior* (pp. 190–211). Cambridge, England: Cambridge University Press.

Brockner, J., Siegel, P. A., Daly, J. P., Tyler, T., & Martin, C. (1997). When trust matters: The moderating effects of outcome favorability. *Administrative Science Quarterly, 42*, 558–583.

Bryk, A. S., & Schneider, B. (2002). *Trust in schools: A core resource for improvement.* New York: Russell Sage Foundation.

Butler, J. K., Jr. (1991). Toward understanding and measuring conditions of trust: Evolution of a condition of trust inventory. *Journal of Management, 17*(3), 643–663.

Butler, J. K., Jr. (1995). Behaviors, trust, and goal achievement in win-win negotiation role-play. *Group and Organizational Management, 20*, 486–502.

Butler, J. K., Jr., & Cantrell, R. S. (1984). A behavioral decision theory approach to modeling dyadic trust in superiors and subordinates. *Psychological Reports, 55*, 19–28.

Clark, M. C., & Payne, R. L. (1997). The nature and structure of workers' trust in management. *Journal of Organizational Behavior, 18*, 802–824.

Cogan, M. L. (1973). *Clinical supervision.* Boston: Houghton Mifflin.

Cogan, M., Anderson, R. H., & Krajewski, R. (1993). *Clinical supervision: Special methods for the supervision of teachers* (3rd ed.). Fort Worth, TX: Harcourt Brace.

Cook, J., & Wall, T. (1980). New work attitude measures of trust, organizational commitment and personal need non-fulfillment. *Journal of Occupational Psychology, 53*, 39–52.

Creed, D. W. E., & Miles, R. E. (1996). A conceptual framework linking organizational forms, managerial philosophies, and the opportunity costs of controls. In R. M. Kramer & T. R. Tyler (Eds.), *Trust in organizations: Frontiers of theory and research* (pp. 16–38). Thousand Oaks, CA: Sage.

Cummings, L. L. (1983). Performance-evaluation systems in the context of individual trust and commitment. In F. J. Landy, S. Zedrick, & J. Cleveland (Eds.), *Performance measurement and theory* (pp. 89–93). Hillsdale, NJ: Erlbaum.

Cummings, L. L., & Bromiley, P. (1996). The Organizational Trust Inventory (OTI). In R. M. Kramer & T. R. Tyler (Eds.), *Trust in organizations: Frontiers of theory and research* (pp. 302–330). Thousand Oaks, CA: Sage.

Darling-Hammond, L. (1997). *Doing what matters most: Investing in quality teaching.* New York: National Commission on Teaching & America's Future.

Deutsch, M. (1958). Trust and suspicion. *Journal of Conflict Resolution, 2*, 265–279.

Deutsch, M. (1960). Trust, trustworthiness and the F-scale. *Journal of Abnormal and Social Psychology, 61*, 138–140.

Deutsch, M. (1962). Cooperation and trust: Some theoretical notes. *Nebraska Symposium on Motivation, 10*, 275–318.

Deutsch, M. (1973). *The resolution of conflict: Constructive and destructive processes.* New Haven, CT: Yale University Press.

Dirks, K. T., & Ferrin, D. L. (2001). The role of trust in organizational settings. *Organizational Science, 12*(4), 450–467.

Fabrigar, L. R., Wegener, D. T., MacCallum, R. C., & Strahan, E. J. (1999). Evaluating the use of exploratory factor analysis in psychological research. *Psychological Methods, 4*(3), 272–299.

Forsyth, P. B. (2008). The empirical consequences of school trust. In W. K. Hoy & M. DiPaola (Eds.), *Improving schools: Studies in leadership and culture* (pp. 1–27). Charlotte, NC: Information Age.

Forsyth, P. B., Adams, C. M., & Hoy, W. K. (2011). *Collective trust: Why schools can't improve without it.* New York, NY: Teachers College Press.

Forsyth, P. B., Barnes, L. B., & Adams, C. M. (2006). Trust-effectiveness patterns in schools. *Journal of Educational Administration, 44*(2), 122–141.

Forsyth, P. B., & Mitchell, R. M. (2004). *Trust, the principal, and student identification.* Paper presented at the annual meeting of the University Council for Educational Administration, Austin, TX.

Fox, A. (1974). *Beyond contract: Work, power and trust relation.* London: Faber & Faber.

Frost, T., Stimpson, D. V., & Maughan, M. R. (1978). Some correlates of trust. *Journal of Psychology: Interdisciplinary and Applied, 99*(1), 103–108. doi:10.1080/00223980.1978.9921447

Fukuyama, F. (1995). *Trust: The social virtues and the creation of prosperity.* New York: Simon & Schuster.

Gabarro, J. J. (1978). The development of trust, influence, and expectations. In A. G. Athos & J. J. Gabarro (Eds.), *Interpersonal behavior: Communications and understanding in relationships* (pp. 290–303). Englewood Cliffs, NJ: Prentice-Hall.

Gambetta, D. (1988). Can we trust? In D. Gambetta (Ed.), *Trust: Making and breaking cooperative relations* (pp. 213–238). Cambridge, England: Basil Blackwell.

Garman, N. (1986). Reflection, the heart of clinical supervision: A modern rationale for professional practice. *Journal of Curriculum and Supervision, 2*(1), 1–24.

Geist, J., & Hoy, W. K. (2004). Cultivating a culture of trust: Enabling school structure, teacher professionalism, and academic press. *Leading and Managing, 10,* 1–18.

Glanz, J. (1999). A primer on action research for the school administrator. *Clearing House, 72*(5), 301–305.

Glanz, J. (2000). Supervision for the millennium: A retrospective and prospective. *Focus on Education, 44,* 9–16.

Glanz, J. (2005). *What every principal should know about collaborative leadership.* Thousand Oaks, CA: Corwin.

Glanz, J., & Sullivan, S. (2003). *Supervision in practice: Three steps to improving teaching and learning.* Thousand Oaks, CA: Corwin.

Glickman, C. D. (1985). *Development as the aim of instructional supervision.* Paper presented at the annual meeting of the Association for Supervision and Curriculum Development, Chicago, IL.

Glickman, C. D. (1998). Educational leadership for democratic purpose: What do we mean? *International Journal of Leadership in Education, 1,* 47–53.

Glickman, C. D., Gordon, S. P., & Ross-Gordon, J. M. (1998). *Supervision of instruction: A developmental approach* (4th ed.). Boston: Allyn & Bacon.

Glickman, C. D., Gordon, S. P., & Ross-Gordon, J. M. (2007). *Supervision of instruction: A developmental approach* (7th ed.). Boston: Allyn & Bacon.

Goddard, R. D., Tschannen-Moran, M., & Hoy, W. K. (2001). Teacher trust in students and parents: A multilevel examination of the distribution and effects of teacher trust in urban elementary schools. *Elementary School Journal, 102*(1), 3–17.

Goldhammer, R. (1969). *Clinical supervision: Special methods for the supervision of teachers.* New York: Holt, Rinehart and Winston.

Goldhammer, R., Anderson, R. H., & Krajewski, R. J. (1980). *Clinical supervision: Special methods for the supervision of teachers.* New York: Holt, Rinehart and Winston.

Goldhammer, R., Anderson, R. H., & Krajewski, R. J. (1993). *Clinical supervision: Special methods for the supervision of teachers* (3rd ed.). New York: Holt, Rinehart & Winston.

Golembiewski, R. T. (1979). *Approaches to planned change.* New York: Marcel Dekker.

Golembiewski, R. T. (1985). *Humanizing public organizations.* Mt. Airy, MD: Lomond.

Golembiewski, R. T., & McConkie, M. (1975). The centrality of interpersonal trust in group processes. In C. L. Cooper (Ed.), *Theories of group processes* (pp. 131–185). London: Wiley.

Hallinger, P. (2003). Leading educational change: Reflections on the practice of instructional and transformational leadership. *Cambridge Journal of Education, 33*(3), 329–351.

Hallinger, P., & Heck, R. H. (1996a). The principal's role in school effectiveness: An assessment of methodological progress, 1980–1995. In K. Leithwood, J. Chapman, D. Corson, P. Hallinger, & A. Hart (Eds.), *International handbook of educational leadership and administration* (pp. 723–783). Dordrecht, the Netherlands: Kluwer.

Hallinger, P., & Heck, R. H. (1996b). Reassessing the principal's role in school effectiveness: A review of empirical research, 1980–1995. *Educational Administration Quarterly, 32*(1), 5–44.

Hallinger, P., & Leithwood, K. (1994). Introduction: Exploring the impact of principal leadership. *School Effectiveness and School Improvement, 5*(3), 206–217.

Henderson, J. E., & Hoy, W. K. (1982). Leader authenticity: The development and test of an operational measure. Paper presented at the Annual Meeting of the American Educational Research Association, New York, New York

Hirschhorn, L. (1997). *Reworking authority: Leading and following in a post-modern organization.* Cambridge, MA: The MIT Press.

Hoffman, J., Sabo, D., Bliss, J., & Hoy, W. (1994). Building a culture of trust. *Journal of School Leadership, 4*, 484–501.

Holland, P. E., & Garman, N. (2001). Toward a resolution of the crisis of legitimacy in the field of supervision. *Journal of Curriculum and Supervision, 15*(2), 95–111.

Hosmer, L. T. (1995). Trust: The connecting link between organizational theory and philosophical ethics. *Academy of Management Review, 20*(2), 379–403.

Hoy, W. K., & Forsyth, P. B. (1986). *Effective supervision: Theory into practice.* New York: Random House.

Hoy, W. K, Gage, C. Q., III, & Tarter, J. C. (2006). School mindfulness and faculty trust: Necessary conditions for each other? *Educational Administration Quarterly, 4*, 236–255.

Hoy, W. K., & Hannum, J. (1997). Middle school climate: An empirical assessment of organizational health and student achievement. *Educational Administration Quarterly, 33*, 290–311.

Hoy, W. K., & Kuppersmith, W. J. (1985). The meaning and measure of faculty trust. *Educational and Psychological Research, 5*, 1–10.

Hoy, W. K., & Miskel, C. G. (2008). *Educational administration: Theory, research, and practice* (8th ed.). Boston: McGraw-Hill.

Hoy, W. K., & Sabo, D. J. (1998). *Quality middle schools: Open and healthy.* Thousand Oaks, CA: Corwin.

Hoy, W. K., Smith, P. A., & Sweetland, S. R. (2002). The development of the organizational climate index for high schools: Its measure and relationship to faculty trust. *High School Journal, 86*(2), 38–49.

Hoy, W., & Sweetland, S. (2000). School bureaucracies that work: Enabling, not coercive. *Journal of School Leadership, 10,* 525–541.

Hoy, W., & Sweetland, S. (2001). Designing better schools: The meaning and measure of enabling school structures. *Educational Administration Quarterly, 37*(3), 296–321.

Hoy, W. K., & Tarter, C. J. (1997). *The road to open and healthy schools: A handbook for change.* Thousand Oaks, CA: Corwin.

Hoy, W. K., Tarter, C. J., & Kottkamp, R. B. (1991). *Open schools/healthy schools.* Newbury Park, CA: Sage.

Hoy, W., Tarter, C. J., & Witkoskie, L. (1992). Faculty trust in colleagues: Linking the principal with school effectiveness. *Journal of Research and Development in Education, 26,* 38–45.

Hoy, W. K., & Tschannen-Moran, M. (1999). Five faces of trust: An empirical confirmation in urban elementary schools. *Journal of School Leadership, 9*(3), 184–208.

Hoy, W. K., & Tschannen-Moran, M. (2003). The conceptualization and measurement of faculty trust in schools: The omnibus T-scale. In W. K. Hoy & C. Miskel (Eds.), *Studies in leading and organizing schools* (pp. 181–208). Greenwich, CT: Information Age.

Jones, G., & George, J. (1998). The experience and evolution of trust: Implications for cooperation and teamwork. *Academy of Management Review, 23*(3), 531–546.

Kee, H. W., & Knox, R. W. E. (1970). Conceptual and methodological considerations in the study of trust and suspicion. *Journal of Conflict Resolution, 14,* 357–366.

Kochanek, J. (2005). *Building trust for better schools: Research-based practices.* Thousand Oaks, CA: Corwin.

Kramer, R. M. (1999). Trust and distrust in organizations: Emerging perspectives, enduring questions. *Annual Review of Psychology, 50,* 569–598.

Kramer, R. M., & Tyler, T. R. (1996). *Trust in organizations: Frontiers of theory and research.* London: Sage.

Leithwood, K., Jantzi, D., & Steinbach, R. (1999). *Changing leadership for changing times.* Buckingham, England: Open University Press.

Lewicki, R. J., & Bunker, B. B. (1995). Trust in relationships: A model of trust development and decline. In B. B. Bunker & J. Z. Rubin (Eds.), *Conflict, co-operation and justice* (pp. 133–173). San Francisco: Jossey-Bass.

Lewicki, R. J., & Bunker, B. B. (1996). Developing and maintaining trust in working relationships. In R. M. Kramer & T. R. Tyler (Eds.), *Trust in organizations: Frontiers of theory and research* (pp. 14–139). Thousand Oaks CA: Sage.

Lewis, J. D., & Weigert, A. (1985). Trust as a social reality. *Social Forces, 63*(3), 967–985.

Likert, R. (1967). *The human organization: Its management and value.* New York: McGraw-Hill.

Luhmann, N. (1979). *Trust and power.* Chichester, England: Wiley.

Luhmann, N. (1988). Familiarity, confidence, trust: Problems and alternatives. In D. Gambetta (Ed.), *Trust: Making and breaking cooperative relations* (pp. 94–107). Oxford, England: Department of Sociology, University of Oxford.

Luke, D. A. (2004). *Multilevel modeling.* Newbury Park, CA: Sage.

Marks, H. M., & Printy, S. M. (2003). Principal leadership and school performance: An integration of transformational and instructional leadership. *Educational Administration Quarterly, 39*(3), 370–397.

Mayer, R. C., Davis, J. H., & Schoorman, F. D. (1995). An integrative model of organizational trust. *Academy of Management Review, 20*(3), 703–734.

McAllister, D. J. (1995). Affect- and cognition-based trust as foundations for interpersonal cooperation in organizations. *Academy of Management Journal, 38*(1), 24–59. Retrieved from http://proquest.umi.com

McKnight, H. D., Cummings, L. L., & Chervany, N. L. (1998). Initial trust formation in new organizational relationships. *Academy of Management Review, 23*, 473–490.

Mertens, D. M. (1998). *Research methods in education and psychology: Integrating diversity with quantitative and qualitative approaches.* London: Sage.

Mishra, A. K. (1996). Organizational responses to crisis: The centrality of trust. In R. M. Kramer & T. R. Tyler (Eds.), *Trust in organizations: Frontiers of theory and research* (pp. 261–287). Thousand Oaks, CA: Sage.

Mishra, A. K., & Spreitzer, G. (1998). Explaining how survivors respond to downsizing: The roles of trust, empowerment, justice, and work design. *Academy Management Review, 23*, 567–588.

Murphy, J. (1990). Principal instructional leadership. In R. S. Lotto & P. W. Thurston (Eds.), *Advances in educational administration: Changing perspectives on the school* (Vol. 1, Pt. B, pp. 163–200). Greenwich, CT: JAI Press.

Newmann, F. M., Smith, B., Allensworth, E., & Bryk, A. S. (2001, January). *Improving Chicago's schools.* Chicago: Consortium on Chicago School Research.

Quinn, D. M. (2002). The impact of principal leadership behaviors on instructional practice and student engagement. *Journal of Educational Administration, 40*(5), 517–537.

Raudenbush, S. W., & Bryk, A. S. (2002). *Hierarchical Linear Models: Applications and data analysis methods* (2nd ed.). Thousand Oaks, CA: Sage.

Rotter, J. B. (1967). A new scale for the measurement of interpersonal trust. *Journal of Personality, 35*, 651–665.

Rousseau, D. M., Sitkin, S. B., Burt, R. S., & Camerer, C. (1998). Not so different after all: A cross-discipline view of trust. *Academy of Management Review, 23*(3), 393–404.

Ryan, R. M., & Deci, E. L. (2000). Self-determination theory and the facilitation of intrinsic motivation, social development, and well-being. *American Psychologist, 55*, 68–78.

Schön, D. (1983). *The reflective practitioner.* New York: Basic Books.

Schön, D. (1984). Leadership as reflection in action. In T. J. Sergiovanni & J. E. Corbally (Eds.), *Leadership and organizational culture: New perspectives on administrative theory and practice* (pp. 36–63). Urbana: University of Illinois Press.

Schön, D. (1987). *Educating the reflective practitioner: Toward a new design for teaching and learning in the professions.* San Francisco: Jossey-Bass.

Sitkin, S. B., & Roth, N. L. (1993). Explaining the limited effectiveness of legalistic "remedies" for trust/distrust. *Organization Science, 4*(3), 367–392.

Tarter, C. J., Bliss, J. R., & Hoy, W. K. (1989). School characteristics and faculty trust in secondary schools. *Educational Administration Quarterly, 25*(3), 294–308.

Tarter, C. J., Sabo, D., & Hoy, W. K. (1995). Middle school climate, faculty trust, and effectiveness: A path analysis. *Journal of Research and Development in Education, 29*, 41–49.

Tschannen-Moran, M. (2001). Collaboration and the need for trust. *Journal of Educational Administration, 39*(4), 308–331.

Tschannen-Moran, M. (2003). Fostering organizational citizenship in schools: Transformational leadership and trust. In W. K. Hoy & C. G. Miskel (Eds.), *Studies in leading and organizing schools* (pp. 157–179). Greenwich, CT: Information Age.

Tschannen-Moran, M. (2009). Fostering teacher professionalism: The role of professional orientation and trust. *Educational Administration Quarterly, 45*, 217–247.

Tschannen-Moran, M., Hoy, A., & Hoy, W. K. (1998). Teacher efficacy: Its meaning and measure. *Review of Educational Research, 58*, 202–248.

Tschannen-Moran, M., & Hoy, W. K. (1998). Trust in schools: A conceptual and empirical analysis. *Journal of Educational Administration, 36*(4), 334–352. Retrieved from http://proquest.umi.com.ezproxy1.lib.ou.edu

Tschannen-Moran, M., & Hoy, W. K. (2000). A multidisciplinary analysis of the nature, meaning, and measurement of trust. *Review of Educational Research, 70*(4), 547–593.

Wahnee, R. L. (2010). *The effect of instructional supervision on principal trust.* (Doctoral dissertation). University of Oklahoma, Norman.

Williamson, O. (1993). Calculativeness, trust, and economic organization. *Journal of Law & Economics, 34*, 453–502.

Zand, D. E. (1971). Trust and managerial problem solving. *Administrative Science Quarterly,* 229–239.

Zucker, L. G. (1986). The production of trust: Institutional sources of economic structure, 1840–1920. In B. M. Staw & L. L. Cummings (Eds.), *Research in organizational behavior, 8* (pp. 55–111). Greenwich, CT: JAI Press.

CHAPTER FIVE

Professional Development and Learning in Schools

Teaching Institutions as Learning Institutions

Lisa Bass

> *Continuing development is the mark of a true professional, an ongoing effort that is never completed. Educators committed to attaining and remaining at the top of their profession invest much energy in staying informed and increasing their skill.* (Danielson, 1996, p. 115)

In an era of increased accountability and emphasis on teacher inputs and student outputs (Mintrop & Sunderman, 2009), effective professional development has become increasingly important. According to Guskey (2000), "Never before in the history of education has greater importance been attached to the professional development of educators. Every proposal for educational reform and every plan for school improvement emphasizes the need for high-quality professional development" (p. 3). Unfortunately, not all professional development is created equal nor is it effective for all schools and teachers.

The traditional structure of schools emphasizes student learning as a function of instruction by teachers (Silins & Mulford, 2002). This emphasis can, and often does, lead to a de-emphasized role of the school as a place of continuous learning and professional development for teachers (Darling-Hammond & McLaughlin, 1995). With respect to schooling, we most often think about the connection between teaching and learning. The anticipated and desired outcome is that there is alignment between teaching objectives and student learning outcomes. When teaching accomplishes this goal, it is said to be effective, as the teacher has attained his or her goal of imparting knowledge to his or her students. Continuous, targeted professional development prepares teachers (Fishman, Marx, Best, & Tal,

2003; Joyce & Showers, 2002) to position and equip students to achieve to their highest academic potential.

Teachers in high poverty schools face challenges and increasingly complex working conditions (de Snyder et al., 2011). As a result, effective classroom management and teaching do not come naturally for many teachers working in high poverty contexts (Siwatu, 2011). Siwatu finds that teachers feel more prepared to teach in [low poverty] suburban settings than in high poverty urban settings upon completion of teacher education. He further suggests that they experience higher levels of self-efficacy in suburban settings.

Teachers in high poverty settings, particularly in the urban context and in some rural contexts, are called upon to respond to the demands of increasing diversity, higher numbers of incidences of school and societal violence, and more disciplinary problems (Knapp, 1995). They must overcome these challenges while contending with increasing pressure to improve student achievement (Mintrop & Sunderman, 2009). To effectively meet the needs of their students, teachers must be prepared to serve successfully in the type of classroom to which they are assigned (Knapp, 1995). As such, the demands of teaching stretch far beyond subject matter knowledge (e.g., Ingersoll, 2007). In order to masterfully deliver their lessons, teachers must be able to connect with their students and manage the classroom in such a way that they maintain control while ensuring students are engaged in the learning process (Corbett & Wilson, 2002). When teachers are adequately prepared to address these challenges, many of the problems associated with classroom discipline are eliminated or avoided all together (e.g., Luiselli, Putnam, Handler, & Feinberg, 2005; Marzano, Marzano, & Pickering, 2003).

Many teachers enter the teaching profession with a basic understanding of the educational process based on their own experiences in school, coupled with what they learn in their pre-service teaching coursework and student teaching practica. Unfortunately, these experiences may not be sufficient to prepare new teachers to work effectively with the schools and communities to which they are assigned, especially when these schools and communities are in socioeconomically challenging environments (e.g., Kennedy, 2010; McKinney, Haberman, Stafford-Johnson, & Robinson, 2008; Siwatu, 2011). As Darling-Hammond and McLaughlin (1995) note:

> The vision of practice that underlies the nation's reform agenda requires most teachers to rethink their own practice, to construct new classroom roles and expectations about student outcomes, and to teach in ways they have never taught before—and probably never experienced as students. (p. 597)

As such, the information gathered from teachers' own schooling and their pre-service teaching may not sufficiently address the knowledge, skills, and disposition (Kennedy, 2010) needed in order to be successful at teaching contemporary youth from high poverty contexts. Hence, when teachers receive inadequate pre-service training, the result is problematic (Grogin & Andrews, 2002; Joyce & Showers, 2002). This lack of preparation is then reflected in their teaching and associated student outcomes. This in turn increases the likelihood that students who are already at risk are further disadvantaged by the very institutions that purport to provide them with the necessary knowledge and skills to be successful both in and outside of school. In this scenario, there are no winners; and unfortunately, students have the most to lose. This is particularly troubling in the current era of accountability in which principals, teachers, and students are judged in large part by measures of student performance (Almy & Tooley, 2012; Balfanz & Mac Iver, 2000; Kennedy, 2010).

While teachers are most likely to spend the bulk of their time in one-on-one and small group interactions with students, school leaders must be prepared to support teachers as they engage in the challenging work of promoting high academic standards while nurturing the social, emotional, and physical needs of their students, especially those from socioeconomically challenged homes and communities (Kennedy, 2010). This requires educators who are able and willing to reach out to students whose own personal needs may differ significantly from the needs of the [middle class] students these educators were previously trained to teach (Almy & Tooley, 2012). If educators do not have an inherent disposition toward nurturing and caring behaviors, schools must work to ensure they receive ongoing professional learning and development aimed at strengthening these dispositions and practices (Almy & Tooley, 2012; Balfanz & Mac Iver, 2000).

The Art of Increasing Teacher Effectiveness

As noted above, the primary purpose of professional development is to provide the necessary training that teachers need in order to be successful in the classroom. Zapeda (2008) cites three relevant characteristics of professional teachers in her discussion of professional development:

1. Knowledge and competence acquired from highly [specialized] training and formal education.
2. The respect and trust of community and peers that lead to a degree of autonomy and self-direction.
3. A set of values, moral and ethical, that allows the performance of the job to become more service-oriented rather than profit-oriented (Zapeda, 2008).

The first characteristic is the most salient and relevant for this discussion of professional development for educators in high poverty schools. In order to effectively teach children from high poverty contexts, teachers must engage in specialized training aimed at assisting them in understanding the needs and experiences of the students they serve, as well as how best to address these unique needs. This includes opportunities to engage with and get to know the home lives of their students, to communicate with individuals and groups from diverse backgrounds, and to teach in ways that are most effective for the students with whom they will work. We believe that by incorporating the appropriate professional learning opportunities, teachers will become better equipped to meet the needs of all children in their charge (Walpole, McKenna, Uribe-Zarain, & Lamitina, 2010). While such learning opportunities should be provided for all teachers, they are especially important in high poverty schools (Domitrovich et al., 2009; Johnson & Fargo, 2010) where a large number of teachers either are new to the profession or are less seasoned than their peers in lower poverty settings (Grissom, 2011).

When teachers are equipped with the professional knowledge to do their jobs, they not only perform more effectively, but also are more likely to remain in the teaching profession for a longer period of time, counteracting the problem of high teacher turnover (e.g., Darling-Hammond, 2003; DuFour & Eaker, 1998; Scherer, 2003). Further, if teachers are treated as professionals whose mentors and supervisors care about their professional growth and development, teachers are more likely to feel cared for and supported, thus encouraged to remain in the field (e.g., Fullan, 2001) and, we would argue, that this increases the likelihood that these teachers will continue to work with the population of students who need them most.

The Principal as Professional Development Facilitator

Assessing School Culture, Climate, and Student-Teacher Performance
The school leader plays a critical role in the development and implementation of professional development opportunities within the school (e.g., Darling-Hammond, 2010). There are several activities that the school leader can undertake in order to evaluate the needs of his or her building and develop a suitable professional development plan. An initial step is to assess the needs of faculty and staff within the school building. According to Zapeda (2008), teachers must be empowered to exercise their voices and school leaders must be responsive to these voices. Zapeda further notes that the principal's role is to assist teachers in finding their 'learning' voices. This occurs as the principal considers and assesses the learning climate of the school and carefully aligns professional development activities to match the organizational learning needs of the school and its staff.

As building level administrator, the principal should be visible within and around the school and should strive to observe a wide variety of settings at different times of the day and school year. This will assist the school leader in assessing school culture and climate (Louis & Wahlstrom, 2011), critical elements in the health and well-being of the school and its students, faculty, and staff (MacNeil, Prater, & Busch, 2009). The extent to which the school represents a warm and welcoming work environment is an important factor in determining the extent to which teachers are satisfied with their work conditions, are confident in their ability to engage in effective teaching, and demonstrate a generally pleasant attitude toward the school and teaching (Cohen, McCabe, Michelli, & Pickeral, 2009; Ellis, 2010; Johnson, Kraft, & Papay, 2012). This is important as research (e.g., Ingersoll, 2001) demonstrates that when school working conditions are poor, teachers are more likely to be unhappy, and their dissatisfaction will result in increased turnover rates. For many schools, the loss of even one teacher can be detrimental, as they not only lose personnel, they also lose the costs associated with initially recruiting and training the teacher. The un-measureable effect of instability on student sense of security in their school environment should also be considered. On the flip side, it is organizationally risky for schools to retain teachers who are dissatisfied with their work environment and whose performance may be compromised by their discontent with the school, and whose students may be negatively impacted by a lack of authentic teacher-student engagement in the classroom.

Thus, an essential element of effective professional development is regular observation and mentoring of new teachers by school leaders and other mentors within the school. Observations allow the school leaders to gauge overall quality and style of teaching, student-teacher engagement, alignment between instructional practices and connectedness to the curricula, and overall classroom climate and culture, as well as the day-to-day management and operation of the classroom; student and teacher behaviors outside the classroom; emergent patterns in regard to attendance, truancy, and tardiness; and disciplinary concerns (i.e., Is there evidence of differential discipline for students from different socio-economic groups? Does the disciplinary system appear equitable?). To the extent possible, the principal should also use these observations and interactions as an opportunity to increase his or her awareness of student-teacher interactions, as well as parent-school interactions, and the extent to which parents and teachers are comfortable engaging with each other in matters related to school. These objectives may also be achieved by engaging in a potentially less intrusive process described as a walkthrough, in which the school leader briefly walks through the classroom, makes note of what he or she observes, and then engages the teacher in a conversation about these observations at a later date (e.g., Kachur, Stout, & Edwards, 2010).

All of this information can then be used as a means of assessing teachers' level of skill and ability, with the goal of addressing gaps in their knowledge, skills, and dispositions, through the development and provision of relevant training and professional development opportunities. In doing so, it is critically important for the school leader not to convey a sense of distrust or lack of confidence in the teacher, but rather to project an authentic desire to support the teacher in whatever ways he or she may need in order to be successful in the classroom.

Assessing Teachers' Professional Development Needs through Surveys and Questionnaires

School leaders can also learn more about their teachers and their professional development needs by administering learning needs surveys. D'Ambrosio, Boone, and Harkness (2004) demonstrate the use of surveys administered simultaneously to students and teachers. The purpose of their survey was to obtain student perceptions of effective teaching as compared with teacher perceptions and current teaching practices. These data were then used to guide the planning of professional development activities. The first part of the survey addressed student needs while the second part of the survey contained questions asking teachers what they needed to know or learn in order to perform more effectively. The use of this type of survey enables the school to design a professional development plan to address areas in need of support, as indicated by survey responses. These responses provide important information regarding ways in which the professional development needs of teachers can be designed to best meet students' learning needs. Surveys can also be used as a tool to assign teacher mentors. Teachers who score well on the survey and demonstrate the ability to meet students' learning needs can then be paired with teachers who need to strengthen their teaching skills.

Use of Data to Drive Professional Development

While informal interactions with and observations of teachers are critical, it is also important to utilize other sources of data to assess the organizational health of the school and its members and to guide the school in designing appropriate professional development activities. Data-driven decision-making (e.g., Goldring & Berends, 2009; Wayman, 2005) enables the school leader to make decisions based on the performance of the school, and to directly link professional development activities to the attainment of school goals and the improvement of areas that are not up to par. These data also allow the school leader to determine the extent to which issues within the school are linked to factors such as race, gender, socioeconomic status, grade levels, courses, teachers, and other variables. Teachers can also use these data to improve their teaching and learning practices and provide targeted assistance to those students who are in need of such assistance. An added benefit of using data to drive professional development and other supportive learning activities is that school leaders and other educators are better able to demonstrate to their colleagues, students, and stakeholders the reasons behind the decisions and practices they are engaging in.

Considerations for Designing Professional Development Plans

School leaders have several considerations in designing professional development plans for their schools. In addition to the building level needs, statewide standards and mandates must be considered. In addition to meeting the needs of students and complying with building level demands, teachers are also required to meet the standards of the profession as determined by the district and state. For some schools, this will include making sure teachers have the necessary credentials and up-to-date certifications and that teachers are trained to administer district- and state-mandated tests appropriately. The challenge is for school leaders to balance the administrative demands engendered by increasing systems of external accountability with the more immediate and often pressing demands of the local school site. This is particularly important in schools serving highly vulnerable children and youth, such as those from high poverty contexts.

Key Features of Professional Development

Darling-Hammond and McLaughlin (1995) discuss key features necessary to ensure that professional development is ongoing, purposeful, and effective. These guidelines are applicable to a wide range of school environments, but are especially important when designing professional development activities for schools in need of improvement. According to Darling-Hammond and McLaughlin, "Effective professional development involves teachers both as learners and as teachers and allows them to struggle with the uncertainties that accompany each role. [Professional development] has a number of characteristics" (p. 598):

1. It must engage teachers in concrete tasks of teaching, assessment, observation, and reflection that illuminate the processes of learning and development.
2. It must be grounded in inquiry, reflection, and experimentation that are participant driven.
3. It must be collaborative, involving a sharing of knowledge among educators and a focus on teachers' communities of practice rather than on individual teachers.
4. It must be connected to and derived from teachers' work with their students.
5. It must be sustained, ongoing, intensive, and supported by modeling, coaching, and the collective solving of specific problems of practice.
6. It must be connected to other aspects of school change.

When training and development are collaborative, focused, and in alignment with the school mission and student needs and learning styles, all stakeholders benefit. Students receive a quality education; parents are satisfied that their children are receiving a quality education, regardless of their socioeconomic status; and teachers are more fulfilled, as they are better prepared to teach and work with the students in their charge.

Professional Development in High Poverty Contexts

As noted above, professional development specific to the issues faced in high poverty contexts is necessary due to the unique issues faced by many students from high poverty backgrounds. In the document *Dispelling the Myth: High Poverty Schools Exceeding Expectations*, Barth et al. (1999) list several characteristics of successful high poverty schools. Among these characteristics is the finding that a greater than average percentage of the budget in these schools is spent on professional development aimed at promoting effective instruction. In addition to improving instruction, teachers should also learn ways in which to better meet the non-academic needs of their students. Discovering students' individualized interests and learning needs before attempting to engage them in the teaching and learning process has the potential to promote student engagement and increase the likelihood that students will be more engaged in the classroom. As teachers work to get to know their students, school leaders can support them in these efforts by working to identify school and community resources needed to address student needs. This is where the principal's connections to the community will be beneficial in helping to provide the necessary resources for students and their teachers. Chapter Six, on school and community resources, discusses this in greater detail.

Regardless of the availability of supportive services and community resources, it is imperative that teachers be able and willing to demonstrate an authentic ethic of care toward their students, their families, and their communities. For some teachers, this will require ongoing support and training. Unfortunately, this aspect of humanity cannot be taught to all; however, teachers can be exposed to activities and information that will increase their awareness, understanding, and empathy for others both inside and outside of the school. The principal can help to facilitate this process by engaging in such simple acts as organizing discussion groups and reading circles; viewing and discussing films and documentaries on issues related to poverty, risk, and resilience; as well as inviting parents and community members come to the school to discuss relevant issues, feelings, and concerns, with an aim to collaborate with the school in designing educational programs and services. When educators come to know, understand, and respect their students and their communities, they are better equipped to serve their students.

Characteristics of Effective Professional Development

Effective professional development for high poverty contexts will likely mirror professional development for other contexts; however, specific topics addressed may differ. According to Easton (2008), the following conditions are necessary for professional development to be effective:

1. Topics addressed in the professional development sessions will match the needs of the school. The school leader facilitates this process by carefully assessing school level needs and developing a plan accordingly.
2. The professional development plan must be implemented with persistence and fidelity. To better facilitate this process, the school leader should develop

a 'report card' of sorts that helps to link school improvement efforts to the design and content of professional development activities. The report card or evaluation serves to monitor and document how well the building leader follows through with implementing both the school improvement and professional development plans.

3. Professional development must be multi-tiered, and ongoing. Further, professional development plans must unfold over time, and be implemented systematically in a variety of ways that continue throughout the school year. For example, one concept may be taught in a variety of formats using multiple methodologies, similar to the concept of differentiated instruction in the classroom.

4. Professional development plans must not overlook 'local talent' for the facilitation of professional development activities. The principal (or other local principals), teachers, or even parents are often the best facilitators of building level professional development facilitation because they are familiar with the intimate details of the school context. This can allow for increased building level cohesiveness and community building, reinforce teacher or parent knowledge, and save funds that might have been used to bring in an expensive expert from the outside, who might not tailor the talk as well as those closer to the issues who are also able to be there for follow-up activities, discussions, and support.

Examples of Ongoing Professional Development Strategies

As noted above by Darling-Hammond (1995) and Easton (2008), professional development strategies should be tailor-made for the individual school. They must also extend beyond one-shot activities and programming. Further, the principal should develop a system of evaluation to assess the results or impact of the professional development. Examples of ongoing professional development strategies that work well in most contexts, including the high poverty context, are mentoring/modeling/shadowing programs, data analysis, case discussions, book clubs, differentiated coaching, critical friends groups, professional portfolios, and journaling. These strategies, taken from *Powerful Designs for Professional Learning*, by Lois Brown Easton (2008), are discussed below.

Mentoring/Modeling/Shadowing. Mentoring programs can be used to increase teacher efficacy and effectiveness, as mentors are assigned to work with teachers whose skill levels are not yet on target. When teachers are paired with their colleagues, the pairing is done specific to the teachers' ability. In assigning mentors, the principal should consider the strengths and weaknesses of each teacher in order to ensure an appropriate match. Teachers not only become aware of their strengths and weaknesses while working with mentor teachers, they also learn strategies for improving their teaching practices. For this process to work, there must be a shared understanding and commitment to the goal of improving teaching for increased learning. While providing emotional support, mentors can also assist newer teachers by:

- Co-planning lessons
- Co-teaching lessons
- Problem solving (instructional, curricular, or student-related dilemmas)
- Modeling strategies
- Inviting mentees to observe their thinking as they develop, deliver, and assess lessons
- Reflecting on practice
- Observing and giving feedback
- Serving as bridges to other faculty members who have valuable resources to share (Easton, 2008, p. 186)

Data Analysis. As previously noted, data analysis provides a tool for principals to use in shaping professional development activities. This tool can also be utilized by teachers at the classroom level. To ensure effective use of data, teachers should be trained on how to use the data from test scores, report cards, attendance records, discipline records, classroom observations, and journaling to tailor their teaching practices to better meet the needs of their students. Research has demonstrated the value of data-driven decision making for improving schools (Wohlstetter, Datnow, & Park, 2008). These data can be utilized to chart patterns of teaching and learning and other classroom behaviors to improve classroom management and increase teaching effectiveness.

Case Discussions. The use of case-based readings is an effective means of engaging new and veteran teachers in discussions of a wide range of issues relevant to the teachers, their students, and their schools. These cases offer examples of class and school level dilemmas that teachers may encounter, without teachers actually experiencing these phenomena firsthand. To be most effective, these cases should be based on educators' real-world experiences and should actively engage teachers in open and honest discussions of how to respond to these dilemmas in their own classrooms and schools (Bassey, 2000).

Book Clubs. Book clubs can serve multiple purposes. They allow teachers not only to learn new material that relates to the profession of teaching, but also to facilitate discussion in a more relaxed environment. If done well, these discussions can help to promote community and cohesiveness among participants.

These discussions can also double as mentoring or instructional opportunities, as the more experienced teachers assess and relate the content of the books to their experiences rather than taking the information found in the books at face value only (Kooy, 2006).

Differentiated Coaching. Differentiated coaching is comparable to differentiated instruction in the classroom. Differentiated coaching can be provided by the principal as well as teacher mentors, and is applied to the style and strengths and weaknesses of the teachers. As such, coaching to improve teaching will differ from one teacher to the next (Stover, Kissel, Haag, & Shoniker, 2011).

Critical Friends Groups. Critical friends groups are formed among groups of educators to deepen their understanding of their craft through conversations and peer mentoring. They are also designed to promote team building and cohesiveness. Critical friends groups can double as mentoring groups or as book club groups. The only requirement is that they meet regularly for the purpose of honing the craft of teaching (Bambino, 2002).

Professional Portfolios. Portfolios for educators can be used to chart professional development and demonstrate teaching philosophy. They can also serve as a snapshot of a teacher's professional journey and philosophy. They can form the basis for discussion among colleagues, as well as the basis for professional learning communities. They can also facilitate, assess, and archive professional learning (Constantino, De Lorenzo, & Kobrinski, 2002).

Journaling. Journals can provide a source of reflection for educators. They are an inexpensive way of monitoring and visibly keeping track of teaching experiences. Journals can be used by teachers to demonstrate growth, as well as professional setbacks, as they are records of activity for educators. Journals can also be used to document specific occurrences, such as classroom management trends, experiences with a new program, or any aspect of teaching or personal reaction to teaching that the educator wishes to document (Tillman, 2003).

Conclusion

This chapter has discussed the importance of establishing appropriate professional development in high poverty schools. As stated in the opening, teaching organizations must be learning organizations—especially in schools that serve students from diverse backgrounds, including those from high poverty backgrounds. Principals and teachers must continuously work on their craft if they are to be successful at reaching students from diverse backgrounds. Much of the training or professional development suggested is universal; however, it is particularly crucial for schools dealing with lowered levels of student achievement and the challenges encountered in teaching and leading in high poverty contexts. In sum, principals from high poverty schools are reminded:

1. To develop a need-based professional development plan.
2. To ensure that the professional development plan is ongoing, utilizing multiple methods of delivery that build upon each other.
3. To ensure that the professional development plan is evaluated and that the results of this evaluation are used to improve and strengthen the design and delivery of subsequent professional learning activities.

Questions to Consider

1. Should professional development be the same for all schools districtwide? Why? Why not? What factors should drive differences in approaches to professional development in schools? How do these factors influence the principal's approach to professional development?
2. Can professional development be used to positively change teaching and learning conditions in high poverty schools? If so, how? Have you witnessed such changes as a teacher or as an instructional leader?
3. What skills/professional development training do you believe to be the most critical for school leaders? For school leaders in the high poverty context? How should this training/professional development be delivered?
4. What are the current professional development needs of your school? Your district?
5. What role do you play in the design and delivery of professional development activities? How might this role be strengthened?
6. How does your school or district assess the effectiveness of professional development activities?
7. To what extent are the professional development activities currently offered linked to the overall goals and needs of your school? Your district?

References

Almy, S., & Tooley, M. (2012). *Building and sustaining talent: Creating conditions in high-poverty schools that support effective teaching and learning.* Washington, DC: Education Trust. Retrieved from http://www.joycefdn.org/assets/1/7/Building_and_Sustaining_Talent.pdf

Balfanz, R., & Mac Iver, D. (2000). Transforming high-poverty urban middle schools into strong learning institutions: Lessons from the first five years of the Talent Development Middle School. *Journal of Education for Students Placed at Risk (JESPAR), 5*(1–2), 137–158.

Bambino, D. (2002). Critical friends. *Educational Leadership, 59*(6), 25–27.

Barth, P., Haycock, K., Jackson, H., Mora, K., Ruiz, P., Robinson, S., et al. (1999). *Dispelling the myth: High poverty schools exceeding expectations*. Washington, DC: Education Trust and Council of Chief State School Officers. (ERIC Document Reproduction Service No. ED 445 140)

Bassey, M. (2000). *Case study research in educational settings*. Buckingham, England: Open University Press.

Cohen, J., McCabe, L., Michelli, N. M., & Pickeral, T. (2009). School climate: Research, policy, practice, and teacher education. *Teachers College Record, 111*(1), 180–213.

Constantino, P. M., De Lorenzo, M. N., & Kobrinski, E. J. (2002). *Developing a professional teaching portfolio: A guide for success*. Boston: Allyn & Bacon.

Corbett, D., & Wilson, B. (2002). What urban students say about good teaching. *Educational Leadership, 60*(1), 18–23.

D'Ambrosio, B. S., Boone, W. J., & Harkness, S. S. (2004). Planning district-wide professional development: Insights gained from teachers and students regarding mathematics teaching in a large urban district. *School Science and Mathematics, 104*(1), 5–15. doi: 10.1111/j.1949-8594.2004.tb17977.x

Danielson, C. (1996). *Enhancing professional practice: A framework for teaching*. Alexandria, VA: Association for Supervision and Curriculum Development.

Darling-Hammond, L. (2003). Keeping good teachers: Why it matters, what leaders can do. *Educational Leadership, 60*(8), 6–13.

Darling-Hammond, L. (2010). *The flat world and education: How America's commitment to equity will determine our future*. New York: Teachers College Press.

Darling-Hammond, L., & McLaughlin, M. W. (1995). Policies that support professional development in an era of reform. *Phi Delta Kappan, 76*(8), 597–604.

de Snyder, V. N. S., Friel, S., Fotso, J. C., Khadr, Z., Meresman, S., Monge, P., et al. (2011). Social conditions and urban health inequities: Realities, challenges and opportunities to transform the urban landscape through research and action. *Journal of Urban Health, 88*(6), 1183–1193.

Domitrovich, C. E., Gest, S. D., Gill, S., Bierman, K. L., Welsh, J. A., & Jones, D. (2009). Fostering high-quality teaching with an enriched curriculum and professional development support: The Head Start REDI program. *American Educational Research Journal, 46*(2), 567–597.

DuFour, R., & Eaker, R. (1998). *Professional learning communities at work: Best practices for enhancing student achievement*. Bloomington, IN: Solution Tree Press.

Easton, L. B. (2008). *Powerful designs for professional learning*. Oxford, OH: National Staff Development Council.

Ellis, R. D. (2010). *The principal's role in defining a student success-based school culture: The impact of specific behaviors on school-level teacher working conditions*. (Doctoral dissertation). Retrieved from http://libres.uncg.edu/ir/asu/f/Ellis,%20Dale_2010_Dissertation.pdf

Fishman, B. J., Marx, R. W., Best, S., & Tal, R. T. (2003). Linking teacher and student learning to improve professional development in systemic reform. *Teaching and Teacher Education, 19*(6), 643–658.

Fullan, M. (2001). *Leading in a culture of change*. San Francisco: Jossey-Bass.

Goldring, E., & Berends, M. (2009). *Leading with data: Pathways to improve your school*. Alexandria, VA: American Association of School Administrators.

Grissom, J. A. (2011). Can good principals keep teachers in disadvantaged schools? Linking principal effectiveness to teacher satisfaction and turnover in hard-to-staff environments. *Teachers College Record, 113*(11), 2552–2585.

Grogin, M., & Andrews, R. (2002). Defining preparation and professional development for the future. *Educational Administration Quarterly, 38*(2), 233–256. doi:10.1177/0013161X02382007

Guskey, T. R. (2000). *Evaluating professional development*. Thousand Oaks, CA: Corwin.

Ingersoll, R. (2001, Fall). Teacher turnover and teacher shortages: An organizational analysis. *American Education Research Journal, 38*, 499–534.

Ingersoll, R. (2007). Short on power, long on responsibility. *Educational Leadership, 65*(1), 20–25.

Johnson, C. C., & Fargo, J. D. (2010). Urban school reform enabled by transformative professional development: Impact on teacher change and student learning of science. *Urban Education, 45*(1), 4–29.

Johnson, S. M., Kraft, M. A., & Papay, J. P. (2012). How context matters in high-need schools: The effects of teachers' working conditions on their professional satisfaction and their students' achievement. *Teachers College Record, 114*(10), 1–39.

Joyce, B., & Showers, B. (2002). *Student achievement through staff development*. Alexandria, VA: Association for Supervision and Curriculum Development.

Kachur, D. S., Stout, J. A., & Edwards, C. L. (2010). *Classroom walkthroughs to improve teaching and learning*. Larchmont, NY: Eye on Education.

Kennedy, E. (2010, December). Improving literacy achievement in a high-poverty school: Empowering classroom teachers through professional development. *Reading Research Quarterly, 45*(4), 384–387.

Knapp, M. S. (1995). Academic challenge in high-poverty classrooms. *Phi Delta Kappan, 76*(10), 770–776.

Kooy, M. (2006). The telling stories of novice teachers: Constructing teacher knowledge in book clubs. *Teaching and Teacher Education, 22*(6), 661–674.

Louis, K. S., & Wahlstrom, K. (2011). Principals as cultural leaders. *Phi Delta Kappan, 92*(5), 52–56.

Luiselli, J. K., Putnam, R. F., Handler, M. W., & Feinberg, A. B. (2005). Whole-school positive behaviour support: Effects on student discipline problems and academic performance. *Educational Psychology: An International Journal of Experimental Educational Psychology, 25*(2–3), 183–198.

MacNeil, A. J., Prater, D. L., & Busch, S. (2009). The effects of school culture and climate on student achievement. *International Journal of Leadership in Education, 12*(1), 73–84.

Marzano, R. J., Marzano, D. S., & Pickering, D. J. (2003). *Classroom management that works: Research-based strategies for every teacher*. Alexandria, VA: Association for Supervision and Curriculum Development.

McKinney, S. E., Haberman, M., Stafford-Johnson, D. S., & Robinson, J. (2008). Developing teachers for high-poverty schools: The role of the internship experience. *Urban Education, 43*(1), 68–82. doi:10.1177/0042085907305200

Mintrop, H., & Sunderman, G. L. (2009). Predictable failure of federal sanctions–driven accountability for school improvement—and why we may retain it anyway. *Educational Researcher, 38*(5), 353–364.

Scherer, M. (2003). Improving the quality of the teaching force, a conversation with David C. Berliner. In M. Scherer (Ed.), *Keeping good teachers* (pp. 14–21). Alexandria, VA: Association for Curriculum and Development.

Silins, H., & Mulford, B. (2002). Schools as learning organisations: The case for system, teacher and student learning. *Journal of Educational Administration, 40*(5), 425–446.

Siwatu, K. O. (2011). Preservice teachers' sense of preparedness and self-efficacy to teach in America's urban and suburban schools: Does context matter? *Teaching and Teacher Education, 27*(2), 357–365.

Stover, K., Kissel, B., Haag, K., & Shoniker, R. (2011). Differentiated coaching: Fostering reflection with teachers. *The Reading Teacher, 64*(7), 498–509.

Tillman, L. C. (2003). Mentoring, reflection, and reciprocal journaling. *Theory Into Practice, 42*(3), 226–233.

Walpole, S., McKenna, M. C., Uribe-Zarain, X., & Lamitina, D. (2010). The relationships between coaching and instruction in the primary grades: Evidence from high-poverty schools. *The Elementary School Journal, 111*(1), 115–140.

Wayman, J. C. (2005). Involving teachers in data-driven decision making: Using computer data systems to support teacher inquiry and reflection. *Journal of Education for Students Placed at Risk, 10*(3), 295–308.

Wohlstetter, P., Datnow, A., & Park, V. (2008). Creating a system for data-driven decision-making: Applying the principal-agent framework. *School Effectiveness and School Improvement, 19*(3), 239–259.

Zapeda, S. J. (2008). *Professional development: What works?* Larchmont, NY: Eye on Education.

CHAPTER SIX

Bringing Together Schools and Communities to Meet the Needs of Students from High Poverty Contexts

Susan C. Faircloth & Lisa Bass

Schools are located in communities, but are often 'islands' with no bridges to the "mainland." (Adelman & Taylor, 2007, p. 7)

Throughout this book, we call for a restructuring and refining of leadership practices in schools serving students from high poverty contexts. These nuanced roles require commitment on the part of the overall school leadership to structure schools in such a way that school personnel are able to move beyond and outside of their traditional roles without fear of being sidelined by their supervisors or peers. This change is premised on the belief that school leaders have a moral and ethical obligation or imperative to provide the services and supports that students need, regardless of their socioeconomic status (Dantley, 2005; Fullan, 2003). As Tillman (2003) so aptly points out,

> Together, school leaders and their communities can provide the vision, structures, and incentives for initiatives that are intended to improve social, emotional and academic growth of all students. These same leaders model attitudes, behaviors, values, purpose and actions that lead to collaborative and successful partnerships between school and the parent community in order to 'get knowledge of the parent population and validate their cultural frames of reference, values and heritage'. (Tillman, 2003, p. 311, as cited in Normore & Blanco, 2006, Enhancing Collaborative Partnerships section, para. 7)

What this quote demonstrates is that families and communities, regardless of the challenges they encounter, their lack of money, or their lack of educational experience, have a wealth of familial, community, and cultural knowledge to be shared with the school, if only the school will open its doors and break down the barriers that traditionally exist between schools and communities. Rather than viewing communities as something from which the school should be shielded, the school must begin to envision ways in which the school and community can partner. In turn, the community members must also be challenged to dream about the future of their children and their education. This requires parents and communities to move beyond the negative experiences often associated with their own formalized education and begin to engage schools on their own terms (e.g., Hill & Taylor, 2004) rather than terms dictated by schools alone. Again, this is not an easy process for either party, but it is necessary if schools are to move beyond practices that have served to alienate schools from families and communities.

Historically, the role of schools has been "to educate the masses and to promote equal access to the opportunity structure" (Jozefowicz-Simbeni & Allen-Meares, 2002, p. 128). Unfortunately, in many cases this has not occurred. Normore and Blanco (2006) argue that

> America has failed to offer substantive measures regarding the poor beyond remediation and meals as well as beyond deficiency-oriented rather than school-discriminatory programs. Cultural and racial diversity and the plight of the poor demand that schools embrace a revised and enlightened view of true community leadership that advocates and achieves unity and respect for differences. However, in order for such an endorsement to be effective, school leaders and their communities must engage in leadership where they re-conceptualize their practice based on social justice agendas, specific moral capacities and responsibilities. (para. 3)

As powerful as this quote is, it raises questions about what exactly a social justice agenda is. What are the moral capacities of school leaders? And, what responsibilities do school leaders have beyond providing basic educational programs and services? Shoho, Merchant, and Lugg (2011) argue that a social justice framework requires us to invite all stakeholders to the table, even when these stakeholders have traditionally been viewed as part of the problem. Most important, this framework requires us to move from talk into action. In sum, leading from a social justice perspective requires us not only to point out inequities in the educational system but also to take action to make amends for these inequities and to set a course toward more equitable and just education for all students and their communities. To act in a socially just way is also to act in a morally just way: one that aims to take into account the peoples and relationships involved and to guide them to act ethically and just even in the face of internal and external pressures to act and lead in ways that may not be in the best interest of those who are served (e.g., Greenfield, 2004).

For families and communities that have historically been successful in the educational system, traditional curricula and leadership structures may be adequate;

however, for families and communities for which education has been used to acculturate, assimilate, or isolate them from the dominant society, traditional practices are often insufficient. Many of these families and their communities are faced with the lingering effects of traumas that are rooted in the past yet continue to wreak their effects across the generations (e.g., Cassiman, 2006). Is it possible to move beyond these traumas? Certainly it is possible, but to deny that these traumas have occurred is to minimize these families' and communities' lived experiences, as well as those of past generations. To adequately meet the educational needs of those most impacted by these traumas, schools and communities must work collaboratively and proactively.

Connecting Families and Communities to Better Serve the Needs of Students from High Poverty Contexts

According to the Packard Foundation (1992),

> The proponents of school-linked services believe poor education, health and social outcomes for children result in part from the inability of current services systems to respond in a timely, coordinated, and comprehensive fashion to the multiple and interconnected needs of a child and her or his family. (As cited in Normore & Blanco, 2006, p. 226)

Recognizing the need for increased and improved partnerships between schools and community, Frick and Frick (2010) urge us to consider an ethic of connectedness, which emphasizes relationships and collaborations between schools and communities, as well as the school's moral and ethical responsibility to serve its community. We concur. We believe that exceptional educational leaders possess the ability and willingness for their schools to actively and meaningfully engage communities in the act of co-constructing a new and reinvigorated vision of education for their children. As Fusarelli and Lindle (2011) write, "Just as the academic development of each student is indivisibly linked to mental and physical health and well-being, schools are inseparable from their community's social and economic health and well-being" (p. 411). What this means is that just as the social and economic vigor of a community has the potential to positively or negatively impact the educational aspirations and subsequent academic achievement of its youth, these same youth, through the power of purposeful and meaningful education, have the potential to rejuvenate and inspire these communities to economic, social, emotional, and physical prosperity—not necessarily to be equated with increased monetary wealth, but with increased potential to envision a future not shaped solely by conditions associated with poverty. Again, this requires collaboration and commitment on the part of both schools and communities (e.g., Warren, 2005).

School-Linked Community Services

According to Jozefowicz-Simbeni and Allen-Meares (2002), "High poverty schools and their neighborhoods need to be linked with resources and infused with talent" (p. 123). One approach to achieving this goal is through the development of school-linked community services. School-linked community services go beyond the notion of the school as the change agent for students from high poverty contexts. What is most exciting about these models is that they understand the intricate relationship between schools, communities, families, and other factors in helping to shape students' educational experiences and subsequent outcomes. In this model, schools work together with mental health agencies, community and recreational programs, businesses, law enforcement agencies, courts, and other organizations to meet the needs of the school and its students. These models also include early intervention services, after-school programs, and partnerships between parents and schools (Jozefowicz-Simbeni & Allen-Meares, 2002). Although programs sponsored by state and federal government agencies provide avenues for spearheading these types of models, schools are also encouraged to think of smaller scale ways in which to engage in these types of activities in the absence of state or federal funding. For example, the school may opt to partner with local social service agencies; sponsor school health fairs, screenings, or nutritional training; or plant a community garden in which students, faculty, staff, and community members have a safe space to tend the land, grow nutritious foods, exercise, talk, and learn together. Senior citizen centers might also partner with schools in an intergenerational initiative aimed at developing the literacy skills of the students and the seniors or improving health and nutrition. Or, the school might partner with local cultural organizations to provide supportive services to students from a particular racial or ethnic group within the school. For example, these organizations could partner together to sponsor cultural awareness events or neighborhood festivals (Jozefowicz-Simbeni & Allen-Meares, 2002).

The school-linked community services model espouses Bronfenbrenner's ecological systems theory (1979), which addresses the interaction among five different systems that impact the ways in which children develop (Fusarelli & Lindle, 2011). These include (1) the microsystem, which represents all the things that directly impact the child (e.g., parents, family, school, extracurricular activities); (2) the mesosystem, which represents the coming together of two or more microsystems (e.g., the child's parents are divorced, live in separate homes, but come together as a family unit during holidays or other special events); (3) the exosystem, which includes both the microsystem and the mesosystem, but does not directly impact the child. For example, the exosystem might include the environment in which a child's parent works. The way in which this work environment is structured impacts the parent, which in turn impacts the way in which the parent interacts with the child. (4) The macrosystem involves societal laws, customs, cultures, and other available resources, which impact the ways in which the micro-, meso-, and exosystems function; and (5) the chronosystem—also referred to as time—which reflects how these systems change over time. In effect, this system depicts the interrelatedness of people, places, organizations, policies, practices, and so forth in determining who and what we are and how we experience life. At the center of this model is the child or other individual. Although this model was originally applied to humans, it can also be applied to the life of the school. When applied to schools, this model demonstrates that schools do not operate in isolation; they impact and are impacted by a number of environmental factors, many of which are beyond the direct control of the school but are important in helping to shape the extent to which various supports and services are needed, within the context of the school, to either build upon or combat the effects of these environmental factors.

Community Schools

Full service schools are also referred to as community schools. According to the Coalition of Community Schools (www.communityschools.org),

> A community school is both a place and a set of partnerships between the school and other community resources. Its integrated focus on academics, health and social services, youth and community development and engagement leads to improved student learning, stronger families, and healthier communities. Community schools offer a personalized curriculum that emphasizes real-world learning and community problem-solving. Schools become the center of the community, and are open to every one all day, every day, evenings and week-ends.
>
> Using public schools as hubs, community schools bring together many partners to offer a range of supports and opportunities to children, youth, families, and communities. Partners work to achieve these results: Children are ready to enter school; students attend school consistently; students are actively involved in learning and their community; families are increasingly involved with their children's education; schools are involved with families and their communities; students succeed academically; students are healthy—physically, socially, and emotionally; students live and learn in a safe, supportive, and stable environment; and communities are desirable places to live. (What Is a Community School?, paras. 1 & 2)

As this definition demonstrates, community schools help to bring together and streamline the provision of a wide array of services for children and their families. As such, they serve both as direct service providers, as well as conduits through which other academic, and non-academic services may be provided. If done well, the provision of such services helps to build and strengthen the resilience of students, as well as their communities and schools, as they strive to move beyond the often overwhelming effects of poverty. The goal then is to ensure that these students are not only successful in school, but that they have the necessary supports and services to be successful in life outside and beyond school.

Schools Need More than Teachers and Administrators

As Bronfenbrenner's ecological systems model suggests, what happens in schools does not happen independently of factors either inside or outside of the school.

Each of these factors is interrelated. Following this same line of logic, the actions of the faculty and staff within the school impact the overall operations and climate of the school. Although autonomy within the classroom has been linked to increased teacher satisfaction and empowerment (e.g., Ingersoll, 1997; Ingersoll & Alsalam, 1997; Little, 1990; Marks & Louis, 1997; Pearson & Moonmaw, 2005; White, 1992), there is a social expectation that the staff as a whole will work together in pursuit of the common goals and mission of the school (e.g., DuFour, 2004). Unfortunately, this does not always occur (e.g., Leonard & Leonard, 2003; Piercey, 2010). In some cases, individuals opt to work autonomously within the school, while others simply choose not to be team players. Either way, their actions or inaction have the potential to negatively impact the school and its students. Thus, for schools to effectively serve their students and communities, they may be required to engage in a reconceptualization of the operational structure and leadership of the school. They are also encouraged to begin thinking about leadership as more than administration. In our view, leadership means taking responsibility for the success of all students and providing the necessary academic, emotional, and physical supports needed for these students to be successful. This goes beyond finances, facilities, and basic operational management. It gets to the heart of leadership for learning.

The Role of the School Counselor

Although principals and teachers are key to reforming schools, as discussed in Chapter Three, we also feel strongly that a key figure in the restructuring of schools to better meet the needs of students from high poverty contexts is the school counselor. Unfortunately, in many cases, this position appears to have become an extension of the administrative and clerical arms of the school rather than providing more care-based forms of counseling and other supportive services (Baggerly & Osborn, 2006; Dahir, 2004). Although these are certainly important functions, failure to provide the necessary emotional, social and mental health-related supports that students need may contribute to their failure in school. Thus, school leaders are strongly encouraged to revisit the role of the school counselor, building on the roles and responsibilities identified by the American School Counselor Association (Johnson & Perkins, 2009). The ASCA describes the roles and responsibilities of the school counselor as centering on the provision of culturally appropriate services and supports to students, parents, communities, and staff members, while addressing the in-school academic, as well as post-school academic, aspirations and personal needs and concerns of students.

Johnson and Perkins (2009) argue that the role of the counselor varies depending upon the grade level of the students and the location of the school (e.g., rural versus urban). At the middle school level, the school counselor is in the unique position of working with students at a time when they are extremely vulnerable to both internal and external forces, which will help to determine whether they stay in school and what pathways they will pursue beyond school. Unfortunately, for many school counselors there is a question of role expectation, with school administrators having one vision of the role of the school counselor and the counselor having a different vision. The challenge then is to reach a compromise in which both parties work to ensure that they are acting in the best interest of the students. This requires that the school leadership view the counselor as a fellow leader but that their notions of what it means to be a leader may need to be revised in the case of the school counselor.

If they are utilized correctly, school counselors can become part of a coordinated "system of support" aimed at meeting the needs of the whole child, not just the academic side of the child (e.g., American School Counselor Association, 2009). According to Amatea and West-Olatunji (2007), for students from high poverty backgrounds, counselors have the potential to play a number of roles, including (1) working as a cultural broker between the school and the students and the students' families; (2) working collaboratively with teachers to make the curriculum more meaningful for these students; and (3) working with teachers to make the school environment more family friendly. We would also add that counselors have the potential to work collaboratively with school leaders in ensuring that students and teachers have the supports and services needed to foster a nurturing school climate conducive to learning.

Need for Meaningful Parent Involvement

Although it is important to build a positive climate within the physical structure of the school, if these efforts are limited to the confines of the school, they will not be fully beneficial. Instead, they must take place in consort with parents, families, and communities. As Jozefowicz-Simbeni and Allen-Meares (2002) point out, "Despite personal and environmental risks and lack of resources or capital, some poor children and families manage well" (p. 126). In effect, they are remarkably resilient. Their ability to overcome social and economic circumstances that are less than optimal is a strength that schools should tap into. There are many lessons to be learned from these parents and families if schools are willing to move beyond the confines of the physical school building to reach out to and involve these communities. It is also important to point out that even though many of these parents and families are resilient and able to succeed with limited school supports, this does not absolve the school from its responsibilities to provide additional supports and services to these children and their families (Jozefowicz-Simbeni & Allen-Meares, 2002, p. 128). As schools move forward in these efforts, school counselors are uniquely positioned to serve as mediators between schools, parents, and communities, helping to establish mutually beneficial and trusting working relationships.

Engaging Parents and Families

There are a number of ways in which schools can work to better engage parents and families in schools. These include building upon families' cultures, meeting one-on-one or in small groups, working to improve communication between schools and families, and providing necessary accommodations to foster increased involvement (e.g., child care, transportation, food, translators, and scheduling meetings within the community rather than always holding these meetings at school) (Boethel, 2003, as cited in Ferguson, 2005; Henderson & Mapp, 2002, as cited in Ferguson, 2005). In writing this chapter, the first author (Susan Faircloth) drew on her own personal experience, as she reflected back on her own mother who worked for more than 37 years in a pork-processing plant in a rural community in the South. Even though her mother cared deeply about her education, she was unable to leave work during the middle of the day to volunteer in her daughter's school as a "room mother" or participate in field trips. However, she made every effort to attend evening parent-teacher meetings, only to find herself among the last to show up for these meetings due to long hours at work and quickly dismissed by the teachers, who had little or no time to extend her assigned meeting hour. For some parents, this would have been enough to break their spirit and prevent them from ever returning to the school. Fortunately for the first author, her mother was persistent and determined that she meet with the teachers, even if only for five minutes. Although this is only one example of how schools have failed to take into account the personal and professional demands placed on parents and communities, it is indicative of what many of our parents and communities encounter. If this is all they experience, it is not surprising that they describe schools as unwelcoming places (e.g., Calabrese, 1990; Epstein & Sanders, 2000; Noguera, 2003).

Barriers to School-Linked Community Services

Unfortunately, the development of school-linked community services has encountered a number of barriers. Examples include:

1. Lack of coordination of services provided by state and federal governments and agencies,
2. Policies and regulations that limit the ability of agencies to provide services at the school level,
3. Lack of a stable pool of funding for these services (Sullivan & Sugarman, 1996), and
4. Lack of available human resources designed to coordinate the provision of these services.

Cibulka (1996, as cited in Fusarelli & Lindle, 2011) also argues that there are four lingering questions that impede the successful development of school-linked community services. These questions include:

1. What is the purpose or function of schools (e.g., social versus academic)?
2. To what extent, if at all, should non-educators be involved in schools?
3. To what extent should schools serve a protective role for children?
4. What is the overall goal of school-linked coordinated services (efficiency versus equal opportunity)?

Another basic, but critically important is, is the issue of governance, particularly at the school level (e.g., Dryfoos, 2002). In order for school-community partnerships to work, each actor must be willing to engage in frank and honest discussions regarding issues of management, leadership and day-to-day operation of programs and services. And, in some cases, individual actors may be required to yield control to their partners. This requires risk-taking, trust, and belief in the power of collaboration and cooperation among multiple stakeholders.

Each of these barriers represents a failure on the part of governmental and public agencies, as well as schools and communities, to commit the time, energies, and funding needed to improve the economic, social, and educational conditions of our nation's most vulnerable populations—socioeconomically disadvantaged youth—and their communities. If schools and communities are to work together to improve the life chances of our youth, they cannot be expected to shoulder these efforts on their own. Without adequate education, children living in high poverty communities and attending high poverty schools will be robbed of their right to the social and economic capital their counterparts in more affluent communities have access to (see Bourdieu, 1996, for a more in-depth discussion of capital).

The Community School Coordinator

As noted above, one of the major challenges in leading a community-focused school is mobilizing the necessary human and physical resources to best meet the needs of students. In order for the model to function effectively a number of human and community resources must work in concert to support students. This requires someone who is charged with establishing and maintaining relationships between the school and other external human service agencies, as well as parents, families, local businesses and other community-based organizations. With the school as the hub of the community, someone in the school must act to coordinate the activities of all of the stakeholders involved in enriching the lives of students. Logistics such as paperwork, scheduling, room assignment, and introductions of various partners must be facilitated well, or the community school arrangement may prove more chaotic than helpful to the school.

The Coalition of Community Schools (www.communityschools.org) describes this role as the *community school coordinator*. Although the establishment of such a position requires the commitment of financial resources on the part of the school and its community partners, it is an essential requirement in establishing and maintaining successful school-community partnerships. If funds are not available at the district or school level, school leaders are encouraged to pursue funding from external organizations, agencies, or foundations to support the work of this integral position (e.g., Dryfoos, 2002). Each district or school will likely conceptualize this role in different ways; however, the job description should ultimately match the needs of the school and community. (See www.communityschools.org for examples of job descriptions for community school coordinators.)

Taking Up the Moral and Ethical Fight against the Effects of Poverty on Schools and Communities

In closing, it is important to acknowledge that the notion of providing supportive services to students via schools is not new. In fact, variations of this model have been in force since the late 1800s (Fusarelli & Lindle, 2011). The challenge of providing such services is to discover how to do so in a coordinated, consistent manner over time while maintaining the flexibility to modify existing services and the ways in which they are provided, depending upon the contextual factors that define the school and the community in which it is located. As Smrekar (1996) writes, "An ecological perspective reinforced by a better understanding of the context of children's lives is expected to result in improved care and enhanced student performance" (p. 4). In sum, the implementation of school-linked services models requires a dramatic shift in the way we think and go about the practice of schooling and leading. It also bears noting that this approach is not a panacea and will not eradicate poverty among parents and families (Jozefowicz-Simbeni & Allen-Meares, 2002). This will require ongoing and concentrated efforts at the federal, state, and local levels. However, while we wait for these broader level policies and practices to take effect, we must continue to ask ourselves what is the moral and ethical thing to do now. Ultimately, school leaders and community members must grapple individually and collectively as we decide what to do in this battle against the oppressive forces of poverty within our schools and communities. Whatever decision we make, we must remember that real change takes time, patience, and fortitude and is not sustainable unless it occurs in community with those most impacted by this change.

Working in partnership with communities sends a strong and clear message that the fight against poverty is not the sole responsibility of an individual or an entity. Foremost, educators are tasked with addressing the academic needs of their students, however, this cannot be successfully accomplished if these students, social, emotional and physical needs are not also attended to. School resources are limited. Teachers and administrators are increasingly called upon to meet the demands of accountability-based reform efforts, causing them to focus on academic skill development and growth. These are clearly important efforts if our students and their schools are to be academically successfully. We believe strongly that educators and schools must be supported in their efforts to meet all of these demands. This requires the community-at large to step up to the plate and support educators and schools in these efforts to nurture the development and growth of our children in a holistic rather than piecemeal fashion. That is the moral and ethical thing to do.

Questions to Consider

1. Identify the key stakeholders both internal and external to your school. How involved are these stakeholders in the day-to-day activities of your school? Are you satisfied with this level and type of involvement? How might you work to promote more active and meaningful involvement of these stakeholders?

2. To what extent is the school involved with the community? Who is responsible for cultivating school-community involvement? Is this an official or unofficial responsibility? What barriers have been encountered as you work to promote school-community involvement? What successes have you experienced?

3. Identify three goals for the next academic year that specifically address school-community relations. Develop an action plan for achieving these goals.

4. What is the role of the counselor in your school? Is he or she a part of the administrative leadership team? If not, why not? How do you envision the role of the counselor in your school?

5. Who addresses the non-academic needs of your students and their families? How are these needs identified? To what extent are parents and families satisfied with services provided?

6. How do you define the role of the parents and motivate them to remain involved when so many resources are provided by the school in the community schools model?

References

Adelman, H., & Taylor, L. (2007). *Fostering school, family, and community involvement: Effective strategies for creating safer schools and communities*. Washington, DC: Hamilton Fish Institute on School and Community Violence.

Amatea, E. S., & West-Olatunji, C. A. (2007). Joining the conversation about educating our poorest children: Emerging leadership roles for school counselors in high-poverty schools. *Professional School Counseling, 11*(2), 81–89.

American School Counselor Association. (2009). Role of the school counselor. Retrieved from http://www.schoolcounselor.org/content.asp?contentid=341

Baggerly, J., & Osborn, D. (2006). School counselors' career satisfaction and commitment: Correlates and predictors. *Professional School Counseling, 9*(3), 197–205.

Barone, D. (2011). Welcoming families: A parent literacy project in a linguistically rich, high-poverty school. *Early Childhood Education Journal, 38,* 377–384.

Bourdieu, P. (1986). The forms of capital. In J. Richardson (Ed.), *Handbook of theory and research for the sociology of education* (pp. 183–198). New York: Greenwood.

Bronfenbrenner, U. (1979). *The ecology of human development: Experiments by nature and design.* Cambridge, MA: Harvard University Press.

Calabrese, R. L. (1990, Spring). The public school: A source of alienation for minority parents. *Journal of Negro Education, 59*(2), 148–154.

Cassiman, S. A. (2006). Toward a more inclusive poverty knowledge. *The Social Policy Journal, 4*(3–4), 93–106.

Dahir, C. A. (2004). Supporting a nation of learners: The role of school counseling in educational reform. *Journal of Counseling & Development, 82*(3), 344–353.

Dantley, M. (2005). Moral leadership: Shifting the management paradigm. In F. English (Ed.), *The Sage handbook of educational leadership: Advances in theory, research, and practice* (pp. 34–46). Thousand Oaks, CA: Sage.

Dryfoos, J. (2002, January). Full-service community schools: Creating new institutions. *The Phi Delta Kappan, 83*(5), 393–399.

DuFour, R. (2004, May). Schools as learning communities. *Educational Leadership, 61*(8), 6–11.

Epstein, J. L., & Sanders, M. G. (2000). Connecting home, school and community: New directions for social research. In M. Hallinan (Ed.), *Handbook of sociology of education* (pp. 285–306). New York: Plenum.

Ferguson, C. (2005, September). Reaching out to diverse populations: What can schools do to foster family-school connections? A strategy brief of the National Center for Family and Community Connections with Schools. National Center for Family & Community Schools. Austin, TX: Southwest Educational Development Laboratory.

Frick, J. E., & Frick, W. C. (2010). An ethic of connectedness: Enacting moral school leadership through people and programs. *Education, Citizenship and Social Justice, 5*(2), 117–130.

Fullan, M. (2003). *The moral imperative of school leadership.* Thousand Oaks, CA: Corwin.

Fusarelli, B. C., & Lindle, J. C. (2011). The politics, problems, and potential promise of school-linked social services: Insights and new directions from the work of William Lowe Boyd. *Peabody Journal of Education, 86*(4), 402–415.

Goldenberg, C. (2001). Making schools work for low-income families in the 21st century. In S. Neuman & D. Dickinson (Eds.), *Handbook of early literacy research* (pp. 211–231). New York: Guilford.

Greenfield, W. D., Jr. (2004). Moral leadership in schools. *Journal of Educational Administration, 42*(2), 174–196.

Hill, N. E., & Taylor, L. C. (2004). Parental school involvement and children's academic achievement: Pragmatic issues. *Current Directions in Psychological Science, 13*(4), 161–164.

Ingersoll, R. M. (1997). *The status of teaching as a profession: 1990–1991* (NCES Publication No. 97-104). Washington, DC: U.S. Department of Education, National Center for Education Statistics.

Ingersoll, R. M., & Alsalam, N. A. (1997). *Teacher professionalism and teacher commitment: A multilevel analysis* (NCES Publication No. 97-069). Washington, DC: U.S. Department of Education, National Center for Education Statistics.

Johnson, A. F., & Perkins, G. W. (2009). What we know about at-risk students: Important considerations for principal and counselor leadership. *NASSP Bulletin, 93*, 122–134.

Jozefowicz-Simbeni, D. H. M., & Allen-Meares, P. (2002). Poverty and schools: Intervention and resource building through school-linked services. *Children & Schools, 24*(2), 123–136.

Leonard, L. & Leonard, P. (2003, September 17). The continuing trouble with collaboration: Teachers talk. *Current Issues in Education, 6*(15). Retrieved from http://cie.ed.asu.edu/volume6/number15/

Little, J. (1990). The persistence of privacy: Autonomy and initiative in teachers' professional relations. *Teachers College Record, 91*(4), 509–536.

Marks, H. M., & Louis, K. S. (1997). Does teacher empowerment affect the classroom? The implications of teacher empowerment for instructional practice and student academic performance. *Educational Evaluation and Policy Analysis, 19*(3), 245–275.

Noguera, P. A. (2003). *City schools and the American dream: Reclaiming the promise of public education.* New York: Teachers College Press.

Normore, A. H., & Blanco, R. I. (2006). Leadership for social justice and morality: Collaborative partnerships, school-linked services and the plight of the poor. *International Electronic Journal for Leadership Learning, 10*(27). Retrieved from http://ijll.synergiesprairies.ca/iejll/index.php/iejll/issue/view/35

Pearson, L. C., & Moonmaw, W. (2005). The relationship between teacher autonomy, stress, work satisfaction, empowerment, and professionalism. *Educational Research Quarterly, 29*(1), 37–53.

Piercey, D. (2010). Why don't teachers collaborate? A leadership conundrum. *Phi Delta Kappan, 92*(1), 54–56.

Shoho, A. R., Merchant, B. M., & Lugg, C. A. (2011). Social justice: Seeking a common language. In F. English (Ed.), *The Sage handbook of educational leadership: Advances in theory, research, and practice* (2nd ed.) (pp. 47–67). Thousand Oaks, CA: Sage.

Smrekar, C. E. (1996). The Kentucky family resource centers: The challenge of re-making family school interactions. In J. Cibulka & W. Krietk (Eds.), *Coordination among schools, families and communities: Prospects for educational reform* (pp. 3–25). Albany: State University of New York Press.

Sullivan, C. J., & Sugarman, J. M. (1996). State policies affecting school linked integrated services. *Remedial and Special Education, 17*(5), 284–292.

Warren, M. R. (2005, Summer). Communities and schools: A new view of urban education reform. *Harvard Educational Review, 75*(2), 133–173.

White, P. A. (1992). Teacher empowerment under "ideal" school-site autonomy. *Educational Evaluation and Policy Analysis, 14*(1), 69–82.

CHAPTER SEVEN

Re-visioning the Future of Education for Youth from High Poverty Contexts[1]

Lessons Learned from Working in the Field of American Indian Education

Susan C. Faircloth

> *Much of the rhetoric of 'rigor' and 'high standards' that we hear so frequently, no matter how egalitarian in spirit it may sound to some, is fatally belied by practices that vulgarize the intellects of children and take from their education far too many of the opportunities for cultural and critical reflectiveness without which citizens become receptacles for other people's ideologies and ways of looking at the world but lack the independent spirits to create their own.* (Kozol, 2005, p. 98)

Originally written as a response to Michael Corbett's *Learning to Leave: The Irony of Schooling in a Coastal Community* (2007), this chapter focuses on the re-visioning or rethinking of ways in which education has been implemented and used with American Indian communities in the United States. This revision of my original response uses a similar argument to call for a re-visioning of the education of youth in high poverty schools and communities.

In *Learning to Leave*, Corbett (2007) argues that (1) education has served as a tool to disassociate—both physically and philosophically—students from the places from which they come, particularly if they are from rural areas, in effect creating an ambivalence toward education; (2) the ways in which individuals express this ambivalence is shaped, in large part, by factors such as socioeconomic status and gender, and I would argue race and ethnicity; (3) the purpose of schooling is often in conflict with the values and beliefs of rural communities (i.e., formal education does not increase students' social or cultural capital or their ability to increase economic capital within the rural context); and (4) the effects of globalization are found in many rural areas as evidenced by increasing access to services typically found in more urban areas, thereby decreasing individuals' need to migrate out of these areas.

Guided by these themes, I was asked to respond to the following questions: (1) How do rural community members, educators, and students resolve the tensions between preparing students for success in an increasingly globalized world and maintaining their commitment to the places from which they come? (2) What does this mean for the sustainability and growth of rural communities and schools? (3) How will this affect rural schools and their relationship with the communities they serve? I attempt to respond to these questions using the tradition of storytelling found in Native communities around the globe. Although these questions were not originally focused on students from high poverty contexts, the fact that many of our nation's poorest students come from rural areas makes this discussion particularly germane to this book.

Our Story[2]

In rethinking the ways in which the education of American Indians has been structured, a predominant theme has been one of encroachment and expansion. In modern times, this has been referred to as globalization. However, for the Indigenous peoples of what is now known as the United States, globalization is not a new concept. We have experienced the encroachment of outside forces on our lands and our peoples for more than 500 years. We have lost or been taken away from our lands, lands that hold the key to who we are in ways that are difficult to describe in words. We've endured the long march of the Trail of Tears in which thousands of Native people lost their lives as they were forced to march in harsh conditions from the mountains of Tennessee and Georgia to the plains of Oklahoma. Educationally, we have witnessed our children forcefully removed from their families and placed in boarding schools operated first by religious groups and then by the federal government. Never were we asked what we wanted for our children or what we dreamed for their future. Instead, our hair was cut, we were dressed in new clothing, our languages were silenced, and our spiritual and religious practices were banned. In spite of the damaging effects of globalization on our tribes and communities, Native people have continued to survive—demonstrating our resilience and determination to thrive in the face of seemingly insurmountable conditions.

My Story

The effects of globalization on Native peoples are glaringly evident among the Native tribes and communities scattered along the eastern coast of the United States. It is these tribes that first encountered the colonizing forces who came from across the seas in search of religious freedoms, land, and more. Encounters with these forces resulted in the loss of life, land, language, and, some would argue, culture, forcing many Native peoples to acculturate, assimilate, or die. Many of those who survived turned to farming and other land-based means of subsistence in rural and remote areas. I am a descendant of one of these tribes—the Coharie People of North Carolina.

Growing up in rural North Carolina, I never imagined that I would one day work in a university far removed from my family and community. To many of my public school teachers, success for me would have been graduating from high school and working in the same meat packing company my mother worked in for 37 years. However, my mother and father had aspirations for me that spanned beyond our local community. There was never any doubt in their minds that I would go to college; it was simply a question of where I would go. Today, I find myself immersed in the day-to-day challenges of navigating academia[3] while striving to do work that is meaningful to me, my community, and the larger field of education. In doing so, my work is informed not only by scholarly and academic research but also by my own personal experiences as an American Indian woman, one of the first in my family to attend and graduate from college, coupled with the Indigenous knowledge[4] and ways of knowing that were introduced to me by the members of my family, tribe, and community. As I do this work, I am often reminded of my own experiences in education as well as the stories of scores of children, both Native and non-Native, who have fallen through the cracks of the educational system. These experiences bolster my commitment to finding ways in which to successfully nurture the emotional, cultural, linguistic, physical, and academic needs of students.

I first came to The Pennsylvania State University (Penn State) as a graduate student in the American Indian Special Education Teacher Training Program. I returned to Penn State twice more, first as a doctoral student and finally as a faculty member in the Educational Leadership Program. My time in academia has been challenging. The more educated I've become, the more distanced I sometimes feel from my community, not so much in terms of physical distance, but in the communal sense of shared identity, beliefs, and values. I am in essence a border crosser—not completely comfortable in either the world of academia or in the community in which I spent the bulk of my childhood and early adulthood. Education has provided an opportunity for me to see and experience a world I had never seen before, but it has also distanced me from the world in which I grew up. As a result, I often find myself asking, "Can I go home? And, if I do go home, what will I do?" More than 15 years after beginning this journey, or what Corbett (2007) would term as my *outward migration*, I continue to grapple with the idea of going home and giving back.

Seven years ago, my niece, Kanani, which means "Beautiful Little One" in Hawaiian, was born. During Kanani's first pow wow, at the age of 5 months, our family danced her into the circle, surrounded by members of our community. Kanani was dressed in regalia made of a Hawaiian print, representing her father's heritage. As the dance ended, my sister performed a giveaway, an American Indian tradition of giving gifts to those who have given of themselves, which included gifts for the elders and candy for the children. For me, this day symbolized not only a blending of cultures but also a type of coming home, back to our roots in rural North Carolina. As I held Kanani on a blanket on the ground, I began to realize that coming home, for me, has as much to do with remembering and reclaiming a sense of place in my heart, spirit, and mind as it does with the land that is attached to that place called home. When I'm struggling with the writing of an academic paper or presentation, I close my eyes and recall the sights, sounds, and scents of my grandmother's kitchen on a Sunday afternoon. That's home for me. However, for many years when I traveled the physical distance back to my home community, I was constantly asked, "When are you getting married and having children and when are you coming home for good?" Having recently married, adopted a daughter, and moved back home to North Carolina, where I am a faculty member at North Carolina State University, I can now answer these questions, but for years I often found myself avoiding them, particularly the question of returning home. How could I tell my family and community members that I might never be able to return home permanently in the physical sense? How could I get them to understand that the work I engaged in was done in the hope that future generations of our children would not be forced to leave their home communities to evade the racism, discrimination, and socioeconomic disparities so rampant in many of our communities, to pursue higher education, or to earn an adequate living?

When I see my niece Kanani at home with my parents, I see a child who has not grown up in our rural community, but who is able to code switch between the urban Hawaiian culture and way of life in which she spent the first six years of her life to the life ways of a rural, American Indian community in North Carolina. She has the social and cultural mobility that I strive to achieve even as an adult. Unfortunately, formal education did not prepare me to navigate the borders between my rural community of origin and the larger world. In contrast, it attempted to reinforce the notion that this rural place in which I was born was my place—a place from which I had no right to venture out. The histories that I learned were those told by the majority—histories that I believed until becoming a history major as an undergraduate and being introduced to the concept of revisionist histories. At that point, I understood for the first time that our people, Native people, were not discovered, but in essence were the discoverers of a conquering force that paved the way for globalization as we know it today. This realization of our true histories made me even more distrusting of the education I had received as a youth.

As I read Corbett's arguments in *Learning to Leave*, I was struck by the notion of how difficult it is for me to make sense of the work we do as educators when education has been used as a tool to colonize and decimate many of our Native life ways, traditions, and lands. As an educator, I understand the importance of learning and knowledge, yet as a Native person, I view learning and knowledge as more than what is presented in a formal classroom environment. For me, my first and most important teachers were my mother and grandmother. My mother nurtured my desire to learn the academic ways of the world, while my grandmother passed down the traditions of our community, not in writing, but in the stories that she told of the old days, as I sat by her side on a Saturday night or Sunday afternoon—stories I fear losing as my grandmother is now in her 90s.

The story I tell here is not simply my story but an example of the stories shared by countless numbers of Native people living in rural and urban areas across the nation, many of whom have struggled and continue to struggle with the inherent contradictions of education. My story is individual, yet not unique or very different from my peers. Many Native youth continue to struggle as they work to navigate the educational system, wondering how they can maintain their sense of self and place while being successful academically. Unfortunately, their stories are seldom heard outside their own communities, as their relatively small numbers have tended to render them statistically insignificant in large-scale studies of the condition of education in both rural and urban settings. As a result, they have recently been referred to as the "asterisk" nation (e.g., Shotton, Lowe, & Waterman, 2013): a group typically noted as an asterisk or footnote in national reports on the condition of education in the United States.

Effecting Change for the Future of Rural Education

Today, there are more than 650 state and federally recognized tribes across the nation (e.g., U.S. Department of the Interior, Indian Affairs 2013; National Conference of State Legislatures, 2012), each with their own culture and many with their own language. Although geographically dispersed, American Indian and Alaska Native students are more likely than their peers to attend schools in rural and remote areas. According to DeVoe and Darling-Churchill (2008), 46% of Native students attend schools in rural areas, compared to 30% of whites, 14% of African Americans, 10% of Hispanics, and 9% of Asian/Pacific Islanders.

To reform the education of American Indian peoples in rural schools and communities, we must reflect on the lessons learned from the eras of self-determination and local control, movements that were in full swing in the 1960s and 1970s. These movements brought with them a call for local control of Indian education—a call that continues to ring strong among Native communities across the nation. Local control and self-determination are founded on the belief that local tribes and communities have the right to determine and shape the future and direction of our children's education. Tribes and communities have a history of educating our children—through songs, dances, and stories, by doing, listening, and watching—yet there have been limited attempts at the federal and state levels to tap into these "funds of knowledge" (Moll, Amanti, Neff, & Gonzalez, 1992; Romero-Little, 2010; Vélez-Ibáñez & Greenberg, 1992).[5] One counter-example is the Montana Indian Education for All Act, enacted in 1999. The cornerstone of this act is referred to as seven essential principles, which include (1) Montana's tribes and reservations; (2) diversity represented among the state's tribes and reservations; (3) traditional beliefs, spirituality, and oral histories; (4) tribal lands; (5) federal Indian policy; (6) Native perspectives of history; and (7) tribal sovereignty[6] (Montana Office of Public Instruction, 2008).

Local-tribal control holds the keys for the design and delivery of a truly Indigenous education for Native youth. Through local control, those who are affected most—rural families, children, and communities—are empowered to define the purpose and direction of education. This requires a change in both philosophy and practice at the federal and state levels. In addition to academic skills, our goal should be to equip all of our beautiful little ones to be proficient in their Native cultures and languages; without these funds of knowledge, the sustainability and growth of our tribes and communities are increasingly at risk. To do this requires what Wildcat (2001) described as the "indigenization" of the educational system—"the act of making our educational philosophy, pedagogy, and system our own, making the effort to explicitly explore ways of knowing and systems of knowledge that have been actively repressed for five *centuries*" (p. vii). In essence, education must be used as a means of decolonizing (i.e., facilitating children's and youths' ability to attain and maintain social, economic, and cultural capital[7] within both the local-tribal and global communities) rather than colonizing (i.e., reducing or diminishing social, economic, and cultural capital) Native children and youth.

Sustainability and Growth of Rural Communities

A return to local control of education will not ensure that all Native youth will be academically successful nor does it ensure that they will remain in their communities of origin. However, it does provide a vehicle by which children and youth have the social, cultural, and economic capital necessary to be successful wherever they choose to reside—both in the physical and philosophical sense. For me, the future of our rural communities is dependent upon our ability and willingness to re-vision, repurpose, and restructure education in ways that enable our youth to utilize the skills they are taught locally as well as globally. In essence, education has the potential to be used as a tool for *learning to leave, learning to stay, and learning to return*—skills that are not at odds but are necessary in an increasingly globalized world.

Applying Lessons Learned to the Education of Youth in High Poverty Schools and Communities

In a similar vein, if education is to be effective with students from high poverty schools and communities, policy makers, school leaders, teachers, parents, community members, and students must engage in an ongoing process of dialogue around the purpose of education. This is a visible demonstration of one's commitment to and embodiment of the ethical imperatives of best interest (e.g., Stefkovich, 2006) and care (e.g., Noddings, 2002) as discussed earlier in this book. Through this process of dialogue, students and their families become equal partners in the construction of their education in a way that is aimed at addressing their goals and concerns rather than focusing on the attainment of goals and objectives derived externally and that are often focused solely on the academic domains rather than on the social, emotional, cultural, and linguistic domains so important to the well-being and prosperity of children, youth, and their communities. Certainly this is not an easy process nor will this process work in all schools and communities. It is highly context dependent, but full of possibilities, if these schools and communities see the evidence that all partners and stakeholders are committed to moving beyond dialogue into meaningful practice and action.

As evidenced in the history of American Indian education, for many communities education has failed to embrace its presumed role as the "great equalizer" (e.g., Glomm & Ravikumar, 2003). The existence of persistent and deep poverty among communities of color—American Indians, African Americans, Hispanics/Latinos, Asian/Pacific Islanders, and other racial and ethnic minority groups, as well as the majority white population—is evidence of this unfortunate reality across this nation. According to the National Center for Children in Poverty, more than 15 million children in the United States live below the poverty level. Startlingly, 36% percent of African American, 34% of American Indian, 33% of Hispanic, 24% of children from other racial and ethnic groups, 15% of Asian, and 12% of white children live in poverty (Wight, Chau, & Aratani, 2011). This poses an important question: Is the purpose of education to equip individuals and groups to achieve to their greatest potential or is it to maintain the status quo? Regardless of the stated or actualized purpose, the fact is that education is not working for all students and communities nor is it moving the masses up the socioeconomic ladder.

Although there are many who argue that education alone is not the antidote to poverty, we believe that it is an essential player in this process. Schools are charged with dealing with the collateral damage poverty inflicts upon children and their communities. Rather than berate schools for their failure to serve these students, our task is to find ways in which to transform these schools into sites of possibility and promise. As educators, we have a moral and ethical obligation to engage in this process. We believe that the school leader can be the catalyst for this change process.

Questions to Consider

1. Reflect upon the call to re-vision the future of education for children and youth from high poverty contexts. What does this mean? What might this process look like? Who are the essential stakeholders who should be involved in this process? What strategies should be used in order to facilitate active and meaningful stakeholder involvement?
2. If the future of education is re-visioned, how can this new vision be implemented at the school level? What opportunities and challenges might be encountered in this process?
3. Consider the demographic diversity of your school. How might students' linguistic and/or cultural diversity impact the day-to-day workings of this school? What unique strengths or funds of knowledge do diverse students bring to your school? How might these strengths be leveraged to positively impact the culture and climate of this school? To what extent does your school acknowledge, value, and incorporate student diversity into the teaching and learning practices currently utilized within your school?
4. To what extent does your school prepare students to pursue a wide array of options for their academic and professional futures? To what extent does the educational system support and promote the cultural and linguistic diversity of its students, and their families and communities?

Notes

1. The original version of this chapter was published as S. C. Faircloth. (2009), Re-visioning the future of education for Native youth in rural schools and communities. *Journal of Research in Rural Education, 24*(9). Available online at http://jrre.psu.edu/articles/24-9.pdf. The author has received permission from the editor of *JRRE* to reprint a revised version of this article in this book.
2. See Lomawaima (1999) for a brief history of Indian education in the United States.
3. Until spring 2012, I served as the co-director and director of a personnel preparation grant from the U.S. Department of Education, Office of Indian Education, aimed at preparing students to assume leadership positions in educational organizations serving American Indian and Alaska Native students. This program was administered by Penn State's American Indian Leadership Program (AILP), the oldest continuously operating leadership program for American Indian and Alaska Native students in the nation. Since 1970, the AILP has graduated approximately 220 Native students. For additional information regarding the AILP, see http://www.ed.psu.edu/educ/eps/ailp.
4. See Battiste and Henderson (2000) for a discussion of Indigenous knowledge.
5. Vélez-Ibáñez & Greenberg (1992) define funds of knowledge as the "strategic and cultural resources . . . households contain" (p. 313).

6. See http://www.opi.mt.gov/pdf/indianed/resources/essentialunderstandings.pdf for additional information.
7. See Bourdieu (1986) for a discussion of economic, social, and cultural capital.

References

Battiste, M., & Henderson, J. S. Y. (2000). *Protecting Indigenous knowledge and heritage: A global challenge.* Saskatoon, SK: Purich.

Bordieu, P. (1986). The forms of capital. In J. Richardson (Ed.), *Handbook of theory and research for the sociology of education* (pp. 241–258). New York: Greenwood.

Corbett, M. (2007). *Learning to leave: The irony of schooling in a coastal community.* Halifax, NS: Fernwood.

DeVoe, J. F., & Darling-Churchill, K. E. (2008). *Status and trends in the education of American Indians and Alaska Natives: 2008* (NCES Publication No. 2008-084). Washington, DC: U.S. Department of Education, National Center for Education Statistics, Institute of Education Sciences.

Glomm, G., & Ravikumar, B. (2003, June). Public education and income inequality. *European Journal of Political Economy, 19*(2), 289–300.

Kozol, J. (2005). *The shame of the nation: The restoration of apartheid schooling in America.* New York: Random House.

Lomawaima, K. T. (1999). The unnatural history of American Indian education. In K. S. Swisher & J. W. Tippeconnic III (Eds.), *Next steps: Research and practice to advance Indian education* (pp. 3–31). Charleston, WV: ERIC Clearinghouse on Rural and Small Schools.

Moll, L. C., Amanti, C., Neff, D., & Gonzalez, N. (1992). Funds of knowledge for teaching: Using a qualitative approach to connect homes and classrooms. *Theory Into Practice, 31*(2), 132–141.

Montana Office of Public Instruction. (2008). *Indian education for all: Essential understandings regarding Montana Indians.* Retrieved from http://www.opi.mt.gov/pdf/indianed/resources/essentialunderstandings.pdf

Noddings, N. (2002). *Educating moral people: A caring alternative to character education.* New York: Teachers College Press.

Romero-Little, M. E. (2010). How should young Indigenous children be prepared for learning? A vision of early childhood education for Indigenous children. *Journal of American Indian Education, 49,* 7–28.

Shotton, H., Lowe, S. C., & Waterman, S. J. (Eds.). (2013). *Beyond the asterisk: Understanding Native students in higher education.* Sterling, VA: Stylus.

Stefkovich, J. A. (2006). *Best interests of the student: Applying ethical constructs to legal cases in education.* Mahwah, NJ: Lawrence Erlbaum.

U.S. Department of the Interior, Indian Affairs. (2013). Tribal Directory. Retrieved from http://www.bia.gov/WhoWeAre/BIA/OIS/TribalGovernmentServices/TribalDirectory/

Vélez-Ibáñez, C. G., & Greenberg, J. B. (1992). Formation and transformation of funds of knowledge among U.S.-Mexican households. *Anthropology and Education Quarterly, 23*(4), 313–335.

Wight, V. R., Chau, M., & Aratani, Y. (2001, March). *Who are America's poor children? The official story.* New York: Mailman School of Public Health, Columbia University, National Center for Children in Poverty.

Wildcat, D. R. (2001). Prelude to a dialogue. In V. Deloria & D. R. Wildcat (Eds.), *Power and place: Indian education in America* (p. vii). Golden, CO: Fulcrum.

CHAPTER EIGHT

Addressing the Needs of High Poverty Latino Students as They Navigate the Terrain of Higher Education

Juanita Vargas

Ninety-five percent of Latino parents wanted their children to go to college but parents lacked access to information on preparing their children for college while in high school. (Pew Hispanic Center & Kaiser Family Foundation, 2004)

Education is an international must, a veritable human right, yet education—especially higher education—in the land of the free is still remarkably elusive. (Capra, 2009, p. 75)

The fastest growing demographic in the United States is Latino Americans (U.S. Census Bureau, 2010). This group falls into the high poverty category because members often work in low-paying, low-status positions, including cleaning, cooking, serving, and landscaping. According the U.S. Census Bureau, the poverty rate for Hispanics and Latinos ranged from a low of 16.2% among Cubans to a high of 26.3% among Dominicans (Macartney, Bishaw, & Fontenot, 2013). If these conditions are to change, educators must recognize that the only way to minimize the cycle of individuals and families living and working in poverty is to ensure higher quality and levels of education be attained. Whether children are legal or illegal residents, schools have a legal obligation to serve all children in this country (U.S. Department of Justice & U.S. Department of Education, 2011). As such, schools all over the country seek strategies for providing the needs of this growing demographic, along with other populations, who live in poverty. A primary goal for Latinos, and others, living in poverty should be college readiness.

This chapter discusses this need for college readiness, along with examples of programs that promote college readiness. Latino students are highlighted because of their prominence in this country, as well as the fact that there have been many organized efforts spearheaded by the Latino community and others who wish for their success in school. Although this chapter focuses on Latino students, it is important to note that these strategies and recommendations are relevant for other communities of diverse learners from high poverty backgrounds who desire to pursue higher education.

College Knowledge for Latino Parents

Like many other states, Texas faces a challenge in the coming decades due to demographic trends, which have resulted in the Latino population becoming the majority ethnic minority group in the state (U.S. Census Bureau, 2010). The changing demographics in Texas and other states are making educators and politicians aware that the fastest-growing ethnic minority is also the least college-going population, and such a trend may have severe economic and social implications for future growth and stability for many states (Heller, 2001; Oliva, 2004; Solomon & Wingard, 1991). To understand why large numbers of Latinos may not be going to college, it is important to recognize the barriers and obstacles faced by Latino students in accessing higher education, to explore the role of parental influence on college-going decisions, to review programs for Latino parents focused on developing college knowledge, and to examine how culturally specific changes can be incorporated in new or existing Latino parent education programs.

Obstacles Facing College-going Latinos

There are a number of obstacles that Latinos face when trying to access college. Some of the obstacles that prevent Latinos from accessing college include poverty, underperformance in school (Oliva, 2004), parental low-level or lack of education (Tornatzky, Cutler, & Lee, 2002; Vernez & Mizell, 2001), parental unfamiliarity of the American school system (Tornatzky et al., 2002; Vernez & Mizell, 2001), lack of college preparation while in school (Swail, Cabrera, & Lee, 2004), and the need for financial aid (Heller, 1997, 2001).

The most challenging obstacle to college access for Latino students is poverty and the complications that accompany it. In 2010, 26.6% of Latinos lived in poverty (U.S. Census Bureau, 2010), compared to 25% in 1998 (Evelyn, 2000). Currently, more than 35% of Latino children live in poverty (U.S. Census Bureau, 2012). One reason many Latinos live below the poverty line is the family's low level of education or lack of education. For example, some parents who attended American schools did not finish their education and some did not have positive experiences while in school (Vernez & Mizell, 2001). Unfortunately, the impact of socioeconomic status (SES) continues to be felt even among those students who do go on to pursue higher education. This manifests itself in terms of how and how often they engage in extracurricular activities while in college, the amount and type of non-academic work they engage in as students, and achievements beyond college completion (e.g., Walpole, 2003).

Another obstacle facing Latinos is underperformance in the K–12 sector. According to Hemphill, Vanneman, and Rahman (2011), Hispanic and Latino students lag behind their peers, particularly white students, in their performance on the reading and math components of the National Assessment of Educational Progress. In addition, the dropout rate for Latinos exceeds 50% and is negatively impacted by testing and other scholastic evaluative practices (Oliva, 2004). Research also shows that many Latino students are not taking courses in school that prepare them for academic course work in college. In one study, 59% of Latino students were not adequately prepared for entrance to postsecondary education compared to 41% of white students (Swail et al., 2004).

In addition to poverty and underperformance in schools, the life of many Latinos is impacted by the fact that many of them have immigrated to the United States, and may have had very little exposure to education in their home countries prior to coming to the United States. Many of them also lack knowledge of the American education system, making it difficult for them to advocate for their children. Research also shows that if parents have limited education, the chances of their children going to college are less than those of children whose parents have earned a college degree (Tornatzky et al., 2002; Vernez & Mizell, 2001).

Another obstacle is Latino student access to and preparation for higher education. According to the Pew Hispanic Center (2004), a lack of knowledge of the education system can have negative repercussions for students and their families as they progress through the educational system. According to a study by Romo and Salas (2003), many Latino parents were not aware that their children needed to take higher-level math or English courses while in high school, nor were they aware that they needed to take standardized entrance exams or that they needed to be prepared to take the SAT. Many of them did not realize they needed to learn and develop higher-level math, writing, studying, and test-taking skills. These students and their families were also unaware of tutors or preparation courses that could help students prepare for SAT exams. They also lacked knowledge of the importance of preparing for the admission application process (McDonough, 1994; Romo & Salas, 2003).

Research also shows that Latino students may not have access to high school counselors to help them prepare for college entrance exams and may not be aware that special consultants can be hired to assist with the selection of colleges and completion of the application process (Gandara, 2002). Emslie, Contreras, and Padilla (1998) and Roma and Salas (2003) found that many Latino students did not know that they needed to develop study skills. As a result, they were not prepared for the changes associated with living away from home and were not prepared for the rigors of college work. These students then became discouraged when they found out they did not have the reading, writing, and computer skills needed to be successful and were devastated when placed in remedial courses.

The final obstacle to the pursuit of higher education is the lack of finances to pay for college. Many Latino families and their children have expressed concern about how they can afford college. Unfortunately, many low-SES Latino students and their families who may qualify for financial aid are not aware that financial aid is available for them (Auerbach, 2004; Downs et al., 2008; Zoppi, 2006), as financial aid allocations have dropped in recent federal administrations. As a result, low-income students who have access to fewer funds to pay for college will most likely not enroll in college. In many cases, the decision to enroll in college is complicated by students' sensitivity to tuition increases and drop in financial aid and its effect on college persistence (Heller, 1997, 2001).

In Texas, there are few programs to provide funds for low-income students who wish to pursue higher education. Though the tuition for Texas institutions is low compared to other states, it still is too high for Latino students whose family income is quite low (Romo & Salas, 2003). Studies show that in 2003 it took 71% of the same quintile's family income to pay for college (College Board, 2003). Many Latino students are also hesitant to enroll in college due to the fear of taking out student loans (Cunningham & Santiago, 2008).

A related financial concern, from a cultural perspective, is the family's dependence on the student's employment while he or she is still in high school. Students hesitate to go to college when they are major contributors to their family's livelihood. If they went to college, they would not be able to contribute financially to the family's well-being (Romo & Salas, 2003).

Parental and Family Influence

Although researchers acknowledge the importance of involving the family in helping their children prepare for higher education, historically, parents of some racial and ethnic minority groups were considered an impediment to children's learning. In the case of some ethnic minority children, governmental agencies intervened by removing children from their families.[1] Later researchers theorized that although socioeconomic class was sometimes an indicator of whether a child went to college, parental and family involvement was irrelevant to the child's decision-making process. Research now identifies parents, siblings, and the extended family as necessary components of a child's educational success. Researchers stress that parental influence and educational involvement are crucial to the child's educational success (for an extended discussion of the above, see Tierney, 2002).

Parental and family involvement is critical in the early years of a child's education. Parents who have benefited from education have the college knowledge to prepare their children for further learning at earlier ages (Tierney, 2002). Recent research shows the involvement of Latino parents is essential in increasing the college-knowledge base and providing support for students (Gandara, 2002; Swail & Perna, 2002). Latino parental involvement regarding college preparation needs to occur not only when students reach high school but also in the formative years (i.e., the elementary and middle school grades) when children are developing their opinions of higher education (Gandara, 2002; Jun & Colyar, 2002; McDonough, 1997). Swail and Perna stress that by the time students reach the 8th grade, it may be too late for intervention programs. Others suggest that policy makers should consider starting intervention programs as early as three years of age, especially for students from minority and low socioeconomic backgrounds (Trent et al., 2003).

Unfortunately, Latino parents and extended family members often lack knowledge of what resources and information are needed to effectively assist in preparing their children for college. This is particularly true when Latino parents are also immigrants and low SES, and have not completed high school or gone to college (Tornatzky et al., 2002). This lack of knowledge means that Latino parents are often unaware that providing access to college requires enhancing the families' social, cultural, and other capital, that is, access to college-education networks and resources, and development of multilevel critical advocacy through parents, families, and communities (Hagedorn & Tierney, 2002).

It is now evident that direct and indirect parental and family involvement for Latino students is important. Parental involvement can include providing emotional and motivational support and guidance. Once family members understand the rigors of college coursework, they can provide household support so students can concentrate on their studies (Jun & Colyar, 2002). Many Latino families have strong family networks that provide support. These networks may also include nonblood relations such as the *madrina* (godmother), *padrino* (godfather), friends, and neighbors (Quintero, 1998; Tornatzky et al., 2002). To effectively serve this student population, college knowledge must be extended beyond the immediate family.

Obstacles Faced by Latino Parents
Many Latino parents face hurdles in trying to provide the necessary support for their children to be successful in school. These hurdles include feelings of alienation due to language barriers and lack of knowledge of school policies and processes (Downs et al., 2008; Emslie et al., 1998; Zoppi, 2006). Some parents speak little or no English and not all schools provide Spanish-speaking personnel. These language barriers are particularly difficult for those parents who lack knowledge of the importance of monitoring or assisting with homework and who may not

be aware of what college preparatory courses their children should be taking while in middle and high school (Brooks & Kavanaugh, 1999; Falbo, Contreras, & Avalos, 2003).

In addition to language barriers, in the case of Latino parents, cultural understandings of education often differ from mainstream Western views and may contribute to a lack of congruence between home and school activities. Even when parents want and choose to be involved, they may do so in ways unanticipated by educators (Garcia, 2001; Jun & Colyar, 2002). For example, Latino parents tend to be more authoritarian (warm and strict) compared to authoritative (strict). When teaching tasks to their children, Latino parents tend to provide solutions rather than use the inquiry approach used by non-Latino parents (Jun & Colyar).

Latino parents need to understand how they can help their children prepare for college, how they can provide encouragement and support to increase their children's motivation to succeed academically, and how they can monitor school attendance and schoolwork (Falbo et al., 2003; Gandara, 2002). However, if Latino parents are to learn how to help their children prepare for college, intervention programs should be developed to overcome the existing obstacles.

Intervention Initiatives for Latino Parents

Some communities have innovative high school programs that support Latino children to prepare for college, such as California's Puente program (Hooker & Brand, 2009; Laden, 1998) and the UCLA Outreach programs (Oakes, Rogers, Lipton, & Morrell, 2002). These programs have a parent component; however, it is voluntary and structured for occasional meetings with the parent. Another program, Parents Teaching Parents, initially started in the state of Washington as an association among Central Washington University, the Highland School District, and Latino parents. This program was designed for Latino parents to share their knowledge of the college planning, application, and admissions processes with parents from similar backgrounds (Downs et al., 2008). Unfortunately, these types of programs are not uniformly found across the United States. The few programs that do exist tend not to involve the parent and/or extended family members, except in a minor role, in providing information on financial aid, SAT preparation, and advising. These programs also begin in the late high school years and not during grade school years.

If society expects Latino students to attend college and be successful, intervention programs need to be initiated to provide information and other support for these students and their parents. The type of information that has been identified as useful includes information on courses and skills needed for students to be successful in school and for them to begin learning these skills as early as the 3rd and 4th grades. Such an early start prepares children for college. Latino parents and families need access to this critical information so they are better able to help their children prepare for college. It is also important to point out that these types of supportive interventions should be designed with cultural integrity in mind (Tierney, 2002).

Cultural integrity acknowledges and uses, rather than ignores or devalues, racial and ethnic backgrounds to enhance learning (Deyhle, 1995, as cited in Tierney, 2002). For any program to be successful, development and implementation must take into account the diversity of the specific Latino culture and community with which the program is to be implemented. A culturally specific program should reflect the traditions and values of the intended population while at the same time ensuring that the mission of the program is being met (Tierney, 2002).

Research indicates that programs such as GEAR UP have reported difficulties maintaining parent interest and involvement (Swail & Perna, 2002). Since these programs target African American and Latino students and their families, the question arises whether these programs have been developed to be culturally specific. It is important to determine the extent to which these programs have been designed to incorporate the parents, their culture, and their values. This information is critical to the success of these types of programs.

In sum, it is imperative parent education programs be designed to provide information and support to Latino parents and extended families so they know how to encourage their children's educational success and college aspirations. Information and other support providers need to be aware of Latino cultural differences and adapt their approach to be culturally sensitive to these differences.

Culturally Specific Programs

Cheng Gorman (1996, as cited in Jun & Colyar, 2002) identifies three categories of parent education programs: *translated, culturally adapted,* and *culturally specific*. A translated program is one that is literally translated into another language without any changes and is commonly found in standardized forms, handouts, and brochures, and at numerous government and educational Internet sites. A culturally adapted program is one designed with the values and traditions of the specific ethnic group in mind. A culturally specific approach is a step beyond culturally adapted; the program is designed to be relevant to the target group by taking into account neighborhood associations, local people and resources, and specific cultural needs.

Educational institutions need to understand and appreciate each culture's unique values, beliefs, and customs (Gorman & Balter, 1997). For example, information providers for Latino parents need to understand and accept that non-traditional child-rearing practices exist. This will affect the way in which parents interact with their children both inside and outside of school. Once this is accomplished, institutions and other support providers can adapt or develop programs that are culturally specific to Latino families (Gorman & Balter, 1997; Tierney, 2002).

Although these efforts are a good start, it is important to point out that simply translating literature, brochures, websites, and institutional policies and procedures into Spanish is not enough. To be culturally sensitive means incorporating the values of the target population. Information providers need to understand that any form of communication for Latino parents should be provided in a way that is reflective of their culture(s) and their value system (Gorman & Balter, 1997). Any informational program needs to be developed with cultural sensitivity in mind by striving to understanding participants' cultural values, building on the strengths of the extended family, and making a personal commitment to learn about Latino cultures. Information providers should personalize their communication with the individual parents by speaking with them in a non-patronizing and non-condescending manner. Positive communication requires taking the time to engage in small talk with family members, calling parents at home, speaking with parents when encountering them in the community, and making home visits. Small talk is especially important in communities that have not traditionally been involved in or successful in the educational system. It is a means of building trusting relationships (Scribner, Young, & Pedroza, 1999).

The *colonias* (neighborhood) project in south Texas is an example of incorporating cultural integrity in educational programming. In this project, *promotores* are an invaluable link to local culture and values. The *promotores* are local people who are bilingual and have become knowledgeable concerning the university system. They make home visits to the residents of the *colonias*, and they provide information to parents and students about resources and services available in the community and at the university. They also provide invaluable input and feedback for culturally specific development of their services and programs for the Latino community (May et al., 2003).

Culturally Specific Programs for Latino Parents

According to Auerbach (2004) there are a number of issues to consider when developing culturally specific parent education programs. These include:

- Start early—no later than the upper elementary grades—to reinforce family college aspirations and introduce the idea of planning for pathways to college.

- Speak parents' language. School and colleges must reach out to Latino parents in both English and Spanish, especially on the Internet and in college directories and catalogues.

- Think small and personal. Parents who do not typically come to the school are more likely to come to meetings of small groups with which they have some connection—such as a class, club, sports team, or church group—rather than large schoolwide events. Make meetings as convenient and comfortable as possible. If large events are necessary, arrange for smaller break-out groups and ways for parents to get to know each other over time. Personal face-to-face or telephone invitations to meetings are often more effective than letters or flyers.

- Invite personal stories from guest speakers of similar backgrounds to help families make sense of complex information and feel comfortable asking questions. Guests can include not only K–16 educators, students, and alumni but fellow parents with children in college.

- Reinforce basic college information often, in a variety of ways. It takes time to absorb new, complex information. Written information campaigns or annual college nights will have only limited impact without sustained contact. Have K–12 students research and present college information to their parents at meetings to attract interest.

- Attend to the specialized information needs of Latino parents, such as worries about children's safety on campus, undocumented status, and loans. These practical issues become barriers to access unless addressed in a sensitive, culturally appropriate way.

- Give parents opportunities to meet individually with school and college representatives who can become additional sources of help. Individual contact allows parents to ask questions that are highly specific or private and helps build trust with institutional agents.

- Help parents move through the college planning process together as a group. The social and emotional mutual support that parents gain from undertaking the experience collectively can reduce 'cooling out' and increase their commitment to the process.

- Acknowledge the barriers to college access for Latinos and encourage parent learning about educational inequality. Frank discussions of barriers recognize the realities that students face, introduce strategies for overcoming them, and contribute to a greater sense of community. (pp. 140–141)

A project designed to address college knowledge for Latino parents would involve developing a research-based intervention that interrupts the status quo in order to improve Latino college outcomes (information and information delivery networks). This could include making the information available on demand via responsive technology, such as the Internet. Parental access to this information is important; thus, it is essential that parents signal the need for the information available and assist in the shaping of information delivery. To ensure resources are truly accessible to parents, efforts should be made to provide instruction to parents on using the Internet, not only for access to the website, but also for utilizing additional resources, information, and services available beyond their community borders. The design of these programs should be a collaborative effort that emphasizes the development of a college knowledge program that is parent centered.

Research has also addressed culturally specific parent education programs (Auerbach, 2004). The bilingual parent education program known as Futures & Families (F&F) was part of the (K–16) Futures Project, a collaboration between the University of California and an urban high school. The mission of this program was to help parents develop confidence, deepen their knowledge base regarding the K–16 system, learn how to support their children's learning environment at school and in the home, and expand family social networks to include other families like them, as well as provide supportive school personnel. This program was designed to meet the needs of Latino parents. It was designed to be small, with only 10 to 15 families volunteering to participate. The monthly programs were culturally specific in that they were conducted in Spanish and English, agendas were designed with parental concerns in mind, and college-related topics were specific to Latino students and addressed their lack of college knowledge. The meetings also allowed time for small-group discussion and hands-on activities. The program was considered successful because it provided information and helped develop parents' confidence in their understanding of how they could support their child at home and also serve as an advocate for their child in the educational system.

Another culturally specific parent education program is Parent Institute for Quality Education (PIQE) in San Jose, California (Golan & Petersen, 2002). This program utilizes a conceptual framework for involving immigrant Latino parents in understanding and supporting their children's education. The approach is from a K–12 perspective, can be adapted in any community, and is designed to be culturally specific. This program takes place over an eight-week period, with a four-month follow-up after the parents complete the program. The program is taught by local instructors and their goals are to:

1. Establish and maintain a supportive learning home environment.
2. Communicate and collaborate with teachers, counselors, and principals.
3. Navigate the school system and access its resources.
4. Encourage college attendance.
5. Identify and avoid obstacles to school success.
6. Support children's emotional and social development.

The PIQE program differs from other parent education programs in that it is not focused on child-rearing education but instead on college knowledge and college preparation. In this program, the teachers make personal contact with the parents, invite them to participate in the programs, and involve people who can share similar experiences and concerns with the parents. PIQE parents receive support from other PIQE graduates and also receive monthly follow-up calls to determine if the parents need help or have questions regarding their newly learned strategies to assist their children in improving their study habits and educational experience. As a result of their involvement with PIQE, teachers have developed a better understanding of and sensitivity to the cultural views and values of Latino parents and family structure. In addition, teachers begin to see the educational development of the student as a collaborative effort between the teachers and parents (Golan & Petersen, 2002).

Successful culturally specific programs involving the Latino parent have incorporated cultural integrity in their development. While there are several distinct characteristics that make these programs culturally specific for Latinos, other characteristics of these programs can also be applied to other cultures. Elements of these programs are outlined below (Golan & Petersen, 2002):

1. Make no assumptions. Approach learning about the community without any preconceived assumptions.
2. The programs should be conducted in English and in the language the parents speak.
3. Define the *family* according to their values and culture and develop the program based on that information.
4. Make the program development a collaborative effort between the organization and the parents and family members. Involving them from the initial stages develops trust and commitment.
5. Schedule the program meeting times for the parents' convenience. Know when they are at work.
6. Create a supportive atmosphere during the program by meeting their needs (e.g., Is there a need for child care?).
7. Meetings should not be too long and should be developed with an agenda that addresses participants' concerns and needs. By speaking with them and learning about their home life and concerns, it will be easier to address these needs.
8. Know your community. Walk around the community, watch, and learn. They are Latino but are they Mexican, Costa Rican, Cuban? Where do they frequent?
9. Know what the parental concerns are. Financial aid, undocumented status, safety concerns? Address those concerns during the meetings.

10. Assess the parents' educational level of knowledge before developing the program.
11. Make personal contact with each household by making a home visit or making telephone calls. Stop and take a moment to speak with parents and family members when you see them in the community or in the school.

Once the organization has learned about the community, the parents, and their concerns, it can develop the program, incorporated with the goals of a culturally specific program that will provide college knowledge to Latino parents and their children. Parental college knowledge needs found in the literature (e.g., Tornatzky et al., 2002) stress the need to:

1. Understand the barriers and obstacles endured by Latino parents and family members.
2. Teach parents how they can help their child be successful in school, knowing what kind of classes are college prep classes, and knowing how parents can provide a learning environment at home.
3. Show parents how they can become advocates for their children.
4. Explain the American education system and what resources are available to them, how these resources can be accessed, and why these resources are important for their child's educational development.
5. Explain the benefits of a college education in the language parents will understand. Compare college with community college, the military, and other alternative career choices.
6. Show respect for the role of parents and respect for their cultural values as a community and as a family.
7. Invite other Latino community members to share their experiences in rearing their own children who are now in higher education.
8. Repeat information as needed, as there is so much information to understand and comprehend. Hands-on activities are also helpful.

Finally, the last culturally specific parent education program identified is Parents Teaching Parents (PTP), a collaborative effort among Central Washington University (CWU), Highland School District, and Latino parents (Downs et al., 2008). College representatives theorized that if Latino parents were involved at the start in developing this program, they would have ownership of the program and continue to operate the program regardless of changes in university and school administration. Downs and colleagues described the process involved in developing this six-week program with CWU and Latino parents. This process included the development of sessions, determination of the time and location of sessions, curriculum, and the selection of parent volunteers who learned how to facilitate the sessions. The parents identified the core topics as college entrance requirements, financial aid, careers, and college testing (Downs et al., p. 234). Although this was a much needed program, the organizers encountered resistance from the school administrators in providing space for the PTP meetings, and school counselors who thought they were already meeting the needs of Latino students.

Conclusion

Although many Latino parents desire to educate their children and to encourage their pursuit of higher education, they often face enormous challenges including the lack of necessary college knowledge and other resources available to them. If these challenges are to be resolved, school leaders and policy makers must be proactive in recognizing and responding to the unique needs and circumstances of the Latino population and the urgency of encouraging Latino students to pursue and complete higher education. School leaders and policy makers need to increase their cultural sensitivity toward this population and begin to develop and fund long-term programs designed to educate Latino parents about the benefits and rewards of a college education, as well as the planning and actions required to make college education possible for their children. These programs need to be culturally specific to attract and retain Latino parents and their children. These programs also need to start as early as grade school, so that parents can learn about the education system and become more active participants in developing their children's educational experiences.

Educating Latino parents and their children about the benefits of a college education, teaching them how to access necessary resources, and showing them how to prepare for college while their children are still in elementary and secondary schools are essential steps in addressing the barriers that face this emerging majority. Although the challenges facing many Latinos are overwhelming at times, education is one way out of these circumstances, including poverty, and can make a significant difference in their lives and in society at large. With culturally specific programs designed to educate Latino parents on how to support their children and develop college knowledge, Latino parents and their families can become more empowered and privileged. By understanding why Latino students are not going to college, recognizing and understanding the barriers faced by Latino parents and their children, and respecting the role family plays in college-going decisions, policy makers and educators can work to create culturally specific programs aimed at effectively educating and supporting Latino parents and their children in accessing college and becoming successful graduates. The future of this nation depends on our ability and willingness to develop the talents of all children and youth, particularly those whose families have been socially and economically disenfranchised.

Questions to Consider

1. This chapter discusses the need to make college accessible for Latino students. As noted in this chapter, Latinos represent the fastest-growing minority group in the United States. As such, it is likely that you will lead a school or district that is [heavily] populated by Latino students. What unique challenges do you foresee in working to enable Latino students from high poverty backgrounds to reach their full academic potential? How have you prepared, as a school leader, to address the diverse needs of Latino students? What types of professional development or learning would be beneficial to you and your teachers in working to better meet the needs of this population?

2. Although Latinos are the fastest growing racial/ethnic group in the United States, it is highly likely that you will also lead a school that is attended by students from other racial/ethnic minority groups. What other racial or ethnic groups do you believe will attend school in the buildings or districts you will lead in the future? To what extent might the recommendations offered in this chapter for working with Latino students be applied to students and families from other racial/ethnic groups?

3. How might you work differently with students and parents from other racial and ethnic groups? In what ways might your leadership style differ depending on the racial/ethnic composition of your school? Do you believe that differences in race and ethnicity will or should impact the school leader's leadership style? Why or why not?

4. Do you feel it is ethical to devote increased time and resources toward assisting students from different racial/ethic minority groups? Why or why not?

5. As noted in this chapter, Latino students, and other students from diverse racial/ethnic groups who have been traditionally underrepresented in colleges and universities across the nation, often need more time and resources than other groups in order to successfully access post-secondary education and to reach their fullest academic potential. This increased need is fueled in large part by financial and other circumstances, such as being new to the country or the area. How will you garner the faculty and staff buy-in necessary to adequately support racially/ethnically diverse students from high poverty backgrounds? How will you justify what may be deemed as preferential treatment of students from diverse and/or high poverty backgrounds to parents of other students within your school/district? How will you garner parent support for these initiatives?

Note

1. In some cases, the Bureau of Indian Affairs (BIA) removed American Indian children from their homes because their parents would leave their children in the care of family or nonblood relations when they left in search of employment. Since doing so was a culturally accepted practice among many Native communities, parents trusted their extended family with their children and could be gone for several months without worrying about their children's welfare. However, the BIA interpreted this practice as abandonment, clearly illustrating a difference in cultural expectations and norms. For additional information, see Hollinger (1992) and U.S. House Report (1978).

References

Auerbach, S. (2004). Engaging Latino parents in supporting college pathways: Lesson from a college access program. *Journal of Hispanic Higher Education, 3*(2), 125–145.

Brooks, A. K., & Kavanaugh, P. C. (1999). Empowering the surrounding community. In R. Reyes, J. D. Scribner, & A. P. Scribner (Eds.), *Lessons from high-performing Hispanic schools* (pp. 61–93). New York: Teachers College Press.

Capra, T. (2009, Fall). Poverty and its impact on education: Today and tomorrow. *Thought & Action,* 75–81.

College Board. (2003). *Trends in college pricing.* New York: Author.

Cunningham, A. F., & Santiago, D. A. (2008, December). *Student aversion to borrowing. Who borrows and who doesn't.* Washington, DC: Institute for Higher Education Policy and Excelencia in Education. Retrieved from http://www.ihep.org/assets/files/publications/s-z/studentaversiontoborrowing.pdf

Downs, A., Martin, J., Fossum, M., Martinez, S., Solorio, M., & Martinez, H. (2008). Parents teaching parents: A career and college knowledge program for Latino parents. *Journal of Latinos and Education, 7*(3), 227–240.

Emslie, J. R., Contreras, J. A., & Padilla, V. R. (1998). Transforming high schools to meet the needs of Latinos. In M. L. Gonzales, A. Huerta-Macias, & J. V. Tinajero (Eds.), *Educating Latino students: A guide to successful practices* (pp. 291–302). Lancaster, PA: Technomic.

Evelyn, J. (2000). Research shows lag in Hispanics' bachelor's attainment. *Black Issues in Higher Education, 17*(3), 16.

Falbo, T., Contreras, H., & Avalos, M. D. (2003). Transition points from high school to college. In H. T. Frierson Jr. (Series Ed.) & D. J. Leon (Vol. Ed.), *Diversity in higher education: Vol. 3. Latinos in higher education* (pp. 59–72). Oxford, England: Elsevier Science.

Gandara, P. (2002). Meeting common goals: Linking K–12 and college interventions. In W. G. Tierney & L. S. Hagedorn (Eds.), *Increasing access to college: Extending possibilities for all students* (pp. 81–103). Albany: State University of New York Press.

Garcia, E. E. (2001). *Hispanic education in the United States.* Lanham, MD: Rowman & Littlefield.

Golan, S., & Petersen, D. (2002, March). Promoting involvement of recent immigrant families in their children's education. Cambridge, MA: Harvard Family Research Project. Retrieved from http://www.hfrp.org/publications-resources/browse-our-publications/promoting-involvement-of-recent-immigrant-families-in-their-children-s-education

Gorman, J. C., & Balter, L. (1997). Culturally sensitive parent education: A critical review of quantitative research. *Review of Educational Research, 67*(3), 339–369.

Hagedorn, L. S., & Tierney, W. G. (2002). Cultural capital and the struggle for educational equality. In W. G. Tierney & L. S. Hagedorn (Eds.), *Increasing access to college: Extending possibilities for all students* (pp. 1–11). Albany: State University of New York Press.

Heller, D. E. (1997). Student price response in higher education: An update to Leslie and Brinkman. *Journal of Higher Education, 68*(6), 624–659.

Heller, D. E. (2001). *The states and public higher education policy: Affordability, access, and accountability.* Baltimore: Johns Hopkins University Press.

Hemphill, F. C., Vanneman, A., & Rahman, T. (2011, June). *Achievement gaps: How Hispanic and white students in public schools perform in mathematics and reading on the National Assessment of Educational Progress.* Retrieved from http://nces.ed.gov/nationsreportcard/pdf/studies/2011459.pdf

Hollinger, J. (1992). *Adoption law and practice: October 1992 supplement.* New York: M. Bender.

Hooker, S., & Brand, B. (2009). *Success at every step: How 23 programs support youth on the path to college and beyond.* Washington, DC: American Youth Policy Forum.

Hooker, S., & Brand, B. (2010). College knowledge: A critical component of college and career readiness. *New Directions for Youth Development, 127,* 75–85.

Jun, A., & Colyar, J. (2002). Parental guidance suggested. In W. G. Tierney & L. S. Hagedorn (Eds.), *Increasing access to college: Extending possibilities for all students* (pp. 195–215). Albany: State University of New York Press.

Laden, B. V. (1998, April). *Celebratory socialization: Welcoming Hispanic students to college.* Paper presented at the American Educational Research Association annual meeting, San Diego, CA. (ERIC Document Reproduction Service No. ED429523)

Macartney, S., Bishaw, A., & Fontenot, K. (2013, February). *Poverty rates for selected detailed race and Hispanic groups by state and place: 2007–2011* (American Community Survey Brief No. ACSBR/11-17). Retrieved from http://www.census.gov/prod/2013pubs/acsbr11-17.pdf

May, M. L., Bowman, G. J., Ramos, K. S., Rincones, L., Rebollar, M. G., Rosa, M. L., et al. (2003). Embracing the local: Enriching scientific research, education, and outreach on the Texas–Mexico border through a participatory action research partnership. *Environmental Health Perspectives, 111*(13), 1571–1576.

McDonough, P. M. (1994). Buying and selling higher education: The social construction of the college applicant. *Journal of Higher Education, 65*(4), 427–446.

McDonough, P. M. (1997). *Choosing colleges: How social class and schools structure opportunity.* Albany: State University of New York Press.

Oakes, J., Rogers, J., Lipton, M., & Morrell, E. (2002). The social construction of college access: Confronting the technical, cultural, and political barriers to low income students of color. In W. G. Tierney & L. S. Hagedorn (Eds.), *Increasing access to college: Extending possibilities for all students* (pp. 105–121). Albany: State University of New York Press.

Oliva, M. (2004). Reluctant partners, problem definition, and legislative intent: K–16 policy for Latino college success. *Journal of Hispanic Higher Education, 3*(2), 209–230.

Pew Hispanic Center & Kaiser Family Foundation. (2004, January). *National survey of Latinos: Education* (No. 3031). Washington, DC: Author. Retrieved from http://pewhispanic.org/files/reports/25.pdf

Quintero, E. (1998). Developmentally appropriate practice: Rethinking the preschool curriculum with Latino families. In M. L. Gonzales, A. Huerto-Macias, & J. V. Tinajero (Eds.), *Educating Latino students: A guide to successful practice* (pp. 63–85). Lancaster, PA: Technomic.

Romo, H., & Salas, J. (2003). Successful transitions of Latino students from high school to college. In H. T. Frierson Jr. (Series Ed.) & D. J. Leon (Vol. Ed.), *Diversity in higher education: Vol. 3. Latinos in higher education* (pp. 107–130). Oxford, England: Elsevier Science.

Scribner, J. D., Young, M. D., & Pedroza, A. (1999). Building collaborative relationships with parents. In R. Reyes, J. D. Scribner, & A. P. Scribner (Eds.), *Lessons from high-performing Hispanic schools* (pp. 36–60). New York: Teachers College Press.

Solomon, L. C., & Wingard, T. L. (1991). The changing demographics: Problems and opportunities. In P. G. Altbach & K. Lometey (Eds.), *The racial crisis in American higher education* (pp. 19–42). Albany: State University of New York Press.

Swail, W. S., Cabrera, A. F., & Lee, C. (2004). *Latino youth and the pathway to college.* Washington, DC: Pew Hispanic Center.

Swail, W. S., & Perna, L. W. (2002). Pre-college outreach programs. In W. G. Tierney & L. S. Hagedorn (Eds.), *Increasing access to college: Extending possibilities for all students* (pp. 15–34). Albany: State University of New York Press.

Tierney, W. G. (2002). Parents and families in precollege preparation: The lack of connection between research and practice. *Educational Policy, 16*(4), 588–606.

Tornatzky, L. G., Cutler, R., & Lee, J. (2002). *College knowledge: What Latino parents need to know and why they don't know it.* Claremont, CA: Tomas Rivera Policy Institute. Retrieved from http://www.trpi.org/PDFs/College_Knowledge.pdf

Trent, W., Owens-Nicholson, D., Eatman, T. K., Burke, M., Daugherty, J., & Norman, K. (2003). Justice, equality of educational opportunity, and affirmative action in higher education. In M. J. Chang, D. Witt, J. Jones, & K. Hakuta (Eds.), *Compelling interest: Examining the evidence on racial dynamics in colleges and universities* (pp. 20–48). Palo Alto, CA: Stanford University Press.

U.S. Census Bureau. (2010). Texas quick facts from the U.S. Census Bureau [Data file]. Retrieved from http://quickfacts.census.gov/qtd/states/48000.html

U.S. Department of Justice & U.S. Department of Education. (2011). *Dear colleague letter. Retrieved from www.justice.gov/crt/about/edu/documents/plylerletter.pdf*

U.S. House Report. (1978). No. 1386, 95th Congress, 2nd Session. *Establishing standards for the placement of Indian children in foster or adoptive homes, to prevent the breakup of Indian families, July 24, 1978.* Washington, DC: United States Government Printing Office.

Vernez, G., & Mizell, L. (2001). *Goal: To double the rate of Hispanics earning a bachelor's degree.* Arlington, VA: RAND. Retrieved from http://www.rand.org/pubs/documented_briefings/DB350.html

Walpole, M. (2003, Fall). Socioeconomic status and college: How SES affects college experience and outcomes. *Review of Higher Education, 27*(1), 45–73.

Zoppi, I. M. (2006). *Latino parental involvement in students' school attendance and achievement.* Region II District of Prince George's County Public Schools Research Report. Maryland Institute of Minority Achievement and Urban Education (MIMAUE), College of Education, University of Maryland, College Park. Retrieved from http://www.education.umd.edu/mimaue/documents/publications/latparinvstd.pdf

CHAPTER NINE

Importance of Exceptional Leadership

One School Leader's Insight on Effective Leadership in a High Poverty School System

Wendell Waukau

> *While western approaches [to leadership] are almost always individual in form, American Indian models are more concerned with how different forms of leadership in different circumstances can serve the community rather than enhance the reward and reputation of their individual embodiment.* (Warner & Grint, 2006, p. 225)

In writing this book, we recognized the importance of infusing not only our experiences as educators and researchers but also the stories of others who have worked and are working in schools and communities confronting high poverty and the associated challenges poverty presents. As demonstrated in this chapter, exceptional educational leadership has the potential to transform these challenges into opportunities not only for students, but also for their families and communities at large. This chapter also demonstrates that exceptional educational leadership rests in the hands not only of the principal but also of district-level leadership who are able and willing to champion the rights of traditionally disenfranchised children and youth. This is the story of Menominee Indian School District and its path toward improving the educational conditions and subsequent academic achievement of a district primarily attended by American Indian students.

Menominee Indian School District

Menominee Indian School District (MISD) was established by the state of Wisconsin in 1976. MISD is unique in that it is one of only two public school districts in Wisconsin to be located almost entirely on American Indian[1] lands.

MISD operates under state laws, guidelines, and standards, which apply to all Wisconsin public school systems. The district serves approximately 850 students, of which 99% are Native American; 81% of the students qualify for free and reduced price meals.[2] MISD currently operates four schools: Keshena Primary School, Menominee Indian Middle School, Menominee Indian High School, and Menominee Indian Adult Learning Center. As a rural school district and one considered to be at risk because of the high level of families and children living in poverty, we do face challenges. However, we do not believe in using those challenges as an excuse for our children not learning. Our priority is to provide our students with the best educational experience available and help them gain the knowledge and skills to succeed in school and life.

Sketch of the Community-Nation

In Menominee County, which is coterminous with the Menominee Indian Reservation, almost 90% of the residents are members of the Menominee tribe. The Menominee Indians are the oldest continuous residents of Wisconsin. We have resided on this land for more than 10,000 years, and our creation stories tell us that we have always been here. The name *Menominee* or O-MAEQ-NO-MIN-NI-WUK means "Wild Rice People," for it has been said that when the Menominee entered an area, the wild rice followed. Our Nation is one of the most beautiful areas of Wisconsin, where there is an abundance of pristine forestland, sparkling waterways, and a variety of wildlife. Our Nation is rich in native culture, tradition, and history, which are integrated into our ceremonies, our beliefs, and our celebrations of success (Menominee Indian Tribe of Wisconsin, 2004).

The educational system on the Reservation includes a tribal day care; Head Start program; MISD, a public school system serving pre-kindergarten through 12th grade; a K–8 tribal school; and a tribal college, the College of Menominee Nation. Menominee County has a very small tax base and faces a number of challenges, including an at-risk school population and a high poverty rate. According to the 2011 County Health Rankings report (University of Wisconsin, Population Health Institute, 2011), Menominee County is currently ranked last out of 72 counties in health outcomes and health behaviors. This has gone unchanged since 2004.

These rankings do not fully reflect the continuous improvement efforts made by our community over the years, but they remain at the forefront. According to Freudenberg and Ruglis (2007), a good education predicts good health, and disparities in health and in educational achievement are closely linked. Improvement efforts have been initiated with the community to confront these rankings, in an attempt to better identify what works and what does not, as we have started the journey to get back to where we were once, a healthy Nation.

Challenges

During the 2003–2004 school year, Menominee Indian High School was notified by the state that it was a "School Identified for Improvement" (SIFI) due to low test participation on the 10th grade Wisconsin Knowledge & Concepts Examination (WKCE). In response, we began to take a very thorough look at the needs of the school district. This also had an unintended consequence—to fight back against the higher standards set forth by the state and federal government. The school board, administration, and teachers were very disappointed with the SIFI identification under the state and federal standards, but the message was clear—test scores needed to improve. The best way to deal with the problem was to find a collaborative approach, involving both the school and the community, to erase the negative perception of a "failing school."

The first step in this approach was to examine our data. An examination of our WKCE test results showed a clear indication that our high school was below many state averages. Reading, language arts, and math scores fell below the state average by 34%, 46%, and 43%, respectively. Truancy rates were at 60% and suspension rates were at 25%, along with the low participation on the 10th grade exam. This told us there was a much more serious problem that needed to be explored: our children, families, and even our community members were disengaged from our school system. The impact of this community disengagement had even bigger implications for our Menominee Community: a less educated workforce, higher crime rates, higher costs of social services for the families of these children, and the threat of losing our state and federal funding. Basically, we were treating our families and the community as clients, not as partners, in our school and community improvement efforts. Our data indicated that we were using a one-way communication system with our stakeholders that involved our community but failed to engage them. These sobering consequences forced MISD to look at the bigger picture in which we realized the solution was multifaceted and that it was going to take time and money. MISD was very fortunate in that it received financial and technical assistance from the Wisconsin Department of Public Instruction through Title I Supplemental Grants and a Statewide System of Support (SSOS). The SSOS process allowed our district to improve the effectiveness of our existing school improvement efforts, but more important and in addition, allowed us to develop and implement new opportunities for our neediest schools.

Opportunity: An Unintended Consequence, the Stirring of a Desire to Fight Back

In their book, *Strategies to Help Solve Our School Dropout Problem*, Schargel and Smink (2001, p. 193) state that schools do not exist in a vacuum; they never did and never will. That was the case at MISD as the problems in our schools were a reflection of the problems we faced in our community. And, we realized, these problems could not be solved by the schools alone. Realizing this was the case for MISD, we decided to revise our school reform efforts and look for a systemic model that could address the challenges in the school as well as the community.

After months of exploring various comprehensive school reform models, we decided that Ruby Payne's model of comprehensive school reform best fit our school and community needs. The two models, *A Framework for Understanding Poverty* (Payne, 2005) and *Bridges Out of Poverty* (Payne, DeVol, & Smith, 2001), were the foundations of our reform efforts. These two models were chosen because they met the following requirements:

1. They were researched and evidenced based.
2. These models had been implemented effectively for a number of years in high poverty schools and communities similar to MISD.
3. These models were able to demonstrate under what conditions they worked most effectively.
4. There were data to demonstrate their effectiveness in improving student achievement and community engagement.
5. We knew how long each model would take to implement and we knew the costs associated with training our staff and community to use these models.
6. We could adapt these models to the unique resources and needs of our Menominee culture.

These six requirements were developed in partnership with Dr. William Swan, a retired professor from the University of Georgia who has worked as a consultant with MISD since 2005. These requirements are used whenever we consider any new model or innovation in our district or in individual schools within the district. Dr. Swan was also instrumental in helping our district conduct a needs assessment, which identified three prioritized needs: site-based leadership teams, positive behavior interventions, and data-driven decision making.

Community Engagement

Robert Balfanz, a leading research scientist from Johns Hopkins University, and associates, stress the importance of knowing the extent of the dropout crisis in one's own community (e.g., Mac Iver, Balfanz, & Byrnes, 2009). The data from our state school performance reports and the county health rankings showed a direct relationship—we were both failing, and the future of our schools and Nation was at stake. Our dropout crisis was, in essence, a public health crisis, thus making the case that our schools and community needed to take action and confront the hard facts. Successfully addressing these crises required a paradigm shift from *doing to* our families and community to *doing with* our families and community. The paradigm shift was couched in a process called *community engagement*. The

Centers for Disease Control and Prevention (CDC) defines it as a process of working collaboratively with groups of people who are affiliated by geographic proximity, special interests, or similar situations with issues affecting their wellbeing (Minnesota Department of Health, 2011). A respected Menominee elder in our community defined it more clearly as "connecting the dots."

Home Visits
The impetus behind this initiative is to build positive relationships with our families for the benefit of our students and their learning. We have found that if we can build a positive relationship with our families, the trust barrier comes down and families feel empowered to engage in the future story of their children. All staff at MISD, including student services, teachers, support staff, and administrators, conduct home visits throughout the school year. Staff is compensated for their time if the visits are conducted outside the school day. Home visits take place year-round, but in the past few years we have placed more emphasis on key transitional times and grades, such as when students enter middle school or high school or if they had academic, attendance, or behavior issues the previous year.

Transitions at Critical Grade Levels
Research (e.g., Hertzog & Morgan, 1998; National Middle School Association, 2003; Reyes, Gillock, Kobus, & Sanchez, 2000) cites the importance of transition services for students moving from middle school into high school. When we developed our 9th Grade Freshman Academy in 2007–2008, the goal was to focus on what we thought was the most critical year for our students in their graduation path. Now that we have improved the passing rate for 9th graders we have expanded our transition initiatives from elementary to middle school and our Head Start to elementary school, including a new kindergarten program for four-year-olds. The bulk of the research describes the graduation and dropout crisis as being more of a process than an event (e.g., Alexander, Entwisle, & Kabbani, 2001; Fine, 1991). In our eyes, transition is the same way. If our students have successful transitions to and from these grade levels then we believe they are more likely to stay in school and not drop out.

Our transition activities and planning efforts are comprehensive in that they take place throughout the school year and summer. Throughout these activities, principals and their staff involve our students, families, and community in providing the targeted interventions our students need to be engaged in school.

One successful initiative includes a win-win situation in which we use upperclassmen to mentor our incoming freshmen students throughout the year. The freshmen benefit because they have a peer who they can talk to about their grades, attendance, and behavior. The upperclassmen benefit because it develops their leadership skills.

Another successful initiative involves visiting the homes of all incoming 6th and 9th grade students to promote the school, learn about the hopes and dreams that families have for their children, and showcase opportunities we have to help them achieve these dreams. Families report this is a positive intervention as their children are not in trouble and the school is reaching out to them.

Early Warning Systems

In keeping the focus on the process versus the event, we relied again on the work of Robert Balfanz and his colleagues Liza Herzog and Douglas Mac Iver (2007). According to these researchers, students start sending disengagement signals in middle school, as early as 6th grade. In response, we provide attention and intervention to students who are

- failing mathematics,
- failing English,
- attending school less than 80% for the year, and/or
- receiving an out-of-school suspension.

At Menominee Indian Middle School (MIMS), students are identified in grades 6 through 8 based on these indicators. Once identified, we establish targeted interventions that we monitor throughout the year through our Reach and Teach initiative, a grant funded by the Office of Justice Assistance. These targeted interventions include tutoring during the day, offering homework club, using teachers as academic coaches, conducting home visits, and doing whatever else it takes to get students back on track. In the first year of implementation, significant progress was made with 57 of the targeted students in grades 6 through 8. For example, data showed that 30 out of 36 students passed their math classes and 27 out of 36 students passed their English classes. While significant progress was made in these two areas for most of the targeted students, the intervention plans for those who did not succeed have been reviewed and revised for the upcoming year.

Leadership at the District Level

In our school district, leadership is evidenced on multiple levels, including the school board. According to the National School Boards Association (2006), school boards are charged with the responsibility of educating all children to their full potential. The MISD School Board understands that educating children to their full potential through community engagement is more important than ever. Through its policy making and budgeting, the board has created the conditions under which effective student performance and teaching can take place. The board recognizes the need (even during times of fiscal restraints) to provide professional development for teachers, administrators, and other staff. Many of our students come from at-risk backgrounds so the board makes it a priority for our staff and schools to receive the resources they need to meet the needs of our students as well as their families.

Leadership at the School Level
Where teacher leadership at our schools once consisted of class advisors, textbook adoption committee members, and union representatives, it has now transformed into grade-level teams, content leaders, leadership teams, positive behavior management teams, graduation coaches, monitoring teams, and more. As a result, principals no longer are leading by themselves; now they are leading with their faculty and staff in identifying and responding to academic and behavioral issues critical to the continuous improvement of our schools in the areas of curriculum, assessment, technology, data analysis, and community engagement. We have excellent teachers and principals who can blend high expectations (for students as well as themselves) with healthy, affirming relationships. This positively impacts our students' attitudes about school and has increased the likelihood that our students will graduate from high school. Relationships are at the core of everything we do at MISD, and it has helped us build trust with our students and families. As Dr. James Comer (1995, as cited in Payne, 2008, p. 48) argues, "No significant learning occurs without a significant relationship."

Culture, Language, and History
The Menominee were one of two tribes terminated[3] by the federal government and forced to join the mainstream of American society through assimilation. This dreadful historic event took place on June 17, 1954, under the Eisenhower administration. Although the Menominee were later restored on December 22, 1973, under the Nixon administration, the devastating economic and social effects (e.g., poverty, unemployment, diabetes, alcoholism) of termination still exist today as is reflected in the Wisconsin County Health Rankings. In spite of these challenges, there was something that did survive, and could not be taken from us—and that was our language, history, and culture.

The Menominee people are committed to keeping these traditions alive and have found the perfect opportunity in our school system. All elementary and middle school students are required to learn our Menominee language. In high school Menominee language is an elective, but all students are required to take Menominee history. In addition, language, culture, and history are integrated into all our classrooms, events, and celebrations, which provide our students with relevant and meaningful learning experiences. You won't find this cultural integration on a day-to-day basis in many public schools across the country; we are proud that we can offer this to our students here at MISD. It is important that our students have the opportunity to experience and learn their history, culture, and traditions so they can someday pass those on to their children.

Results

As a result of these efforts, MISD has achieved the following:

- Meeting Adequate Yearly Progress for five consecutive years (2006–2011) in all MISD schools: Menominee Indian High School, Menominee Middle School, and Keshena Primary School.
- Significantly decreasing the dropout rate. In 2009–2010, MISD had a dropout rate of 1.19%, compared to the state average of 1.60%. In 2005–2006, MISD had a dropout rate of 6.96%.
- Three-time award winner (2009, 2010, and 2011) Exemplary Middle School, by the Association of Wisconsin School Administrators (AWSA).
- Menominee Indian Middle School received the 2010 Breakthrough School Award from MetLife Foundation–National Association of Secondary Schools (NASSP). This award is part of NASSP's Breakthrough School Project,[4] which identifies, recognizes, and showcases middle schools and high schools that serve large numbers of students living in poverty and are demonstrating high achievement or dramatically improving student achievement.
- Keshena Primary School received the 2011 Wisconsin School Health Award. This award is given to schools in recognition of their efforts to develop programs, policies, and resources that support students' academic achievement and long-term physical health. "These schools include parents and the community in efforts to improve the long-term health of all students, and they demonstrate leadership in developing and maintaining quality school health programs" (Wisconsin Department of Public Instruction, 2011).

Lessons Learned

- Positive relationships with students and families come first. When they trust us, learning becomes relational.
- Schools are for kids. The superintendent, principals, assistant principals, faculty, and staff must differentiate and adapt teaching and learning in all areas to meet the learning styles and needs of students.
- "No Kid Walks." We don't give up on kids; all students have the right to learn and grow from their mistakes.
- The dropout problem isn't just a school problem. Schools must collaborate with families, agencies, and the community to provide effective education for all students. This is called *community engagement*.
- The problem needs to be addressed at the lowest possible level—high school is too late. We start intervening as early as pre-K and kindergarten.
- The focus is on key transition points: grades 3, 6, and 9.

- Continuous improvement is what moves our schools and community ahead. We assess, set goals and objectives, develop action plans, monitor, assess again, evaluate, continue, and refine improvements, and we know when to quit doing something because it is not working.
- Culture needs to be embedded in everything we do in our schools. When we were terminated as a tribe in 1954 and later restored in 1976, it was our culture that enabled us to survive and once again begin a new journey to economic progress through self-sufficiency.

Recognition of Exceptional Leadership

In 2012, the White House identified Menominee Indian School District Superintendent Wendell Waukau as a "Champion of Change," one of twelve "school turnaround leaders" across the nation. He was honored for his work in "building expectations, improving instruction, creating safe environments, for learning, and fostering professional collaboration." According to the district's website (*www.misd.k12.wi.us/*),

> Seven plus years ago, MISD embarked on a school improvement plan that involved teachers, students, staff, administrators, parents, government and community agencies, as well as the public. While academics are a focus, the effort extends beyond that to include healthy eating, physical activity, positive behavioral interventions, Menominee language culture and on site health care services. The result is that there have been dramatic gains in graduation rates, student learning and test scores, student attendance and retention, and vastly improved student behavior.
>
> Upon receiving this award, Mr. Waukau commented,
> It is an honor to be recognized. It's an honor, I gladly share with everyone in our district. . . . In order to be successful in turning things around, you have to design your plans to fit your own community. We have certainly done that and the results in areas like higher graduation rates, better student retention and higher test scores show our plan is working. We're not done yet, but it's great to have educational leaders recognize our efforts. (White House Office of Communications, 2012)

School Board president David "Jonesy" Miller also remarked, "It's also an honor that should be shared by everyone in our community. This kind of change doesn't happen without a lot of hard work on everyone's part." This point is summed up by the principal of Menominee Indian Middle School, who writes, "Change like ours doesn't happen overnight. We went through some rough times along the way, but one thing never wavered: our belief in the kids. If you keep that as your goal, there's nothing you can't accomplish" (Menominee Indian Middle School, 2010).

Concluding Thoughts

In this chapter, the author illustrates the potential for widespread change to occur if school leaders are committed to initiating this change. This commitment is sparked in large part by the belief that one's socioeconomic status alone need not be an indicator or determinant of one's lifelong potential for learning, achieving, and living healthy and productive lives both within and outside of school. While some might argue that the use of Payne's *A Framework for Understanding Poverty* lends itself to a deficit approach to serving students from high poverty backgrounds, what MISD has demonstrated is that different approaches are required dependent upon the context in which these approaches are implemented. In this case, the author's deep understanding of and involvement in the Menominee Indian community enables him to assist this school district in implementing educational strategies in a culturally relevant and effective manner that acknowledges the needs of the school and its students, while simultaneously affirming their strengths and potential for success. The important takeaway is that school leaders must initiate change, but they alone cannot effect real and lasting change. They need the support and buy-in of their schools and communities.

Questions to Consider

1. As this chapter demonstrates, superintendents and other district-level personnel play essential roles in schools. Reflecting on your district, consider how district-level leadership might be leveraged to effect positive change at the school level for schools serving students from high poverty contexts.

2. To what extent does linguistic and/or cultural diversity play a role in the day-to-day life of your school? Of your district? (i.e., How diverse is your school? Your district?) How is this diversity reflected in the mission, vision, and related goals of your school?

3. What does success mean for the students in your school?

4. To what extent is your school or district successful in achieving high academic outcomes among students from socioeconomically, linguistically, and/or culturally diverse groups? What factors contribute to this success? What might you do to foster increased success?

Notes

1. The terms *American Indian* and *Alaska Native* are used interchangeably in this chapter to refer to the Indigenous peoples of what is now known as the United States.
2. High poverty schools are considered those in which 75% or more of the student enrollment qualify for free or reduced price lunch (see http://nces.ed.gov/programs/coe/supnotes/2012-n01.asp for additional information regarding the number of students qualifying for this service nationally). Using this definition, it can be deduced that the majority of students in MISD qualify for free or reduced price lunch.
3. Under the termination policy of the 1950s, the federal government determined that it no longer recognized the sovereign status of a tribal nation. The Menominee Nation was not formally recognized again until the 1970s. For additional information, see Herzberg (1978).

4. For additional information, including an interview with the principal of Menominee Indian Middle School, see http://www.principals.org/tabid/3899/default.aspx#menom.

References

Alexander, K. L., Entwisle, D. R., & Kabbani, N. S. (2001). The dropout process in life course perspective: Early risk factors at home and school. *Teachers College Record, 103*(5), 760–822.

Balfanz, R., Herzog, L., & Mac Iver, D. (2007). Preventing student disengagement and keeping students on the graduation track in high-poverty middle-grades schools: Early identification and effective interventions. *Educational Psychologist, 42*(4), 223–236.

Fine, M. (1991). *Framing dropouts: Notes on the politics of an urban high school.* Albany: State University of New York Press.

Freudenberg, N., & Ruglis, J. (2007). Reframing school dropout as a public health issue. *Preventing Chronic Disease, 4*(4). Retrieved from http://www.cdc.gov/pcd/issues/2007/oct/07_0063.htm

Hertzog, C. J., & Morgan, P. L. (1998). Breaking the barriers between middle school and high school: Developing a transition team for student success. *NASSP Bulletin, 82*(597), 94–98.

Herzberg, S. J. (1978). The Menominee Indians: Termination to restoration. *American Indian Law Review, 6*(1), 143–186. Retrieved from http://www.jstor.org/stable/20068052

Mac Iver, M. A., Balfanz, R., & Byrnes, V. (2009, October). Advancing the "Colorado graduates" agenda: Understanding the dropout problem and mobilizing to meet the graduation challenge. The Center for Social Organization of Schools, Johns Hopkins University. Retrieved from http://acyi.org/sites/default/files/Colorado%20Graduates%20Initiative%20%28Center%20for%20Social%20Organization%20of%20Schools,%20Johns%20Hopkins%20University%29.pdf

Menominee Indian Middle School. (2010, May). *A community school with voice and heart.* Retrieved from http://www.principals.org/Content/158/PLMay10_menominee.pdf

Menominee Indian Tribe of Wisconsin. (2004). *Facts and figures reference book.* Retrieved from http://www.menominee-nsn.gov/mitw/pdf/facts%20figures%20with%20supplement.pdf

Minnesota Department of Health. (2011). Overview: What is community engagement? Retrieved from www.health.state.mn.us/communityeng/intro

National Middle School Association. (2003). *This we believe: Successful schools for young adolescents.* Westerville, OH: Author.

National School Boards Association. (2006). *Becoming a better board member.* Alexandria, VA: Author.

Payne, R. (2008, April). Nine powerful practices. *Educational Leadership, 65*(7), 48–52. Retrieved from http://www.ascd.org/publications/educational-leadership/apr08/vol65/num07/Nine-Powerful-Practices.aspx

Payne, R. K. (2005). *A framework for understanding poverty.* Highlands, TX: aha! Process.

Payne, R. K., DeVol, P. F., & Smith, T. D. (2001). *Bridges out of poverty: Strategies for professionals and communities.* Highlands, TX: aha! Process.

Reyes, O., Gillock, K. L., Kobus, K., & Sanchez, B. (2000). A longitudinal examination of the transition into senior high school for adolescents from urban, low-income status, and predominantly minority backgrounds. *American Journal of Community Psychology, 28*(4), 519–544.

Schargel, F., & Smink, J. (2001). *Strategies to help solve our school dropout problem.* Larchmont, NY: Eye on Education.

University of Wisconsin, Population Health Institute. (2011). County health rankings. Mobilizing action toward community health. Retrieved from http://www.countyhealthrankings.org/wisconsin/downloads-and-links

Warner, L. S., & Grint, K. (2006). American Indian ways of leading and knowing. *Leadership, 2*, 225–244.

White House Office of Communications. (2012, August 20). White House to honor local school turnaround leader Wendell Waukau as "Champion of Change." Retrieved from http://www.misd.k12.wi.us/pages/Menominee_Indian

Wisconsin Department of Public Instruction. (2011). 2011 Wisconsin school health awards announced. Retrieved from eis.dpi.wi.gov/files/eis/pdf/dpinr2011_51.pdf

CHAPTER TEN

Bridging High Poverty Schools and Communities—Implications and Conclusions

Where Do We Go from Here?

Susan C. Faircloth

> *Like a bridge across a powerful river, successful approaches to change enable people to make the journey from one place of action to another.* (Wilson, 2010, p. 21)

As we bring this book to a close, we would like to reflect on what we believe are the common characteristics of exceptional educational leaders in high poverty schools. These characteristics include:

1. willingness to embrace change,
2. ability to coalesce support for change,
3. ability and willingness to delegate power and control to a wide range of individuals including teachers, students, parents, and community members,
4. willingness to take risks (e.g., Carter, 2002, as cited in Mulford et al., 2008)
5. willingness to assume responsibility for difficult decisions and the consequences of these decisions,
6. understanding and appreciating the culture and context of the school and community with which he or she is working,
7. willingness to engage external partners in providing necessary supports and services to students, families, and teachers,

8. leading from the ethics of justice, care, critique, community, and the best interest(s) of students, both collectively and individually (e.g., Shapiro & Stefkovich, 2011; Stefkovich, 2006), and

9. belief in the ability of all children/students to learn and achieve (e.g., Bishop, 2006, as cited in Mulford et al., 2008;[1] Harris & Chapman, 2002, 2004, as cited in Mulford et al., 2008).

These characteristics reflect leaders who are not afraid of or averse to change. They are rooted and grounded in the belief that leadership is a calling not simply a job. They are truly exceptional.

We believe that all schools, not only those in high poverty contexts, need and deserve exceptional leaders who are effective in leading, managing and sustaining change in the face of challenging conditions. Studies have consistently cited effective leadership as the key element in the success of high poverty schools (e.g., Bishop, 1999, as cited in Mulford et al., 2008; Fullan, 2001; Mortimore, 1993, as cited in Mulford, Silins, & Leithwood, 2004; Thomson & Harris, 2004, as cited in Mulford et al., 2008; Townsend, 2007, as cited in Mulford et al., 2004).

Although the leader is critical to the success or failure of a school, the practices that the leader engages in and embraces are equally important. For example, research identifies a number of policies, programs, and services that have been successful in ensuring equity in educating students from high poverty contexts. One such initiative involves the provision of extended learning opportunities and summer school programs. A 2005 publication by the Council of Chief State School Officers presents examples of five successful high poverty schools that utilize such programs. These schools include Charles R. Drew Elementary School operated by the Gary Community School Corporation, Gary, Indiana; East Silver Spring Elementary School, operated by Montgomery County Public Schools, Silver Spring, Maryland; John B. McFerran Preparatory Academy operated by Jefferson County Public Schools, Louisville, Kentucky; Tarrallton Elementary School operated by Norfolk Public Schools, Norfolk, Virginia; and Weil Technology Institute operated by Pittsburgh Public Schools, Pittsburgh, Pennsylvania. Among these schools, seven common (best) practices were evidenced:

1. Leadership experienced at all levels—from parents to teachers to school and district-level leaders.

2. Emphasis on teaching and learning.

3. Equitable, adequate, and consistent funding provided, with fee waivers available for students unable to pay for services.

4. Integration of data collection and analysis as a key element in evaluating the effectiveness of programs and services.

5. Professional development sessions targeted toward the needs of the teachers and the goals of the program. Teachers are compensated for attending professional development sessions.
6. Active involvement of community groups, parents, and families encouraged. Student input sought. Incentives provided to students who maintain perfect attendance during the program.
7. Summer program designed as an extension of the district's overall plan for improvement (Council of Chief State School Officers, 2005).

What these practices demonstrate is the existence of shared leadership, emphasis on equity, use of data, meaningful professional development, engagement of community partners, and extended learning tailored to meet student needs.

Lyman and Villani (2004) also speak to the importance of effective leadership in turning around high poverty schools. Each of the schools in their study recognized the need to build the capacity of the school to effect change. To achieve this goal, members of the research team recommended "train[ing] and recruit[ing] leaders to guide school improvement efforts." They pointed out that this process requires the appointment of "leaders with a definite vision for school improvement who are not paralyzed by obstacles facing high-poverty schools and who are willing to make changes that respect a school's unique context" (p. 7). In addition to the school leader, the research team also emphasized the need to build the capacity of teachers and students, thus acknowledging the importance of distributed leadership and the collaborative nature of improving schools to ensure long and lasting change.

Recommendations for Future Research

As professors of educational leadership, we would be remiss if we did not acknowledge the need for ongoing research into the relationship between effective high poverty schools and school leaders. As noted by Thomson and Harris (2004, as cited in Mulford et al., 2008), there is an urgent need for new research that addresses the following questions:

1. How do the day-to-day pressures and responsibilities of the principalship impact school leaders?
2. What does the instructional leadership role of school leaders look like?
3. Other than the principal, who plays a key role(s) in the leadership of high poverty schools?
4. How do principals lead in the face of severe criticism and lack of support?

In addition, Keys and colleagues (2003, as cited in Mulford et al., 2008) and Bishop (2004, as cited in Mulford et al., 2008) call for studies that examine the ways in which varying school contexts help to shape one's leadership practices. Given the wide array of diversity reflected in schools and students in high poverty contexts, we also recommend that the number of schools and school leaders in future studies be expanded to better reflect this diversity.

Although we have cited several examples of areas in need of further research, we concur with Machtinger (2007), who raises an important question regarding the power of research to influence public policy. Machtinger asks, "How does research enter public consciousness and gain influence in a tumultuous political environment?" (p. 7). This question is central to our work as educational leadership faculty. In this role, we are charged with preparing the next generation of school leaders. Although we acknowledge the importance and place of both qualitative and quantitative research methodologies, we are concerned about the ability of the results of these studies to be translated into practice at the school and district levels. As Kaestle (1993) points out, educational research has historically been difficult to translate into practice due to a number of roadblocks including philosophical disagreements regarding the utility of research to the field and the politicalization of education and education research. In spite of these challenges, Kaestle reminds us that we have an obligation to move beyond these obstacles and work more closely with school level educators to effect change. One of our aims in writing this book is to assist in making these important conversations around poverty and schooling more accessible to those who are ultimately responsible for making schools more effective for all students—school leaders and other educators. One way to do this is to demonstrate to school leaders the ways in which research can be translated into practice at the school level. For example, practitioners and academics can engage in action inquiry projects aimed at promoting improved communication and relationships between parents, families, communities, and schools. Doctoral students and other emerging researchers should also be encouraged to conduct research that addresses the most pressing issues for today's schools. This research should be designed and conducted in collaboration with schools and communities. To conduct such research well requires researchers to work collaboratively with schools and communities to identify research problems, construct research methodologies, and analyze and disseminate the results of this research in such a way that the nonacademic audience is able to utilize the research findings. Otherwise, research will continue to be conducted for academic purposes rather than the larger purpose of fostering a more socially just and equitable educational system (Furman & Shields, 2005).

Implications for Practice

If school leaders are to be successful in promoting change within their schools, they must be willing to take risks and to valiantly champion the students, families, and communities they serve. Building on the work of Freire (e.g., 1970, 1993,

2000), Miller, Brown, and Hopson (2011) argue that in order to effect change, leaders are called to move beyond the confines of the structural and physical world within which they traditionally work. This requires school leaders to talk with and get to know the people they serve in order to understand the conditions within which they live and the factors that help to create and sustain these conditions.

Reflecting back on the school-linked community services approach described in Chapter Six, school leaders are also reminded of the importance of thinking about schools in terms of what happens beyond the school doors. Unfortunately,

> despite the pervasive influences of poverty, racism, and other such debilitating factors, educational leadership discussions have largely remained limited to that which occurs within school walls. Such bounded conceptualizations are evident in the ways that theories of educational leadership have been engaged in recent years, as witnessed in common descriptions of transformational, participative, collaborative, distributed, and servant leadership which have primarily focused on place-attached and/or principal leadership. (Spillane, 2006, as cited in Miller et al. 2011, p. 1081)

Harris (2007) reminds us that "accountability and other solutions will be undermined if they do not recognize that schools are not the only or main cause" (p. 370) of poor student achievement and outcomes. Again, this underscores the importance of partnering with communities and community agencies to effect change.

Finally, Jacobson (2011) encourages us to consider what happens when a successful school leader leaves a school. Are policies, procedures, and, equally important, institutional commitment sufficient such that the positive changes encouraged by the departing school leader are able to sustain themselves? In other words, is change leader specific or can the school and community sustain promising practices even in the face of leader turnover? Does being successful in one school guarantee that the leader will be successful in another school? In effect, is successful leadership context dependent?

Legal and Political Implications of Failing to Effectively Lead High Poverty Schools

As previously discussed, schools have a moral and ethical responsibility to act in the best interest (Stefkovich, 2006) of all students, including those from economically disadvantaged backgrounds. Beyond that, they have a legal and political responsibility to ensure equity and equality of programs, services, and opportunities for these students. As Scutari (2009) writes, "Educational equality is indeed a crucial prerequisite for an oppressed group's ability to compete for equal access to the institutional and economic power controlled by the dominant group" (p. 930). Unfortunately, not all schools are created equal; thus some schools can be changed only by force of law or threat of legal action. Our hope in writing this book is that we as school leaders, educators, parents, and community members will be encouraged to do the right thing—work together to envision and plan for the future of our children's education—even when it is not the easy thing to do, because it is in the best interest of our students. Once legal action is taken, it is difficult to repair relationships, both within and outside of the school, that have been damaged as a result of this action. In the end, our children and communities continue to suffer while we wait to litigate or legislate change.

Recent data (e.g., Aud et al., 2010) indicate we cannot afford to continue to wait to address the needs of high poverty schools. For example, during the 2007–2008 academic year,

1. 17% (more than 16,000 schools) of public schools were identified as high poverty schools (i.e., at least 75% of the students received free or reduced price lunch);
2. a disproportionate number of the secondary schools identified as high poverty also served students in need of alternative educational services and special education;
3. higher numbers of elementary students (20%) attended high poverty schools than did secondary students (6%);
4. minority students (Black, Hispanic, American Indian/Alaska Native) attended high poverty schools at higher rates than did their white or Asian/Pacific Islander counterparts;
5. high poverty schools also served a larger number of English Language Learners;
6. 21% of all principals were assigned to high poverty schools;
7. there were marked differences in educational credentials (lower levels of education) between secondary principals in high poverty schools and their counterparts in low poverty schools;
8. 21% of elementary teachers worked in high poverty schools;
9. teachers in high poverty schools tended to have lower levels of education than did their counterparts in low poverty schools;
10. students in high poverty schools tended to score lower on the National Assessment of Education Progress (NAEP) in reading and math, as well as music and visual arts;
11. students in high poverty schools tended to have lower rates of graduation (68% vs. 91%) and college attendance (28% vs. 52%) than their peers in wealthier schools; and

12. students in high poverty schools were more likely than their peers to experience violence on campus.

As these figures demonstrate, the effects of poverty are felt in schools across the nation.

Implications for Policy

Although we have emphasized the role of the principal in creating effective schools in high poverty contexts, real change also requires the support and work of teachers. Research tells us that teachers are critically important to student success (e.g., McCaffrey, Lockwood, Koretz, & Hamilton, 2003, as cited in Hightower et al., 2011; Rivkin, Hanushek, & Kain, 2000, as cited in Hightower et al., 2011; Rowan, Correnti, & Miller, 2002, as cited in Hightower et al., 2011; Wright, Horn, & Sanders, 1997, as cited in Hightower et al., 2011). However, in high poverty schools the ability to recruit and retain highly qualified teachers is often constrained by the challenges these teachers face once they enter these schools (e.g., Peske & Haycock, 2006; Smith & Ingersoll, 2004). This is evidenced by a disproportionate percentage (40%) of all teacher turnover occurring in high poverty schools than would be expected given the percentage of all schools, approximately 25%, classified as high poverty (e.g., Ingersoll & Merrill, 2010).

At the federal, state, and local levels, it is important to develop and implement policies that incentivize working in these schools and that help to support teachers who choose to remain in these schools. An essential element of these policies is the recruitment and retention of highly qualified and committed principals. This is important given the link between principals and teacher turnover. Research indicates that principals make a difference in the hiring of quality teachers (e.g., Baker & Cooper, 2005). A legal analysis of high poverty schools in North Carolina also found that "one of the mechanisms by which highly rated principals with longer tenure in their schools improve students' achievement is through their ability to reduce teacher turnover and to staff their schools with more qualified teachers" (Clotfelter, Ladd, Vigdor, & Wheeler, 2006, p. 1376).

Implications for Educational Administration/Leadership Faculty

The ways in which we approach the teaching of school leadership is shaped in large part by our own experiences as individuals, community members, educators, and leaders. We evidenced this fact most clearly as we began to write this book. Although we recognized that a number of scholars have written on the characteristics of high poverty schools (e.g., Blank, 2005; Brooks-Gunn, Duncan, & Aber, 1997; Carlson, 2006; U.S. Department of Education, National Center for Education Statistics, 2011), as well as techniques and strategies for leading effectively in these schools (e.g., Finnigan, 2012; Giles, Johnson, Brooks, & Jacobson, 2007; Jacobson, 2008; Picucci, Brownson, Kahlert, & Sobel, 2002), we felt strongly that many school leaders continued to miss the mark in terms of reshaping their leadership craft to be responsive to the unique contexts of their schools. We also reflected on the ways in which we as educational leadership faculty approached the teaching of aspiring leaders. While Lisa considered the implications of the origins of poverty, re-visioning the traditional roles of educational leaders specific to high poverty contexts and the importance of developing a specialized professional development plan to accomplish set objectives, Susan focused on issues of diversity, students with disabilities, and the moral and ethical implications of school leadership. Individually, we felt that our approaches to leadership development were somewhat deficient, but collectively they began to touch on the multilayered entity that is school—an entity located within the community, built for the community, yet isolated in many ways from the community. We believed strongly that there was something unique or exceptional about those leaders who were able to transcend the boundary between school and community on their journey to transform schools into sites of possibility, promise, and hope rather than vehicles through which cycles of poverty and despair were re-created and reinforced.

Through the process of conceptualizing and writing this book, our belief in the following has been strengthened: *When working with aspiring school leaders, it is important to link theory to practice, incorporate practical life experiences into the classroom, and engage in assignments that are problem-based.* In some cases, this requires taking the learning process beyond the bounded walls of the traditional classroom. One way to introduce aspiring school leaders to the concept of exceptional leadership and high poverty schools is to facilitate ongoing discussions around issues of practice encountered in these schools. To help facilitate these discussions, a number of case studies from the *Journal of Cases in Educational Leadership* are cited below. As a word of caution, while these cases should be used as a launchpad for discussions and as tools for applying the theoretical and philosophical constructs discussed in class, these cases are best utilized as supplemental tools rather than taking the place of real-life experiences with and in high poverty schools and communities.

Journal of Cases in Educational Leadership

Each of these cases addresses issues related to leadership in high poverty schools. The questions and activities included in these selected cases are geared toward aspiring school leaders and others pursuing graduate degrees in educational administration and leadership. At the school and district level, these cases may be used to facilitate discussion around the ways in which leaders can best respond to issues and dilemmas involving the education of students from high poverty contexts. The goal is for practitioners to reflect upon their current beliefs and responses with an eye toward teaching and leading in a more responsive and appropriate manner. For additional guidance on how to use these cases in class, see Bass, Garn, and Monroe (2011).

Allen, L. A. (2005, March). Hard times in Harmony School District: A case study. *Journal of Cases in Educational Leadership, 8*(1), 1–5.

Cortez, M. T., Sorenson, R. D., & Coronado, D. (2012, March). A case study of a new high school principal: Instructional challenges and administrative interventions relating to immigrant students and teacher apathy on the U.S./Mexico border. *Journal of Cases in Educational Leadership, 15*(1), 7–24.

Ingle, W. K., & Rutledge, S. A. (2010, March). Selecting the "best applicant(s)" with limited options and policy constraints. *Journal of Cases in Educational Leadership, 13*(1), 37–47.

Jacobson, S. (2012, August). Principal leadership: Sustaining and deepening school improvement in low-income communities in North America. *Journal of Cases in Educational Leadership, 14*, 7–10.

Rodriguez, M. A. (2012, March). "But they just can't do it": Reconciling teacher expectations of Latino students. *Journal of Cases in Educational Leadership, 15*(1), 25–31.

Salmonowicz, M. J. (2007, June). Scott O'Neill and Lincoln Elementary School: Preventing a slide from good to worse. *Journal of Cases in Educational Leadership, 10*(2), 28–37.

Salmonowicz, M. J., & Levy, M. K. (2009, March). Turning around Maple Shade Middle School: A principal's initial reform efforts. *Journal of Cases in Educational Leadership, 12*(1), 26–37.

Schulte, D. P., & Hong, S. S. (2011, December). Portraits of leaders: Striving for a fuller humanity. *Journal of Cases in Educational Leadership, 14*(4), 31–46.

Next Steps: Taking Up the Challenge

Freire (1993, p. 39, as cited in Miller et al., 2011, p. 1086) challenges us to envision education as an institution "that transforms the space where children, rich or poor, are able to learn, to create, or to take risks, to question, and to grow." Freirian leadership is built upon the need for change, the pursuit of equity and justice. According to Kaak (2011), Freirean leadership educators will ask questions, and more questions, such as:

- Does the way I determine class content communicate that I trust and value my students' experience and expertise?
- Does the way I talk to my students illustrate that I respect them as co-learners and even as co-leaders in the classroom?

- Do my pedagogical methods lead students closer to confidently claiming their leadership identity and responsibility?
- Does my approach to teaching help students to see for themselves the problems and needs of society, as well as the strengths and potential in others? (p. 134)

This approach moves beyond simply teaching future school leaders about the philosophical, theoretical, and historical underpinnings of school leadership. This approach requires educational leadership faculty to encourage and require their students to engage in the messy and often uncomfortable act of problematizing their role, as educators, and the role of the educational system at large in helping to sustain and promote poverty. This is not to say that these acts of sustainment and promotion are intentional, for as a former student once said, "none of us goes into the business of education to do harm to our students." In contrast, this is a call to action to revisit, re-vision, and reframe our leadership practices in ways that help to move us all beyond simplistic discussions of why individuals, families, and communities live in poverty to how schools can play a real and lasting role in decreasing poverty and its effects and equipping students to do and become whatever they dare to dream. That is the moral and ethical thing to do. As Machtinger (2007) so aptly writes,

> Our challenge, in reality, is whether we seriously mean to bring all children, including those in high poverty schools, into a global community of learning and work or remain content to relegate high poverty students to the bottom of the global market place where their only comparative advantage lies in the low cost of their labor. (p. 7)

We believe that school leaders have a professional, moral, and ethical responsibility to do much more than this.

Summary

As we end this book, we acknowledge that we have not presented a one-size-fits-all model for transforming high poverty schools or communities nor for ending poverty. Poverty has and will continue to persist in places driven by market economies, global conflict, and institutional and societal notions of class-based societies. Nonetheless, we believe as Freire (2003, 2000, as cited in Kaak, 2011) did, that we, as educators and educational leaders, have a moral and ethical duty to lead in ways that mirror our beliefs regarding the power of education and schools as tools and sites of social, political, and ideological change. Leaders who embrace Freire's teachings will reflect upon the extent to which they demonstrate to their students that they "trust and value" what they bring to the learning process; engage in the process of co-construction and co-leadership; foster leadership among students; encourage students to problematize and problem solve issues around them; and acknowledge the "strengths and potential" of those around them (Kaak, 2011, p. 134). Freirian leadership educators will also make their students aware of the potentially oppressive nature of traditional leadership practices, acknowledge and value the knowledge they bring to the classroom, engage them in the process of problem posing and problem solving, and work to establish a healthy sense of and respect for authority. At the programmatic level, this type of approach requires restructuring the way in which our leadership preparation programs are designed and delivered so that they are "learner-driven," "life-embedded," and supportive of co-constructed learning processes (Kaak, 2011).

Kaak (2011) calls on us to

> help [our] students to see for themselves the problems their generation of leaders will be called on to solve. Use questions and practice being okay with having no set answers. Provide yourself with evidence that learning is powerful, even when solutions are not forthcoming from the teacher's lips. (p. 140)

Kaak (2011) also reminds us that "education is an act of love and courage. To avoid being a farce, it cannot fear the analysis of reality or avoid creative discussion" (p. 141). In sum, if real change is to occur in schools, simultaneous change must occur within colleges and universities that prepare educators and school leaders; this requires change among those who inhabit and work within these spaces. Aspiring school leaders look to their mentors and teachers to guide them as they embark upon their leadership journeys. If we simply teach them about leadership from the limited scope of formulaic texts, traditional theories and beliefs, and canned lectures, we will have failed our students, our students' students, their schools, and their communities. In sum, we are left to respond to a critically important question as posted by Everson and Bussey (2007, p. 179): "How can educational leadership programs prepare their students to lead schools or school districts effectively without directly addressing the moral obligation to educate every child, regardless of economic status?"

References

Aud, S., Hussar, W., Planty, M., Snyder, T., Bianco, K., Fox, M., et al. (2010). *The condition of education 2010* (NCES Publication No. 2010-028). Washington, DC: U.S. Department of Education, National Center for Education Statistics, Institute of Education Sciences.

Baker, B. D., & Cooper, B. S. (2005, August). Do principals with stronger academic backgrounds hire better teachers? Policy implications for improving high-poverty schools. *Educational Administration Quarterly, 41*(3), 449–479.

Bass, L., Garn, G., & Monroe, L. (2011). Using JCEL case studies to meet ELCC standards. *Journal of Cases in Educational Leadership, 14*(1), 1–12.

Blank, R. M. (2005). Poverty, policy, and place: How poverty and policies to alleviate poverty are shaped by local characteristics. *International Regional Science Review, 28*(4), 441–464.

Brooks-Gunn, J., Duncan, G. J., & Aber, J. L. (Eds.). (1997). *Neighborhood poverty: Context and consequences for children*. New York: Russell Sage Foundation.

Carlson, K. T. (2006). Poverty and youth violence exposure: Experiences in rural communities. *Children & Schools, 28*(2), 87–96.

Clotfelter, C., Ladd, H. F., Vigdor, J., & Wheeler, J. (2006). High-poverty schools and the distribution of teachers and principals. *North Carolina Law Review, 85*, 1346–1379.

Council of Chief State School Officers. (2005, February). *Summer learning opportunities in high-poverty schools*. Washington, DC: Author. Retrieved from http://www.ccsso.org/Documents/2005/Summer_Learning_2005.pdf

Everson, S. T., & Bussey, L. H. (2007, December). Educational leadership for social justice: Enhancing the ethical dimension of educational leadership. *Catholic Education*, 176–187. Retrieved from *http://ejournals.bc.edu/ojs/index.php/catholic/article/view/1004*

Finnigan, K. S. (2012, March). Principal leadership in low-performing schools: A closer look through the eyes of teachers. *Education and Urban Society, 44*(2), 183–202.

Freire, P. (1970). *Pedagogy of the oppressed*. New York: Continuum.

Freire, P. (1993). *Pedagogy of the city*. New York: Continuum.

Freire, P. (2000). *Pedagogy of the oppressed* (30th ed.). New York: Continuum.

Fullan, M. (2001). *The new meaning of educational change* (3rd ed.). New York: Teachers College Press.

Furman, G. C., & Shields, C. M. (2005). How can educational leaders promote and support social justice and democratic community in schools? In W. A. Firestone & C. Riehl (Eds.), *A new agenda for research in educational leadership* (pp. 119–137). New York: Teachers College Press.

Giles, C., Johnson, L., Brooks, S., & Jacobson, S. L. (2007, September). Building bridges, building community: Transformational leadership in a challenging urban context. *Journal of School Leadership, 51*(5), 519–545.

Harris, D. N. (2007). High-flying schools, student disadvantage, and the logic of NCLB. *American Journal of Education, 113*(3), 367–394.

Hightower, A. M., Delgado, R. C., Lloyd, S. C., Wittenstein, R., Sellers, K., & Swanson, C. (2011, December). *Improving student learning by supporting quality teaching: Key issues, effective strategies*. Bethesda, MD: Editorial Projects in Education.

Ingersoll, R., & Merrill, L. (2010, May). Who's teaching our children? *Educational Leadership, 67*(8), 14–20.

Jacob, B. A., & Ludwig, J. (2009, Fall). Improving educational outcomes for poor children. *Focus, 20*(2), 56–61.

Jacobson, S. (2011). School leadership and its effects on student achievement. *International Journal of Educational Management, 25*(1), 33–44.

Jacobson, S. L. (2008). Leadership or success in high poverty elementary schools. *Journal of Educational Leadership, Policy and Practice, 23*(1), 3–17.

Kaak, P. A. (2011, Winter). Power-filled lessons for leadership educators from Paulo Freire. *Journal of Leadership Education, 10*(1), 132–144.

Kaestle, C. F. (1993, January–February). The awful reputation of education research. *Educational Researcher, 22*(1), 23, 26–31.

Lyman, L. L., & Villani, C. J. (2004). *Best leadership practices for high-poverty schools*. Lanham, MD: Scarecrow.

Machtinger, H. (2007, February–March). What do we know about high poverty schools? Summary of the high poverty schools conference at UNC–Chapel Hill. *High School Journal, 90*(3), 1–8.

Miller, P. M., Brown, T., & Hopson, R. (2011). Centering love, hope, and trust in the community: Transformative urban leadership informed by Paulo Freire. *Urban Education, 46*(5), 1078–1099.

Mulford, B., Kendall, D., Ewington, J., Edmunds, B., Kendall, L., & Silins, H. (2008). Successful principalship of high-performance schools in high-poverty communities. *Journal of Educational Administration, 46*(4), 461–480.

Mulford, W., Silins, H., & Leithwood, K. (2004). *Educational leadership for organisational learning and improved student outcomes.* Norwell, MA: Kluwer.

Peske, H. G., & Haycock, K. (2006). Teaching inequality: How poor and minority students are shortchanged on teacher quality. A report and recommendations by the Education Trust. Washington, DC: The Education Trust. Retrieved from http://www.edtrust.org/sites/edtrust.org/files/publications/files/TQReportJune2006.pdf

Picucci, A. C., Brownson, A., Kahlert, R., & Sobel, A. (2002). *Driven to succeed: High-performing, high-poverty, turnaround middle schools: Vol. 1. Cross-case analysis of high-performing, high-poverty, turnaround middle schools.* Austin: Charles A. Dana Center, University of Texas at Austin.

Scutari, M. (2009). "The great equalizer": Making sense of the Supreme Court's equal protection jurisprudence in American public education and beyond. *Georgetown Law Journal, 97,* 917–943.

Shapiro, J. P., & Stefkovich, J. A. (2011). *Ethical leadership and decision making in education: Applying theoretical perspectives to complex dilemmas* (3rd ed.). Mahwah, NJ: Lawrence Erlbaum.

Smith, T. M., & Ingersoll, R. M. (2004, Fall). What are the effects of induction and mentoring on beginning teacher turnover? *American Education Research Journal, 41*(3), 681–714.

Stefkovich, J. A. (2006). *Best interests of the student: Applying ethical constructs to legal cases in education.* New York: Taylor & Francis.

U.S. Department of Education, National Center for Education Statistics. (2011). *The condition of education 2011* (NCES Publication No. 2011–033). Washington, DC: U.S. Government Printing Office.

Wilson, D. G. (2010). Building bridges for change: How leaders enable collective change in organizations. *Development and Learning in Organizations, 24*(1), 21–23. doi: 10.1108/14777281011010488

Contributors

LISA BASS is Assistant Professor of Education at North Carolina State University. Her research broadly focuses on issues that encourage school reform for disenfranchised students—especially students from high poverty backgrounds. Her work is dedicated toward discovering and presenting effective learning conditions, as well as broadening educational opportunities for this target population. Her work can be found in the *International Journal of Qualitative Studies in Education, Education Policy, Journal of School Public Relations, The Journal of Educational Research, Education Sciences, The Journal of Cases in Educational Leadership,* and *Teacher Education and Practice.*

SUSAN C. FAIRCLOTH (a member of the Coharie Tribe of North Carolina) is Associate Professor of Education at North Carolina State University. Her research explores factors that account for the disproportionate referral and placement of American Indian and Alaska Native students in special education programs and services, the preparation of school leaders, and the moral and ethical dimensions of school leadership. She has been published in *Educational Administration Quarterly, Harvard Educational Review, The Journal of Special Education Leadership, International Studies in Educational Administration, Values and Ethics in Educational Administration, Tribal College Journal of American Indian Higher Education, Rural Special Education Quarterly,* and *Journal of Disability Policy Studies.*

JUANITA G. VARGAS is Assistant Professor at The University of Oklahoma. The focus of her work is community colleges and leadership. Vargas (a member of the Comanche and Kickapoo tribes) is currently conducting a longitudinal study on Latina marginalization intersecting with class, gender, ethnicity, and age within the framework of White oppression and privilege. Future research interests involve the psychological and sociological experiences of Mexican-American males at elite public and private colleges.

ROBBIE WAHNEE (a member of the Comanche Tribe) holds a PhD in Educational Leadership and Policy Studies, a Master's in Secondary Education Administration, a Bachelor's in Sociology/History, and a 5-year standard Oklahoma teaching certification. She has worked in Human Resource Management for 24 years, is currently Director of Talent and Organizational Development in Housing & Food Services, and Adjunct Professor of Human Relations, at The University of Oklahoma. Her passion is providing employee enrichment and engagement, and studying the effects of trust in organizations. Wahnee is also a certified civil mediator with the American Society of Training & Development.

WENDELL WAUKAU (a member of the Menominee Nation) is the superintendent of Menominee Indian School District (MISD), a predominantly American Indian district, in Wisconsin. He has been an educator for more than 20 years. Under his leadership, MISD has been nationally recognized for its efforts to improve the academic outcomes of its students, while also incorporating, honoring, and celebrating students' culture and heritage.

Index

9th Grade Freshman Academy, 153–154

ability, 71
  see also competence
academic exploration, 51, 53
accountability, 93
achievement, academic
  and expectations, 49
  and general building management, 40
  and health, 150
  in high poverty schools, 4
  and poverty, 22
  and urban poverty, 20
action, and caring, 49
Adams, C. M., 74
African Americans, poverty among, 15
Alaska Natives. see American Indians
Allen, L. A., 169
Allen-Meares, P., 109, 113
Amatea, E. S., 113
American Indians
  as "asterisk" nation, 125
  control of education of, 125–126
  effect of education on, 123, 124, 125
  effects of globalization on, 122–125

  local control, 125–126
  Menominee Indian School District (MISD) (see Menominee Indian School District)
  Montana Indian Education for All Act, 126
  reformation of education of, 125
  self-determination, 125–126
  structure of education of, 122
  termination policy, 158n
  use of education in communities, 121
  use of term, 158n
American Indian Special Education Teacher Training Program, 123
American School Counselor Association (ASCA), 49–50, 112
assistance, direct, 76, 79, 81
Auerbach, S., 138
authenticity, of principal/leader, 68
authority, administrative, 77
authority, and trust, 74
autonomy, teacher, 112

Balfanz, R., 152, 154
Barth, P., 98
Barton, A. W., 21
Bass, L., 48, 168, 169

Bates, A., 30
Battiste, M., 128n
Begley, P. T., 7
benevolence, 32, 70, 73
best interest, ethic of, 127
Bishop, P., 163
Blanco, R. I., 108
Blase, J., 64, 76
Blase, J., 64, 76
Bomer, R., 49
book clubs, 100–101
Boone, W. J., 96
border crossers, 123
Bourdieu, P., 129n
Breakthrough School Award, 156
Bridges Out of Poverty (Payne, DeVol, and Smith), 152
Bronfenbrenner, U., 110, 111
Brown, D. L., 21
Brown, T., 165
Bryk, A. S., 32, 73
Bunker, B. B., 67, 72
bureaucracy, 67
Bureau of Indian Affairs, 145n
Bussey, L. H., 171

California, 136, 140
California, University of, 140
Canada, G., 36
capital, cultural, 14, 37
care, ethic of, 48–54, 98, 127
care/caring
  and action, 49
  and expectations, 49
  as motivation, 48
  necessary for principals, 29–30
  and parents' trust, 33
  in policies and practices, 30
  in school culture, 47
  training in, 98
  and zero tolerance policies, 47
career exploration, 50, 51, 53–54
caring, institutional, 30
Carlson, K. T., 21, 22
case discussions, 100
case studies, 168–169
Annie E. Casey Foundation, 20
Cassidy, W., 30
Centers for Disease Control and Prevention (CDC), 153
Central Washington University (CWU), 136, 142–143
change
  effecting, 164–165
  and leaders, 128, 158, 161, 162
  need for community buy-in, 158
  need for effective leadership in, 163
  questions regarding, 158
  and teacher preparation, 171
  through legal action, 165–166
change agent, school as, 30, 110
children
  development of, 110–111
  number of in poverty, 3, 127
Child Trends, 2
Chronic Poverty Research Center (CPRC), 15
chronosystem, 110
Cibulka, J. G., 115
Clements, S. K., 30, 35, 46
climate, school, 94–95
coaching, differentiated, 101
Coalition of Community Schools, 111, 116
Coharie People, 123
  see also American Indians
college
  affording, 134
  effects of socioeconomic status in, 133
college access
  barriers to for Latino Americans, 132–136, 139
  questions regarding, 144
college readiness
  goal of, 131
  intervention programs, 135, 136–143
  need for, 132
colonias, 138
Comer, J., 155
communication
  importance of, 71
  in MISD, 151
  in negotiating community partnerships, 39
  with parents, 138
  by principals, 30
  and trust, 32, 73
communication, positive, 138
community
  disengagement of, 151
  engagement with, and dropout rate, 156

engagement with, in MISD, 152–153
impact on youth, 109
involvement of in successful high poverty schools, 163
community partnerships
in fight against poverty, 116
need for, 36–37, 108, 109–110, 165
negotiating, 39
questions regarding, 117
community school coordinator, 115–116
community schools
benefits of, 37
defined, 111
support provided by, 37, 39
community schools facilitators, 39–40
community services, school-linked, 110, 114–115
see also support services
compassion
in policies and practices, 30
in principal trust, 32
competence, 32, 71
see also ability
completion, school. see dropout rate; graduation
confidence, 69–70
conflict resolution, 47
connectedness, ethic of, 109
consequences, 52
consistency, 32
context
and leadership, 55, 165
need for understanding of, 55
contracts, 72–73
Contreras, J. A., 133
control, local, 125–126
Cook, J., 69
coordinator, community school, 115–116
coping strategies, 47, 51–52
Corbett, M., 8, 121, 123, 125
Coronado, D., 169
Cortez, M. T., 169
Council of Chief State School Officers, 162
counselors/counseling
access to, 133
need for, 54
role of, 49–52, 53, 112–113
critical friends groups, 101
cultural capital, 14, 15, 37

cultural integration, 155
cultural integrity, 137, 141
cultural mobility, 124
culture
importance of in MISD, 157
need to understand, 35
culture, school
assessing, 94–95
caring in, 47
culture of poverty
Payne on, 46
use of term, 2
cycle of poverty, 15–16, 35

D'Ambrosio, B. S., 96
Darling-Churchill, K. E., 125
Darling-Hammond, L., 92, 97, 99
data
use of by successful high poverty schools, 162
using in professional development, 96, 100
Davis, J. H., 68
Davis, R., 24n
decolonization, 126
deficit thinking, 46, 49, 158
Deutsch, M., 69
DeVoe, J. F., 125
diet, and poverty, 17–18
see also health
direction, need for, 37
discipline, and relevancy, 53
disengagement, 154
Dispelling the Myth (Barth et al.), 98
diversity, questions regarding, 128, 158
Charles R. Drew Elementary School, 162
dropout rate
and community engagement, 156
extent of crisis in, 152
of Latino Americans, 133
in MISD, 156
Strategies to Help Solve Our School Dropout Problem, 151
see also graduation
Duncan, C. M., 20

Easton, L. B., 98, 99
East Silver Spring Elementary School, 162
ecological systems theory, 110–111
economic capital, 115

education
  ambivalence toward, 121
  benefits of, 143
  cultural understandings of, 136
  effects of on American Indians, 123, 124, 125
  failure of as equalizer, 127
  in fight against poverty, 127
  goals of, 54
  and health, 150
  indigenization of, 126
  level of, 16, 133
  as means of decolonizing, 126
  and opportunity, 18
  purpose of, 127
  quality of, 16
  re-visioning of, questions regarding, 128
  sociopolitical contexts of, 55
Educational Leadership Program, 123
effectiveness, teacher, 93
emergencies, in high poverty contexts, 34
emotions, dealing with, 51–52
employment, gainful, 16
Emslie, J. R., 133
Enabling School Structure Scale (ESS), 76, 77
environment, 19–20, 35
environmental scanning, 23, 24n
equality, educational, 165
ethic of best interest, 127
ethic of care, 48–54, 98, 127
ethic of connectedness, 109
ethic of profession, 46–48
ethics
  of educational leaders, 46–47
  and promoting equality of opportunity, 54–57
  questions regarding, 57
evaluation, performance, 73
Everson, S. T., 171
exchanges, repeated, 73
exosystem, 110
expectations, 35–37, 49
extended learning opportunities, 162

Faircloth, S., 114, 122–125, 168
family
  definition of, 141
  and educational success, 134–135
  expectations, 145n
  involvement of in successful high poverty schools, 163
  need to engage, 114
  relationships with, 153, 156
  see also community; parents
feedback, constructive, 52
financial aid, 134
flexibility, importance of, 34
food insecurity, 17
A Framework for Understanding Poverty (Payne), 152, 158
Freire, P., 164, 169, 170
Freudenberg, N., 150
Frick, J. E., 109
Frick, W. C., 109
Furman, G. C., 54
Fusarelli, B. C., 109
Fusarelli, L. D., 55
Futures & Families (F&F), 140
Futures Project, 140

Garn, G., 169
GEAR UP, 137
Glickman, C. D., 64, 80
globalization, 122–125, 126
Goldberg, M. F., 5
Gordon, S. P., 64
Gorman, C., 137
graduation
  in high poverty schools, 4
  and poverty, 16
  see also dropout rate
Greenberg, J. B., 128n
Grissom, J. A., 40
grocery stores, 17
guidance, 49–52
Guskey, T. R., 91

handbooks, 73
Harkness, S. S., 96
Harlem Children's Zone (HCZ), 36–37
Harris, A., 163
Harris, D. N., 165
HCZ (Harlem Children's Zone), 36–37
health
  and dropout crisis, 152
  and education, 150
  of Menominee, 155
  Wisconsin School Health Award, 156

see also well-being
health care, in rural areas, 20
Hemphill, F. C., 133
Henderson, J. E., 68
Henderson, J. S. Y., 128n
Herzberg, S. J., 158n
Herzog, L., 154
Hibpshman, T., 30, 35, 46
hierarchy, 66–67, 81–82
Highland School District, 136, 142–143
Hippocratic oath, 56
Hispanics
　poverty among, 15
　see also Latino Americans
history, 124
Holiday Elementary School, 73
Hollinger, J., 145n
home visits, 153
honesty, 71
Hong, S. S., 169
hope, 50
hopelessness, 22
Hopson, R., 165
housing, and quality of education, 16
Hoy, W. K., 65, 66–67, 68, 69–70, 77

identification, school, 47
Indians, American. *see* American Indians
indigenization, 126
information, sharing of, 71
Ingle, W. K., 169
Instructional Supervision Scale (ISS), 76
Instructional Supervision Survey, 78–79
integration, cultural, 155
integrity, cultural, 137, 141
interdependence
　and competence, 71
　and reliability, 70
　and trust, 66, 69
Internet, instruction in, 140
interpersonal skills
　development of, 31
　needed by principals, 30–31
　in negotiating community partnerships, 39
involvement, parent. *see* community; family; parents

Jacobson, S., 169
Jacobson, S. L., 45, 165

Johns Hopkins University, 152
Johnson, A. F., 112
Johnson, B. L., 23, 24n
journaling, 101
Journal of Cases in Educational Leadership, 168–169
Jozefowicz-Simbeni, D. H. M., 109, 113

Kaak, P. A., 169, 171
Kaestle, C. F., 164
Kanani, 123–125
Kannapel, P. J., 30, 35, 46
Keys, W., 163
Kochanek, J., 64, 72, 73
Kruse, S. D., 23, 24n
Kupersmith, W. J., 68

Ladson-Billings, G., 56
language, in culturally specific programs, 138
language, Menominee, 155
Latino Americans
　barriers to college access for, 132–136, 139
　college preparation of, 133–134
　culturally specific programs for, 138–143
　cultural understandings of education, 136
　dropout rate of, 133
　family networks of, 135
　information needs of, 139
　parental educational levels, 133
　parental involvement and success of, 135
　population of, 132
　poverty rate for, 131, 132
　questions regarding, 144
　school performance of, 133
leaders
　and change, 128, 158, 161, 162
　counselors as, 113
　ethics of, 46–47
　identifying, 40
　need to understand environment, 19–20
　practices of, 162–163
　support for, 21
　ultimate goal of, 45
　see also principals
leaders, instructional
　principals as, 32, 64
　questions regarding, 82–83
　see also supervision, instructional
leadership

as calling, 162
as context dependent, 165
Journal of Cases in Educational Leadership, 168–169
in MISD, 154–155
as more than administration, 112
recognition of, 157
research on, recommendations for, 163–164
style of, and context, 55
teaching of, 167–169
see also principals
leadership, authoritative, 74
see also supervision, instructional
leadership, district-level, 154
leadership, exceptional educational
characteristics of, 22–23, 29–40, 161–162
concept of, 6
defined, 5
leadership, Freirian, 169–171
learning, emphasis on, 91
Learning to Leave (Corbett), 8, 121, 125
Levy, M. K., 169
Lewicki, R. J., 67, 72
Lindle, J. C., 109
Loeb, S., 40
Lomawaima, K. T., 128n
Lugg, C. A., 108
Lunenberg, F. C., 30
Lyman, L. L., 163

Machtinger, H., 164, 170
Mac Iver, D., 154
macrosystem, 110
management, general building, 40
Mann, H., 18
Mayer, R. C., 68, 70, 72
McAllister, D. J., 68, 72
John B. McFerran Preparatory School, 162
McLaughlin, M. W., 92, 97
Menominee County, 150
Menominee Indian Middle School, 154, 156
Menominee Indian Reservation, 150
Menominee Indians
description of, 150
termination of tribe, 155, 158n
Menominee Indian School District (MISD)
challenges to, 151
community engagement in, 152–153
cultural integration in, 155

description of, 149–150
disengagement interventions in, 154
district-level leadership in, 154
dropout rate in, 152, 156
home visits in, 153
importance of culture in, 157
language requirement in, 155
Reach and Teach, 154
results of reform in, 156
school-level leadership in, 155
transition services in, 153–154, 156
Menominee Indian School District (MISD) School Board, 154, 157
mentoring, 50, 52, 95, 96, 99–100, 101
Merchant, B. M., 108
mesosystem, 110
microsystem, 110
migration outward, 123
Miller, David "Jonesy," 157
Miller, P. M., 165
minority groups
questions regarding, 144
see also American Indians; Latino Americans
MISD (Menominee Indian School District).
see Menominee Indian School District
mobility, cultural, 124
mobility, social, 124
modeling. *see* mentoring
Monroe, L., 169
Montana Indian Education for All Act, 126
Morrison, J. L., 24n
motivation
care as, 48
of principals, 30
and relevancy, 53

National Assessment of Educational Progress, 133
National Center for Children in Poverty, 127
National Center for Education Statistics, 4
National School Boards Association, 154
Native Americans. *see* American Indians
No Child Left Behind (NCLB), 4
Noddings, N., 7, 30, 48
Normore, A. H., 108
norms, cultural, 21
North Carolina, 123

observation, 95

Omnibus Trust Scale, 76–77
openness, 32, 71
opportunity
  and education, 18
  equality of, promoting, 54–57
  exposure to, 50
  and need for support services, 55
  and school reform, 4

Padilla, V. R., 133
Parent Institute for Quality Education (PIQE), 140–141
parents
  access of to information, 139–140
  communication with, 138
  culturally specific programs for, 137–143
  educational levels of, 133
  and educational success, 134–135
  involvement of, facilitating, 33
  involvement of, need for, 113, 114
  involvement of in successful high poverty schools, 163
  perspective of, 33
  relationships with, 33–34
  see also community; family
Parents Teaching Parents (PTP), 136, 142–143
Payne, R. K., 46, 158
Pennsylvania State University, 123
Perkins, G. W., 112
Perna, L. W., 135
Pew Hispanic Center, 133
PIQE (Parent Institute for Quality Education), 140–141
policies, punitive, 47
policy
  care and compassion in, 30
  influence of research on, 164
portfolios, professional, 101
poverty
  definitions of, 14
  difficulty of conceptualizing, 13–14
  economic perspective on, 14
  effects of on educational institutions, 3
  factors in, 15
  failure to eradicate, 4
  persistence of, 2
  questions regarding, 23–24
  socio-cultural-economic perspective on, 14
  understanding conditions behind, 46
  and well-being, 3, 15
poverty, culture of, 2, 46
poverty, cycle of, 15–16, 35
poverty, intergenerational, 15–16, 35
poverty, rural, 20, 21, 23
poverty, urban, 20, 21, 23
power asymmetry, 64, 69, 73
Powerful Designs for Professional Learning (Easton), 99
power symmetry, 66, 79
practices
  care and compassion in, 30
  of successful high poverty schools, 162–163
  translating research into, 164
principals
  authenticity of, 68
  characteristics of, 29–40
  demographics of, 3
  importance of, 63
  as instructional leaders, 32, 64 (see also supervision, instructional)
  motivation of, 48
  preparation of, questions regarding, 41
  as professional development facilitator, 94–99
  responsibilities of, 64
  roles of, 66, 80
  roles of, questions regarding, 40
  trust of (see trust, principal)
  see also leaders; leadership
Principal Trust Scales, 77
prison, school as pipeline to, 56
profession, ethic of, 46–48
professional development
  book clubs, 100–101
  case discussions, 100
  characteristics of, 98–99
  critical friends groups, 101
  data analysis in, 100
  development of plan for, 94–97
  differentiated coaching, 101
  evaluation of, 99
  features of, 97
  in high poverty contexts, 97–98
  importance of, 91, 94, 154
  journaling, 101
  mentoring, 50, 52, 95, 96, 99–100, 101
  observation, 95
  portfolios, 101

principal as facilitator of, 31–32, 94–99
questions about, 102
and standards, 96–97
in successful high poverty schools, 163
for teachers in high poverty contexts, 93–94
using data to develop, 96
Program Coherence (PC), 76
programs, new, 31
proxies, 73
Puente program, 136

Rahman, T., 133
Reach and Teach, 154
reciprocity, 37–39
reform
  and instructional supervision, 64
  models for, 152
  and opportunity, 4
relevancy, 52–53
reliability, 32, 70
research, 163–164
resourcefulness, 34
resources, exposure to, 50
responsibilities, and trust, 80
risk, 69, 71
rituals, cultural, 21
Rodriguez, M. A., 169
Romo, H., 133
Ross-Gordon, J. M., 64
Rotter, J. B., 71
Ruglis, J., 150
rules, 73
rural communities
  access to employment in, 16
  American Indians in, 125
  commitment to, 122
  education in, 8
  effects of education in, 121–122
  and globalization, 122, 126
  health care in, 20
  need to re-vision education in, 126
  poverty in, 20, 21, 23
  substance abuse in, 20
  see also Menominee Indian School District; poverty, rural
Rutledge, S. A., 169

Salas, J., 133
Salmonowicz, M. J., 169

Schargel, F., 151
Schneider, B., 32, 73
school culture, 47, 94–95
school experience, 16
school identification, 47
schools, community. *see* community schools
schools, high poverty
  defined, 3, 158n
  difficulties facing, 5
  lack of preparedness for, 92–93, 171
  leaders of, 3 (*see also* leaders; principals)
  location of, 4
  need for effective leadership in, 162, 163
  statistics regarding, 166–167
school/schooling
  as change agent, 30, 110
  connectedness to, 47
  historic role of, 108
  impact of systems on, 111
  obligations of, 131
  purpose of, 50
  teachers' experience with, 92
school structure, 91, 107
school structure, enabling, 76, 77
Schoorman, F. D., 68
Schulte, D. P., 169
Scutari, M., 165
self, student view of, 38–39
self-determination, 125–126
service learning, 38, 39
services. *see* support services
shadowing. *see* mentoring
sharing, 71
Shields, C. M., 54
Shoho, A. R., 108
Siddle-Walker, V., 30
Siwatu, K. O., 92
Smink, J., 151
Smrekar, C. E., 116
Snarey, J., 30
social capital
  absence of transfer of, 15
  need for, 37
  right to accumulate, 14, 115
social justice agenda, 108
social mobility, 124
social similarity, 72, 73
society, position in, 14
Sorenson, R. D., 169

SSOS (Statewide System of Support), 151
stability, and general building management, 40
standards, and professional development plans, 96–97
Starratt, R. J., 56
Statewide System of Support (SSOS), 151
Stefkovich, J., 7, 46, 56
Strategies to Help Solve Our School Dropout Problem (Schargel and Smink), 151
strengths, assessing, 52
structure, school, 76, 77, 91, 107
substance abuse in rural areas, 20
success, questions regarding, 158
summer school programs, 162, 163
supervision, instructional
  definitions of, 64
  direct assistance, 76, 79, 81
  functions of, 81
  importance of, 63, 81, 82
  measures of, 75–76
  practice of, 66
  and principal trust, 64–82
  questions regarding, 82–83
  and reform, 64
  sample in study of, 78
  views of, 79–80
supervisors, transformational, 80
support services
  community school coordinator, 115–116
  at community schools, 37, 39
  counseling, 49–52, 112–113
  in fight against poverty, 116
  at HCZ, 36
  need for, 31, 37, 55–56
  obligation to provide, 107
  and professional development, 98
  questions regarding, 40–41
  school-linked community services, 110, 114–115
  and school structure, 107
  transition services, 153–154
surveys, to assess professional development needs, 96
Swail, W. S., 135
Swan, W., 152
Swanson, L. E., 21
Sweetland, S., 66–67, 77
systems, ecological, 110–111

Tarrallton Elementary School, 162
Taylor, D., 30, 35, 46
teachers
  assessing, for professional development, 94–96
  autonomy of, 112
  characteristics of, 93
  connecting with, 32–33
  effectiveness of, 93
  in high poverty schools, characteristics of, 3–4
  preparation of, 92–93, 171
  recruitment of, 167
  relationships with, 31–33 (*see also* trust, principal)
  retention of, 94, 95, 167
  schooling experiences of, 92
  supervision of, 66 (*see also* supervision, instructional)
teaching, effective, 91
teaching, pre-service, 92–93
Tebo, M. G., 47
test scores, in high poverty schools, 4, 151
Texas, 134, 138
Thomas, P. S., 24n
Thomson, P., 163
Tickamyer, A. R., 20
Tillman, L. C., 107
Title I districts, 3
Title I Supplemental Grants, 151
transition services, 153–154, 156
transportation, 16, 17
trust
  and caring, 33
  definitions of, 69, 71
  descriptions of, 65, 67–68
  elements of, 32
  establishment of, 32, 33
  Hoy's work on, 65–66 (*see also* Hoy, W. K.)
  importance of, 67, 156
  and interdependence, 66, 69
  need for, 31
  and responsibilities, 80
  and risk, 69
  types of, 67–68, 72
  and vulnerability, 68
trust, affect-based, 68, 72
trust, behavioral, 65
trust, calculus-based, 67, 72

trust, character-based, 72
trust, cognition-based, 65, 68, 72
trust, conditional, 67
trust, identification-based, 67, 72
trust, institutional-based, 73
trust, knowledge-based, 67, 72, 73
trust, principal
   and authoritative leadership, 74
   components of, 68–72
   defined, 65
   development of, 72–73
   measures of, 76–77
   relationship with instructional supervision, 64–82
   research methods in study on, 74–79
trust, relational, 32
trust, unconditional, 67–68
Tschannen-Moran, M., 32, 69–70

unions, 72
urban areas, 20
   see also poverty, urban

Vanneman, A., 133
Vélez-Ibáñez, C. G., 128n
Villani, C. J., 163
violence, 21, 22
Vodicka, D., 32
vulnerability, 68, 69, 71, 72

Wahnee, R. L., 32, 65
Wall, T., 69
Washington, 136, 142–143
water insecurity, 17
Waukau, W., 157
weaknesses, assessing, 52
Weil Technology Institute, 162
well-being, 3, 15
   see also health
West-Olatunji, C. A., 113
Wildcat, D. R., 126
Wisconsin. *see* Menominee Indian School District (MISD)
Wisconsin Department of Public Instruction, 151
Wisconsin Knowledge and Concepts Examination (WKCE), 151
Wisconsin School Health Award, 156
working conditions, 95

youth, potential of, 109

Zapeda, S. J., 93, 94
zero tolerance, 47, 48
Zucker, L. G., 72, 73

M. Christopher Brown II. *General Editor*

The *Education Management: Contexts, Constituents, and Communities* (EM:c³) series includes the best scholarship on the varied dynamics of educational leadership, management, and administration across the educational continuum. In order to disseminate ideas and strategies useful for schools, colleges, and the education community, each book investigates critical topics missing from the extant literature and engages one or more theoretical perspectives. This series bridges the gaps between the traditional management research, practical approaches to academic administration, and the fluid nature of organizational realities.

Additionally, the EM:c³ series endeavors to provide meaningful guidance on continuing challenges to the effective and efficient management of educational contexts. Volumes in the series foreground important policy/praxis issues, developing professional trends, and the concerns of educational constituencies. The aim is to generate a corpus of scholarship that discusses the unique nature of education in the academic and social spaces of all school types (e.g., public, private, charter, parochial) and university types (e.g., public, private, historically black, tribal institutions, community colleges).

The EM:c³ series offers thoughtful research presentations from leading experts in the fields of educational administration, higher education, organizational behavior, public administration, and related academic concentrations. Contributions represent research on the United States as well as other countries by comparison, address issues related to leadership at all levels of the educational system, and are written in a style accessible to scholars, educational practitioners and policymakers throughout the world.

For further information about the series and submitting manuscripts, please contact:

Dr. M. Christopher Brown II | em_bookseries@yahoo.com

To order other books in this series, please contact our Customer Service Department at:

(800) 770-LANG (within the U.S.)
(212) 647-7706 (outside the U.S.)
(212) 647-7707 FAX

Or browse online by series at www.peterlang.com

www.ingramcontent.com/pod-product-compliance
Ingram Content Group UK Ltd.
Pitfield, Milton Keynes, MK11 3LW, UK
UKHW022239230426
12048UKWH00018BA/1354